Teaching Copyright

Teaching Copyright

Practical Lesson Ideas and Instructional Resources

Sara E. Wolf

Foreword by Carol Simpson

BLOOMSBURY LIBRARIES UNLIMITED
NEW YORK • LONDON • OXFORD • NEW DELHI • SYDNEY

Online resources to accompany this book are available at https://www.bloomsbury.pub/teaching-copyright. If you experience any problems, please contact Bloomsbury at: onlineresources@bloomsbury.com

BLOOMSBURY LIBRARIES UNLIMITED
Bloomsbury Publishing Inc
1385 Broadway, New York, NY 10018, USA
50 Bedford Square, London, WC1B 3DP, UK
29 Earlsfort Terrace, Dublin 2, Ireland

BLOOMSBURY, BLOOMSBURY LIBRARIES UNLIMITED and the Diana logo are trademarks of Bloomsbury Publishing Plc

First published in the United States of America 2025

It is important for readers to understand that the definitions, information, and lesson ideas presented in this text are only applicable to United States copyright law. Readers must conduct their own due diligence to be sure that the lessons within this book and the resources on the accompanying website are applicable to their locale.

Cover image: V3rc4/Shutterstock

Library of Congress Cataloging-in-Publication Data
Names: Wolf, Sara E., author.
Title: Teaching copyright : practical lesson ideas and instructional resources / Sara E. Wolf.
Description: New York : Bloomsbury Libraries Unlimited, 2025. | Includes bibliographical references and index.
Identifiers: LCCN 2024024341 (print) | LCCN 2024024342 (ebook) | ISBN 9781440880926 (paperback) | ISBN 9798216184362 (epub) | ISBN 9781440880933 (pdf) Subjects: LCSH: Copyright. | Copyright–Study and teaching.
Classification: LCC K1420.5 .W65 2025 (print) | LCC K1420.5 (ebook) | DDC 346.04/82071--dc23/eng/20240602
LC record available at https://lccn.loc.gov/2024024341
LC ebook record available at https://lccn.loc.gov/2024024342

ISBN: PB: 978-1-4408-8092-6
ePDF: 978-1-4408-8093-3
eBook: 979-8-216-18436-2

Typeset by Deanta Global Publishing Services, Chennai, India
Printed and bound in the United States of America

Contents

Foreword

Copyright is a topic that is seldom understood in education. Educators and administrators vary in understanding from "You can use anything as long as you aren't selling it" or "It's for the good of the students" to "If it is copyrighted, run away." Clearly, neither extreme is always the truth, but most educators (including administrators who have likely taken a course in school law) don't understand how to begin to assess the rights and risks of using copyrighted material. As a school attorney, I had to help clients navigate choppy copyright waters when teachers posted copied study guides on open websites, cafeteria managers went image shopping on the internet to illustrate tasty dishes, or coaches posted inspirational poems on Twitter/X accounts. Having a reasonable background in copyright can protect schools and individuals from copyright infringement actions.

Sara E. Wolf has been curious about copyright law for a number of years and was a manuscript reviewer for several copyright books before she co-authored *Copyright for Schools: A Practical Guide* (6th ed.). She has used innovative teaching techniques to reinforce copyright foundations and concepts for her undergraduate and graduate students at Auburn University. She understands that teaching copyright involves the diligent study of extremely complex ideas and explaining the balancing of two worthy rivals: the copyright owner and those who would use the owner's creation to advance "Science and useful Arts" (U.S. Const. art. I, § 8, cl. 8). This book is a passion project—an outgrowth of her learning and teaching. While there are some good copyright reference works on the market, there have been no texts that guide teachers who educate their students about the nuances of copyright law. Until now.

In this work, you will find lessons that are flexible enough to teach basics to older elementary students and deep enough for graduate students to get a rich understanding of copyright's nuances—all from the same lesson. You can teach one lesson or a group of lessons. Creative teachers may want to modify the lessons to suit their topics and audiences, and Sara grants such permission. Additionally, this work is teacher-friendly. She has provided plentiful supplemental resources for each lesson, such as assessments, test item banks, and an online repository of PowerPoint slides. For those readers who must submit annotated lesson plans, each lesson includes time estimates and guides to Bloom's Taxonomy. Each lesson references the common education/library copyright hornbooks that summarize and explain the law, so no matter what your copyright reference might be, these lessons will complement it.

One feature of this book found in few others on this topic is the Concordance. A concordance is an alphabetical index of the principal words or phrases of a book (or section of a book), so if you know a word of a case or a concept, the concordance will point you to every time that word or phrase appears within the text. Concordances are not common outside of religious texts, so this feature is remarkable in educational texts or legal texts. If you already have some familiarity with copyright concepts or cases, the Concordance can take you to an on-point discussion of those topics without having to do a hit-or-miss search of the chapters and lessons.

You will find this book works hand in hand with curriculum and administration, and you'll have ample options to teach your students. There is no reason to avoid teaching and discussing complicated copyright; this work will set you up for success.

Carol Simpson, Ed.D., J. D.
May 2024

Acknowledgments

This book couldn't have come into existence without the love and support of my mom and dad. Dad is deceased, but while he was with our family, he instilled an innate sense of awe and wonder in the knowing of all things interesting. Mom is the source of my affinity for the spoken and written word. She was my first example of an avid, prolific reader. They were my first teachers. Without them, I wouldn't have learned to appreciate humor and sarcasm, ride a bike, drive a standard transmission car, boil an egg, make pancakes, and an entire lifetime of other skills. I've never doubted that they were proud of my work, even when they sometimes didn't always understand it. My sister, Catie, says that I was her first teacher. That means that she was my first student. Her advice to me on how to interact with her children, to "tell the truth, using language as simple as possible," resonates with me whenever I teach—regardless of the age of the students.

Without the trust that Carol Simpson gave me by inviting me to co-author with her, I certainly would never have endeavored to write this title. I've admired her work ever since my first graduate school program, trusted her advice and guidance as a peer, and enjoyed her humor and friendship as a peer. She is one of my most generous friends, without whom my understanding of copyright would be woefully incomplete.

My colleagues Sheri Downer and Carey Andrzejewski have provided invaluable support to me during my writing process. Whenever I needed a sanity check on a logical conundrum, or a sounding board to use in times of frustration, they were both there. Between the two of them, I need never open a thesaurus ever again; their vocabularies are that large and varied. I couldn't have gotten where I am without their friendship and support.

Special thanks go to my friends and family, as well as the visitors to the Bloomberg Digital Solutions booth at ALA 2022, who graciously agreed to let me use their names as characters throughout this text. The scenarios and examples in the text are fictitious and do not in any way represent the actual behavior or decision making that the actual people would exhibit when faced with situations similar to those described herein.

Carey Andrzejewski, AL
Carol Mahoney, MD
Carol Simpson, TX
Cassandra Cuppy, NY
Catie Murphy, VA
Charlotte Murphy, VA
Chris Bearinger, MI
Chris Murphy, VA
Dwayne Clark, AL
Eileen Burnell, ME
Ericka Patillo, TN
Evelyn Bearinger, MI
Garmina Chaturvedi, MD
Georgia Murphy, VA
Ignacio (Nacho) Pecina, TX
Jamie Becker, MO
Jean Overman, VA
Jenell Steis, VA
Jess Shelleman, PA
Jill Corcoran, Wash., DC

John Budd, MO
Kaili Clark, AL
Kellan Burnell, ME
Kyle Burnell. ME
LeNessa Clark, SC
Natalie Bearinger, MI
Rex Bearinger, MI
Richard Ashby, PA
Rosalind Lett, GA
Sara-George-Ann Pecina, TX
Steve Cohen, IL
Susan Bannon, AL
Susie Wolf, VA
Tiernan Burnell, ME
Yousuf Jalel, MD

1 Introduction and Organization

Before You Begin

One of the aspects of copyright that many people do not understand is that there is no universal, all-encompassing copyright law applicable everywhere in the world. Copyright law is unique to each country. While some conceptual definitions do cross international borders, others do not. In fact, more of them don't cross borders than do. The concept of authorship is defined differently in different areas of the world, as is the concept of fair use. The fact that these two foundational concepts, as well as others relating to copyright, have different definitions depending on the laws of a particular country makes creating instructional resources and lessons that apply to anyone in any location impossible. Therefore, it is important for readers to understand that the definitions, information, and lesson ideas presented in this text are only applicable to US copyright law. Readers in other countries who are reading this book will want to be sure to conduct their own due diligence to ensure that the lessons within this book and the resources on the accompanying website are applicable to their locale.

Who Should Use This Book?

If you have purchased this book, you are interested in teaching your students about copyright. You may be a faculty member at a college or university; an administrator of a department, unit, school, or district; or a teacher or school librarian in a K–12 school. You likely have at least a passing knowledge about the basic concepts associated with copyright, such as fair use, public domain, or possibly the classroom exceptions. However, you might want some guidance on ways to teach about these and other concepts relating to copyright. You may just want some ideas or "starters" to spark your own instructional creativity as you design instructional activities for your students. After all, teachers, professors, and administrators are busy people, and having some ready-made plans and ideas for lessons about copyright can be useful in managing an already busy schedule.

This book is written with the following assumptions about the people who will purchase it:

- You are a teacher or instructor in some form, whether by training, vocation, or job description.
- You have an interest or need to teach about copyright.
- You are NOT a legal scholar, professor, or expert.

- You may or may not have available to you textbook or textbook-type materials about copyright, but not necessarily lessons for how to teach it.
- You have a basic understanding of copyright, but specifics and nuances may be unfamiliar to you.
- You would benefit from recommended reading to deepen your own understanding of copyright and related concepts.

How Should This Book Be Used?

This book should be used as a resource for lesson ideas. It is not a text about copyright. Authors such as Rebecca Butler, Kenneth Crews, Carrie Russell, Carol Simpson, and several others have published extensively about copyright law. This book should not supplant their very thorough work. Rather, it is a companion to those works. It is written from a text-neutral perspective. Regardless of the text that you prefer as your primary reference/resource, the lessons and activities in this book will provide references to commonly used copyright textbooks and cases so that you can read, research, assign, and so on, as is appropriate for your teaching situation.

I hope that you are able to use the lessons in this book the same way that you are able to use other teacher guides or instructional units. That is, I hope that if you find the lessons appealing and useful as they are written, you will implement them with fidelity to the plans provided. If, however, you find that a particular lesson needs tweaking or adjustment in order to better fit your particular teaching situation, please do so with my blessing. If your modification works better for you, and you'd like to share it with others, I'd also love to hear from you so that I can include it in future revisions of the text as they are completed.

How Is This Book Organized?

The lesson ideas in this book are organized according to broad concepts within copyright. Lessons are well annotated in terms of related texts or readings that might be assigned as well as supporting materials that might be used for lesson implementation. Additionally, each lesson contains annotations that will help you modify it to best fit your own instructional context. These revisions include ways to make lessons simpler or more complex, as appropriate for different learners, ways to shorten or extend the time needed for lessons, and ways to vary practice or assessment activities within the lesson.

The chapters following the lessons present the **Test and Scenario Banks** as well as the annotated supplemental resources for use with the lessons or as stand-alone items. Please note that online resources are volatile in nature. Their presence is not guaranteed from one day to the next. The URLs that are provided are accurate, to the best of my knowledge, as of the date of the printing of the text.

Each lesson, stand-alone activity, and supplemental resource will be annotated to provide you with the following information:

- A brief overview/summary of the item.
- A connection to Bloom's Taxonomy to indicate the cognitive level being addressed.
- A link to lessons within the book (in the case of supplemental materials) that would appropriately use that item as a part of the lesson implementation.

How Do I Choose Which Lesson Choice/Type to Deliver?

Making instructional decisions for a specific group of students in a particular learning context is inherently a personal undertaking. Every faculty member and teacher that I know uses a slightly different personal algorithm to make these decisions. That being said, I can offer the following suggestions regarding how to select a particular lesson or activity from those presented for you in this work:

- Each lesson will have an estimated time for completion as a part of the plan. Use these estimates to determine which one best suits your instructional needs. Each of the lessons is designed to be implemented in multiples of 15 minutes. If you need or want to segment or combine lessons into shorter or longer workshops, you have natural places for breaks if needed.
- Each lesson will also have an index for the main level of Bloom's Taxonomy that it addresses with regard to the types of objectives it is designed to address. These levels can also provide valuable information for making decisions about which activity you'd like to implement.
- Use the list of instructional goals/objectives that are provided to determine which lessons/activities address each one. Review the indicated lessons/activities and select the ones that best fit your instructional needs.

How Do I Connect the Lessons to My Curriculum?

Each lesson has broadly written learning goals (Smith & Ragan, 2005; Zook, 2001) that can be used to help you correlate the lessons with the course of study/curriculum that you are responsible for teaching in your school. For those instructors who teach outside of a K–12 school or who are providing professional development for teachers rather than students, these learning goals can be used to track learner mastery of key copyright concepts.

For those teachers who teach students in K–12 school settings, connecting the lessons with your state's course of study/curriculum may be more appropriate for your documentation at the building level. Each state places copyright concepts in a different location in their courses of studies. Periodically, these courses of study are revised, thus possibly changing where copyright is expected to be taught to students. When you are searching for course of study/curriculum items to use with these lessons, you may need to search in a variety of subjects in your state's course of study/curriculum. Below, I list the locations where you will likely find copyright-related objectives. I am not including individual objectives, as subsequent revisions within the states would render the list obsolete. Therefore, use this list as an initial starting point for your search of appropriate course of study/curriculum objectives.

Curriculum Standards for US States and Territories

State/Territory	**Course of Study URL**
Alabama	https://alex.state.al.us/browseStand.php
Alaska	https://education.alaska.gov/standards
Arizona	https://www.azed.gov/standards-practices
Arkansas	https://dese.ade.arkansas.gov/Offices/learning-services/curriculum-support/arkansas-academic-standards
California	https://www.cde.ca.gov/be/st/ss/index.asp
Colorado	https://www.cde.state.co.us/standardsandinstruction
Connecticut	https://portal.ct.gov/SDE/CT-Core-Standards/Materials-for-Teachers
Delaware	https://delaware.gov/guides/school-k-12/
Florida	https://www.cpalms.org/public/search/Standard
Georgia	https://www.georgiastandards.org/
Hawaii	https://www.hawaiipublicschools.org/TeachingAndLearning/StudentLearning/Pages/standards.aspx
Idaho	https://www.sde.idaho.gov/academic/standards/
Illinois	https://www.isbe.net/Pages/Standards-Courses.aspx
Indiana	https://www.in.gov/doe/students/indiana-academic-standards/
Iowa	https://iowacore.gov/standards/iowa-core-standards
Kansas	https://www.ksde.org/Agency/Division-of-Learning-Services/Career-Standards-and-Assessment-Services/CSAS-Home/Curricular-Standards
Kentucky	https://kystandards.org/home/ky-acad-standards/
Louisiana	https://www.louisianabelieves.com/resources/library/academic-standards
Maine	https://www.maine.gov/doe/learning/content
Maryland	https://marylandpublicschools.org/about/Pages/DCIPL/index.aspx
Massachusetts	https://www.doe.mass.edu/frameworks/current.html
Michigan	https://www.michigan.gov/mde/services/academic-standards
Minnesota	https://education.mn.gov/mde/dse/stds/

State/Territory	Course of Study URL
Mississippi	https://www.mdek12.org/OAE/college-and-career-readiness-standards
Missouri	https://dese.mo.gov/college-career-readiness/curriculum/missouri-learning-standards
Montana	https://opi.mt.gov/Educators/Teaching-Learning/K-12-Content-Standards
Nebraska	https://www.education.ne.gov/contentareastandards/
Nevada	https://doe.nv.gov/Standards_and_Instructional_Support/
New Hampshire	https://www.education.nh.gov/who-we-are/division-of-learner-support/bureau-of-instructional-support/career-and-college-ready-standards
New Jersey	https://www.nj.gov/education/cccs/2020/
New Mexico	https://webnew.ped.state.nm.us/bureaus/instructional-materials/new-mexico-content-standards/
New York	http://www.nysed.gov/curriculum-instruction
North Carolina	https://www.dpi.nc.gov/districts-schools/classroom-resources/academic-standards/standard-course-study
North Dakota	https://www.nd.gov/dpi/districtsschools/k-12-education-content-standards
Ohio	https://education.ohio.gov/Topics/Learning-in-Ohio/OLS-Graphic-Sections/Learning-Standards
Oklahoma	https://sde.ok.gov/oklahoma-academic-standards
Oregon	https://www.oregon.gov/ode/educator-resources/standards/pages/default.aspx
Pennsylvania	https://www.education.pa.gov/Teachers%20-%20Administrators/Curriculum/Pages/default.aspx
Rhode Island	https://www.ride.ri.gov/InstructionAssessment/ContentStandards.aspx
South Carolina	https://ed.sc.gov/instruction/early-learning-and-literacy/early-learning/standards/
South Dakota	https://doe.sd.gov/contentstandards/
Tennessee	https://www.tn.gov/education/instruction/academic-standards.html
Texas	https://tea.texas.gov/academics/curriculum-standards
Utah	https://www.schools.utah.gov/curr/utahcorestandards
Vermont	https://education.vermont.gov/student-learning/content-areas
Virginia	https://www.doe.virginia.gov/testing/index.shtml Links to individual subject areas provide detailed documents organized by grade-level and subject
Washington	https://www.k12.wa.us/student-success/learning-standards-instructional-materials
Washington, D.C.	https://dcps.dc.gov/publication/curriculum-dcps

State/Territory	Course of Study URL
West Virginia	https://wvde.us/tree/
Wisconsin	https://dpi.wi.gov/standards
Wyoming	https://edu.wyoming.gov/for-district-leadership/standards/
Territories and Other US School Systems	
American Samoa	https://www.doe.as/District/Department/14-Office-of-Curriculum -Instruction/1313-Content-Standards-Benchmarks.html
Guam	https://www.guamservicelearning.com/sites/default/files/guam_ contentstandardsfinaljune152010.pdf
Northern Mariana Islands	At the time of publication, an online source for this curriculum was unable to be located
Puerto Rico (Note: *These links reflect Language Arts and English only, not the entire curriculum.*)	https://dedigital.dde.pr/pluginfile.php/145102/mod_resource/content/6 /Est%C3%A1ndares%20y%20Expectativas%20Programa%20de%20Ingl %C3%A9s.pdf or https://www.uprm.edu/ppm/wp-content/uploads/sites/47/2018/01/ estandares_de_ingles_2014.pdf
US Virgin Islands	At the time of publication, an online source for this curriculum was unable to be located
Department of Defense Education Activity (DoDEA)	https://www.dodea.edu/Curriculum/index.cfm

How Are the Test Bank Items, Lessons, and Activities Classified?

In order to organize the lessons, activities, and Test Bank items in a manner that is most useful to educators from a variety of backgrounds, I have elected to use the Revised Bloom's Taxonomy of Cognitive Processes (Anderson & Krathwohl, 2001) as the metric. As many educators are aware, the original taxonomy (Bloom et al., 1956) had six levels, each of which described a level of cognitive thought. These levels were (from lowest level to highest level):

1. Knowledge
2. Comprehension
3. Application
4. Analysis
5. Synthesis
6. Evaluation

During the mid-1990s, however, former students of Benjamin Bloom reexamined his classic taxonomy and revised it. Their revision brought the names of the cognitive levels into grammatical parallelism and swapped the labels for the highest two levels, as well as more deeply examined the knowledge constructs that weren't heavily discussed by Bloom in his original work. The result of this revision is a knowledge/construct matrix that I've used to index the Test Bank items as well as activities within each lesson. The revised taxonomy (Anderson & Krathwohl, 2001) reads as follows:

1. Remembering
2. Understanding
3. Applying
4. Analyzing
5. Evaluating
6. Creating

The knowledge dimensions are being used as they are applied to the nature of the content being examined. In other words, if the information is factual in nature, or can be recalled or named, or can complete a statement that begins with the words "I know that . . .," that content is being classified as *factual knowledge*.

Conceptual knowledge is defined as the "knowledge of categories and classifications and the relationships between and among them . . ." (Anderson & Krathwohl, 2001). This may take the form of basic definitions (e.g., which of the following statements best describes the concept of Fair Use) or the form of application-level questions (e.g., using fair use as a context, determine whether the decision described in this scenario would be considered permissible).

Procedural knowledge questions and activities ask the learner to demonstrate the ability to do something, such as requesting permission to use copyrighted materials.

Finally, *metacognitive knowledge* questions are primarily embedded in the scenarios. They require the learner to demonstrate an awareness of the information that is provided or omitted from a scenario or to describe a decision-making scheme to make a desired determination. These questions allow the learner to demonstrate to the teacher an awareness of not only how information is interrelated throughout the scenario but also how that information is used by the learner in a thinking process.

Every effort has been made to ensure that each item is appropriately formatted to be useful as either a pre- or a post-test item. Individual instructors may find that some items are more useful in one setting than the other; you should feel free to use items in the manner that is most useful to you. Some types of items are represented by multiple choices, while others have a single item. The number of items in any one type is incidental and does not reflect the relative importance of that item type.

Each of the 231 items is classified according to the table below. Classifications for individual items are provided in Chapter 5's concordance for your reference and aid in selecting items for use with your students. The distribution of items within the context of Bloom's Taxonomy is shown on the next page.

The Knowledge Dimension	**The Cognitive Process Domain**					
	1. Remember (Retrieve relevant knowledge from long-term memory.)	**2. Understand** (Construct meaning from instructional messages, including oral, written, and graphic communication.)	**3. Apply** (Carry out or use a procedure in a given situation.)	**4. Analyze** (Break material into constituent parts and determine how parts relate to one another and to an over all structure or purpose.)	**5. Evaluate** (Make judgments based on criteria and standards.)	**6. Create** (Put elements together to form a coherent or functional whole; reorganize elements into a new pattern or structure.)
A. Factual (The basic elements students must know to be acquainted with a discipline or solve problems in it.)	49 items	50 items	13 items	2 items	1 item	2 items
B. Conceptual (The interrelationships among the basic elements within a larger structure that enable them to function together.)	3 items	40 items	16 items	12 items	16 items	3 items
C. Procedural (How to do something, methods of inquiry, and criteria for using skills, algorithms, techniques, and methods.)	0 items	0 items	0 items	7 items	1 item	7 items
D. Metacognitive (Knowledge of cognition in general as well as awareness and knowledge of one's own cognition.)	0 items	1 item	1 item	0 items	0 items	7 items

Based on the taxonomy table (Anderson & Krathwohl, 2001, pp. 28, 29, and 31)

In addition to the Bloom Classification code shown in the concordance, each item is associated with the lesson or lessons for which it might be used.

Should you wish to explore the relationship between the levels associated with the revised taxonomy, you may find the representation that Heer (2021) created useful to explore. His work is also available in text-only and responsive design formats on the Iowa State University Center for Excellence in Learning and Teaching website, Revised Bloom's Taxonomy (http://www.celt.iastate.edu/teaching-resources/effective-practice/revised-blooms-taxonomy/).

Where Are Supplemental Resources Located?

Throughout Chapter 2, you will see references to items within the "resources" section of individual lesson plans. Items in the resources section of the lesson plans can be found on the companion website for the book at https://bloomsbury.pub/teaching-copyright. Except as otherwise noted on the file or item itself, all items on the companion website are for your personal instructional use only. A mouse icon (see the icon next to this paragraph) will indicate resources and files found on the companion website.

The companion website contains the following types of files:

- **Starter Slides**: I have created skeleton PowerPoint™ files that include a basic structure that you can revise and customize for your personal instructional use.
- **Scaffolds**: Several of the appendices are printed versions of scaffolds and other tools that you may find useful, particularly for teaching students how to analyze copyright problems and scenarios. Full size, reproduceable versions of these scaffolds are available for your personal instructional use. Some scaffolds are also Creative Commons licensed. If applicable, you will find relevant licensing statements on the document itself.
- **Objective Item Test Bank**: In Chapter 3, I've included a set of questions that you are welcome to use to create tests or quizzes for your students. The companion website contains a file that is formatted to be used within common learning management systems such as Canvas or Moodle. This file includes a set of distractors and the correct answer for each item.
- **Scenario Bank, Annotated**: In Chapter 3, I've included a set of brief scenarios that you can modify for use as practice or test items. They represent a variety of potential situations. The companion website contains a file of annotated extended scenarios that correlate with the brief scenarios in the printed text. The annotations include the affected rights of the copyright holder, the types of infringement represented, key concepts represented, and suggestions to make them simpler or more complex, as the needs of your learners dictate.

Terminology and Acronyms Found in This Book

Throughout this text, I've used the terms "student(s)" and "learner(s)" to indicate the recipients of the lessons. You should not infer any meaning based on which of these terms I use. Also, you will notice that I've used acronyms at times to refer to guidelines, laws, organizations, or other commonly shortened terms. Those acronyms are all defined in the glossary, rather than spelling them out at the first usage. As acronyms may be used in several different lessons, placing the long version of them in the glossary is a more efficient manner to communicate what they mean.

2 Lessons Organized by Topic

You will find fourteen different lessons in this chapter. The first one is the most broad, as it represents a traditional interactive lecture format of direct instruction. The other thirteen lessons are designed to focus on one of eight specific aspects of copyright. While some topics contain a single lesson, others are broken into sub-topics, each of which corresponds to one lesson, resulting in more than one lesson in that topic. Within each lesson you will find suggested readings for learners, suggested directions to learners when appropriate for specific activities, and suggestions for how to modify the lessons to make them appropriate for learners of different skill levels. Some areas of differentiation within the lesson plan may occur in:

- Preparatory readings assigned to students
- Vocabulary level of instructional materials
- Bloom's Taxonomy level of target learning goals
- Complexity of test item and/or scenario
- Other areas as appropriate

Topics Covered:

1. What is copyright?
2. What is Fair Use?
3. How do licenses influence how I am permitted to use copyrighted materials?
4. What exceptions to the copyright law affect my teaching/learning?
5. How do I determine whether what I want to do/use is permissible?
6. What are the important laws and guidelines that affect my use of copyrighted materials?
7. What significant court cases have influenced copyright law?

Lesson Template

The following template is used to organize information about the lesson ideas. You should feel free to modify the specifics of content within the sections to meet your specific needs. When possible, suggestions for modifications will be provided to guide your decision-making process. The template includes information about the contents that you will find within each section of the plan.

Title/Topic

Each lesson will have either a title or a broad topic that describes it. Titles are used only to differentiate one lesson from another, and are not in any way indicative of what may be appropriate for you to title the lesson for your students or in your lesson planning documents that you may submit to your administration.

Approximate Length of Lesson/Topic

Each lesson will have an estimated time needed to complete the activities as written. These estimates are broadly determined and may easily be modified to reflect the needs of your particular students. Younger or more novice learners will commonly need more time for activities than older or more accomplished learners, especially those activities that require collaboration, discussion, or decision making.

Intended Audience

The intended audience for each lesson will be described in terms of expertise in learning (novice vs. accomplished) as well as reading levels. You should use your professional judgement in determining whether any one individual lesson or activity is appropriate for the students you are teaching.

Learning Goals

Each lesson will have learning goals that are written using the style recommended by Zook (2001). **The internal capability verb is bolded in each learning goal**.

Materials/Resources/Suggested Reading(s)

Reading(s)

Suggested reading options will be listed in either a list or table format. Suggested readings may take the form of textbook chapters, online documents, or other appropriate sources of information.

Resources

Links to online documents, tools, or other ancillary information will be provided in this section. Some teachers may find resources to also work as "readings" for their students; others may not. In general, I have categorized things like online games, tools where teachers can create items for use within lessons (card games, worksheets, etc.), and videos or animations that may be useful in the direct instruction or review for students as a resource rather than a reading.

Materials

Items that **teachers will need to gather or may choose to gather** for each lesson will be listed in this section. Commonly found items in most learning environments, such as writing surfaces and utensils, or display/white boards, are assumed to be available in each learning environment as appropriate. The assumption that these materials are ubiquitously present results in reference being made to them in the procedures section of each lesson.

Procedures/Activity

Activity Summary

A short overview of the lesson activities is provided in this section. The description is high level and does not contain small details for the implementation of the lesson. The activity summary is useful for teachers by providing information that they may use to verify the estimated time for the length of the lesson, especially as it might be modified to more appropriately meet the learning needs of the specific class in front of them at any one time.

Activity Preparation

Students

Activities, readings, or other tasks that **students should do prior to the implementation of the lesson.** Some teachers might refer to these sorts of activities as "pre-homework," while others may not have a special name for them. Teachers should feel free to assign these tasks in a way that works best for their own classrooms, whether that means students will complete them prior to the lesson or that a period of time during regular instructional time will be provided for students to complete the tasks.

Teacher

Tasks that the teacher will need to complete in order to implement the suggested activity procedures of the lesson. Common tasks include the gathering of items listed in the materials section of the lesson plan, arranging the classroom furniture if needed or customizing the starter slides that might be used in a lesson.

Environment

Special **environmental modifications** that might be needed for lessons. MOST lessons will not require special environmental or classroom modifications. Teachers should feel free to consider any suggestions in this section within the totality of their classroom and implement, revise, or discard them as appropriate.

Activity Procedures

Step-by-step description that teachers can follow to implement the lesson. Special issues and considerations that are relevant to lessons are also provided here. Specific concerns that teachers should keep at the forefront of their minds while teaching are also placed in this section.

This book was written under the assumption that those using the lessons possess reasonable management skills for classroom culture, so will not belabor issues such as behavior. However, as readers' experience in teaching is likely to vary, some experienced teachers may find the procedures section to be more detailed than they would otherwise prefer. Those teachers are encouraged to use the procedures as a guide for their own implementation of the lessons. Less experienced teachers may find the step-by-step procedures helpful as they organize their teaching time.

Assessment and Evaluation Suggestions

Suggestions have been provided for measuring student mastery of the learning goals listed at the beginning of each lesson. Sometimes, more than one option is listed. Teachers should feel free to use any, all, or none of the suggestions provided. Again, more experienced teachers may find that these suggestions are extremely detailed, while less experienced teachers may find them to be quite useful.

References to the Test Bank and the Scenario Bank are listed in this section of the lesson plan. Access to the Test and Scenario Bank is available via the companion site for this text found at https://bloomsbury.pub/teaching-copyright.

Suggested Scoring Criteria

Some lessons may have assessment and evaluation suggestions that lend themselves to atypical scoring criteria. Therefore, suggested "pass rates" for objective item tests or quizzes have not been provided. Those thresholds are much more appropriately decided by teachers, using guidelines of their own institutions as a basis for their decision-making processes.

Sample Rubric for Subjectively Scored Projects

Some assessment and evaluation suggestions will have students creating projects or products that are typically scored on subjective scales, rather than objective ones such as 75 percent = pass or 9/12 points = pass.

In these subjectively scored situations, you will find a set of guiding criteria that teachers can use to be the basis for rubric scoring. Teachers are strongly encouraged to customize the rubric suggestions so that they are most useful to them and their students.

You will also find an operational explanation for the rubric column headings for those rubrics that are present. See the next section for details of that explanation.

	Excellent	Good	Poor	Missing

Rubric Heading Explanations

Research papers, projects, and other written work are, by nature, holistic endeavors. By that, I mean that the reader can't "pull out" the grammar, or the introduction, and have the remainder of the assignment be complete. That's what allows readers of novels to say "the book was good" or "the book was scary" or "I didn't like it" and refer to the entire title, rather than just a single chapter or introduction. On the other hand, teachers must have a way of assigning credit to the work that each student does for project-based assignments. Teachers must also have a way to help students identify their strengths and weaknesses within a project according to the expectations and criteria that the teacher established when it was assigned.

That being said, each section of the sample rubrics for suggested projects or assessment items contained in the lessons and Test Bank can be used as a holistic guide in the assessment of student work. To reduce student work to a frequency count of spelling errors, citations, or other artificial methods of evaluating projects would trivialize the importance of being able to craft a cohesive paper, project, or assignment.

Therefore, I have established the following operational definitions as a guide to holistic grading of student project work:

1. Teachers should answer each question asked in the rubric with either a "yes" or "no."
2. If the answer is "no," the work is **MISSING**. Students would receive no credit for that particular question or criterion. Alternatively, teachers could establish a "lowest possible points" value for items that are deemed missing from a project.
3. If the answer is "yes," teachers should ask which one of the following statements is true:
   - "Yes," but it was **POOR** work. Students would receive credit according to the point-value or grading convention established by the teacher.
   - "Yes," and it was **GOOD** work. Students would receive credit according to the point-value or grading convention established by the teacher.
   - "Yes," and it was **EXCELLENT** work. Students would receive credit according to the point-value or grading convention established by the teacher.

There will be times when this might cause the math of the assignment to get quite detailed, but it is the most efficient way that I have found over the years to provide feedback and assessment to students on projects that are creative/written/non-test in nature.

The "Missing/Poor/Good/Excellent" naming convention is one that I use frequently as a grading mechanism. It is helpful, then, that everyone understands how I use these terms. Please refer to the following chart for my operational definitions for these terms:

Missing	• The item or criterion is completely absent from the project. • The section or element is not addressed (in multi-part assignments).
Poor	The item or criterion is present, but . . . • is defined, used, or implemented incorrectly or inadequately. • there are so many errors that the reader's understanding is inhibited. • lengthy and/or involved conversations between the student and instructor would be required in order for adequate corrections to be made to bring the quality of the work up to "Good." This meeting would have to be via voice or face-to-face to ensure adequate understanding of the nature of the problem as well as the requirements for correcting the work.
Good *MOST work tends to fall into this category*	The item or criterion is present, and . . . • is used or defined properly. • the student has provided sufficient numbers/quantity to meet the basic requirements of the project, section, or element. • the reader can understand the student's work with little difficulty. The nature of the work meets the MINIMUM requirements of the project, section, or element. While errors may be present, they are of a superficial nature and would require little more than editing or a brief exchange between the instructor and the student. Email would be sufficient to communicate the requirements for correcting the work. The reader/evaluator might make recommendations or comments to improve the work, but they would serve to expand the quality of the work rather than correct deficiencies.
Excellent	The item or criterion is present, and . . . • is used or defined properly, and with particular insight or creativity. • in situations of quantity, the student has exceeded the basic requirements of the project, section, or element. • the reader can understand the student's work with no difficulty. The nature of the work **EXCEEDS** the minimum requirements of the project, section, or element. The reader/evaluator might make comments on the student's work of a thought-provoking nature, or as asides to the work. The work could stand on its own, except for stylistic differences in formatting, presentation, and/or voice (in cases of narrative).

By all means, you should use a grading convention or set of rubric criteria that match your teaching philosophy and the needs of your instructional goals. I offer these suggestions as an option that has worked well for me in the past as well as leaving room for personalization on an as-desired basis.

Now that the structure of the lesson plans and the naming conventions for rubric headings are clear, you are ready to explore the lessons in the seven different topics. After the first lesson, the interactive lecture, each topic will be indicated with "Topic: *Topic title listed here.*" The beginning of each lesson will be indicated with "Lesson #: *Lesson title listed here.*" These indicators will help you remain oriented as you explore the text.

Lesson 1: Comprehensive Interactive Lecture (Copyright, Fair Use, Public Domain, Plagiarism, Exclusive Rights of Copyright Holder)

Approximate Length of Lesson/Topic

60–120 minutes

Intended Audience

HS–Adult

Learning Goals

- Learners will be able to **apply** the concept of Fair Use to authentic scenarios.
- Learners will be able to **identify** the six exclusive rights of a copyright owner.
- Learners will be able to **classify** items as either copyrighted, trademarked, or patented.
- Learners will be able to **classify** items as either Public Domain or Protected by Copyright.
- Learners will be able to **discriminate** between Plagiarism and Copyright Infringement.
- Learners will be able to **define**:
    - Fair Use
    - Public Domain
    - Plagiarism
    - Copyright
    - Six exclusive rights of a copyright owner

Materials/Resources/Suggested Reading(s)

Reading(s)

The following suggested readings correspond to popular texts about copyright law. The readings are organized by broad topics addressed in the learning goals for the interactive lecture.

	Simpson and Wolf (2021)	Crews (2020)	Russell (2023)	Other
Copyright Law Basics	Chapter 1 (pp. 1–40)	Part I (pp. 3–50)	Chapters 1 and 2 (pp. 1–38)	
Fair Use	Chapter 4 (pp. 55–72)—fair use "Proper"; p. 80—details of Kastenmeier Report (the print guidelines); pp. 103–109—details of A/V guidelines; pp. 137–140—details of music guidelines; pp. 153–156—details of multimedia guidelines; pp. 169–175—details of the TEACH Act (Distance Education)	Part III (p. 95–150)—for a complete reading of fair use; for LG1: Chapters 11 and 12 (pp. 103–126)	Chapter 3 (pp. 39–56)	
Public Domain	Chapter 2 (pp. 41–44)	Part I (pp. 1–22)—for a complete reading of the extent of copyright and works that are protected; for LG4: Chapters 4 and 5 (pp. 33–50)	Broadly, Chapter 2 (pp. 15–38)	
Plagiarism	pp. 216; 247–248			
Copyright Exclusive Rights	pp. 2–9	Part II (pp. 51–94)—for a complete reading of the rights of copyright owners; for LG2: Chapters 7 and 8 (pp. 61–82)	pp. 18–19	

Resources

- Lecture starter slides
- Plicker cards and questions (see Appendix L for additional suggested Plicker questions)
- Poll everywhere questions (see Appendix L for additional suggested Poll Everywhere questions)
- Copyright scenarios

Materials

- "Stoplight" Cards (teacher created)
    - Green—copyright
    - Yellow—trademark
    - Red—patent

Procedures/Activity

Activity Summary

One of the most common methods for delivering instruction is the lecture. However, lectures are frequently "tuned out" by the target audience because of the unidirectional nature of the communication. The interactive lecture format can provide the benefit of student–student interaction and student–instructor interaction while also maximizing the use of a limited time for the instructional activity.

Poll Everywhere and Plickers are two tools that can be used to formatively assess whether students are grasping the concepts being presented. Both allow anonymous responses, thus removing the stigma of "wrong answers" from the activity. The anonymous responses also tend to prompt discussion about the question/topic at hand, thus allowing the teacher to provide specific corrections to misunderstandings among the students.

Activity Preparation

Students

Complete readings as assigned by the instructor. Be prepared to participate in the lecture by applying the concepts addressed in the readings to questions and scenarios within the lecture.

Teacher

- Practice with the Plicker and Poll Everywhere tools. Select one to use for your own lesson, particularly if your instructional time is shorter rather than longer. For longer sessions, using both tools is possible, especially as the specific kinds of questions that each can handle are quite different.
- Create your Poll Everywhere questions or Plicker questions inside your accounts for those tools. See Appendix L for recommended questions.
- Print the appropriate set of Plicker cards (if appropriate).

Environment

The free account in Poll Everywhere permits up to forty responses per poll (question) using the educator's version of the tool. Plickers provide up to sixty-three Plicker cards for printing. Depending on whether the teacher elects to have students respond individually or in pairs, the largest target audience could contain as many as 126 learners using Plickers and 80 using Poll Everywhere. A small seminar size audience of approximately ten learners is the smallest that would best accommodate the interactive lecture. Many fewer than ten learners would likely benefit more from an interactive workshop design for the same content.

Any type of indoor learning space will work, as long as the instructor is able to scan the Plicker cards (if appropriate) with a smart device. Plickers provides a large format set of cards that should be used in venues much larger than a standard classroom-sized room. Lighting is important, as in order for the Plicker cards to be read, there must be sufficient lighting for the smart device's camera to "see" the cards.

Appropriate equipment:

- Computer and projector/screen/interactive whiteboard
- Smart device (for scanning Plicker cards)
- Printed Plicker cards (if appropriate)
- Learner owned/borrowed devices (phones, tablets, computers, etc.) if using Poll Everywhere
- Reliable internet connection

Activity Procedures

1. **Introduce learners to the use of the tools that will be used during the lecture**. Most students will have had some experience with Poll Everywhere's method of data collection, as it's similar to the "voting" that is done on television shows. However, students may not have experience with Plicker cards. Be sure to provide practice with the question types that will be used throughout the presentation. Both tools permit the creation of multiple choice/true-false questions. Plickers are limited to questions having four distractors. Poll Everywhere, however, has several different types of questions that can be created. Some of these questions are open ended, while others permit clicking on images. Respondents can also "vote up" some responses in some question types in Poll Everywhere.
2. **Deliver the lecture**. Structure your lecture delivery in a manner that best fits your instructional style. I've had the most success with a distributed practice method of interactive lecture delivery. By distributing formative questions throughout the lecture (approximately every four to six slides), I am able to gauge the level of understanding in the audience members.
   - **a)** Use the starter slides to begin building your lecture. Note the use of builds and animations to draw learner attention to important information. Also note the need to find relevant images for your set of learners.
   - **b)** A note about timing: the starter slides provided are intended to fill a two-hour lecture-like period of time. Feel free to sub-divide the lecture into smaller parts to fit your instructional time frame.
   - **c)** Personalize your lecture slides with links/addresses to local sources of help and information.
3. **Assess immediate and long-term retention of lecture content**. See chart below for suggestions.

Assessment and Evaluation Suggestions

Unlike more formal ways of assessing student mastery of content, the embedded Plicker questions in the presentation for this lesson are informal ways to determine whether students are making adequate progress toward their understanding of the concepts being taught. Each of the embedded questions within the presentation has correct, and in some cases "more or less" correct, answers. The questions and answers are provided here for your convenience. As they function as informal assessment items, they do not appear in the Test Bank. Select objective items from the Test Bank for use in a formal written test/quiz.

Practice Plicker Questions

Six Rights

Which one of these is NOT one of the exclusive rights of a copyright holder?

A. Right of reproduction

B. Right of public display

C. Right of monetary gain

D. Right of distribution

Answer:

C: Copyright owners do not have the right to actually gain any money from their work. They can only control one of six actions: reproduction, distribution, adaptation, public display, public performance, and public performance by digital audio transmission.

Preamble Recitation

As a part of the annual convocation, the ROTC unit recites the preamble to the US Constitution as the opening activity/welcome for the students.

Is this activity permissible under the copyright law?

A. Yes

B. No

Answer:

A: The preamble is a part of a federal document, and therefore is in the public domain. It was also written well before January 1, 1928, and therefore, if it were not a federal document, it would also be part of the public domain on that basis.

Webpage Usage

You want to post an informative news article (related to your department's mission) on your department's webpage (so that current and future visitors to your page can read it right from your page without having to download anything) and have written to the publisher for permission to do so. It has been four weeks since you requested permission, and you have not heard anything Do you post the article? Which of the following choices is the best/safest option?

A. Yes, without hesitation.

B. No, no way!

C. No, but I post a synopsis and citation.

D. Yes, but if I hear from the publisher that the answer is "no," I will take it down.

Answer:
B: This is the safest, but it also is the most restrictive.
C: This is a very safe option, as well as representing knowledge of fair use.

Student Publication

In your work with the student grievance committee, you hear that in a college class about the "methods of teaching" requires students to create lessons and lesson ideas on a variety of topics. Students are mandated/required to submit those ideas for grading via a published and publicly accessible website owned/managed by the professor. Is the publication requirement of the assignment a copyright infringement?

A. Yes, absolutely, no other way to look at it.

B. No, it's perfectly fine.

C. No, but it might be problematic according to some other law.

D. Yes, but there might be a way students could protect their work.

Answer:
D: This is the most correct answer. The intent of having student work published for peer review within the purview of a course is laudable. However, having that work published on an open website as a required aspect of the course is troublesome. Many learning management systems have tools/features that allow this sort of sharing of student work in a way that maintains the privacy of students as well as permitting them to control the use of their work in terms of the six exclusive rights of a copyright holder.

HR Workshop Materials

As part of the transition to a new student information system, you ask a member of the faculty to design, develop, and implement the training for all personnel who will access the new system. You pay the faculty member for her work above and beyond her regular salary. When the initial training during transition is complete, your office asks her to turn over all training documents that she created so that they can be used by members of the HR training staff for the onboarding of future employees. She declines to share the documentation, asserting that she is the copyright owner and should be able to keep them. Is she correct?

A. Yes

B. No

C. Maybe, I need more information to decide (the information I need is: ____)

Answer:

C: There isn't quite enough information in the scenario to make a "for sure" determination about the request. It might be that the work is considered to be a work made for hire, but in order to qualify as this, the institution would have to have signed documentation to that effect prior to the work starting. Also, while you may have paid the designer above and beyond her salary, her contract might have stipulations that control what work is considered to be a normal part of her job. So, you'd likely need to see if there are any policies at the institution level that would govern this sort of extra work for faculty members, in addition to finding out whether there was a separate signed work-made-for-hire contract on file for the project.

Topic: What Is Copyright?

Lesson 2: How Do I Keep Someone Else from Using My "Stuff"? (Understanding the Basics of Copyright)

Approximate Length of Lesson/Topic

60–75 minutes

Intended Audience

Learners of all ages and levels of experience

Learning Goals

- Learners will be able to **describe** the types of works that are eligible for copyright protection.
- Learners will be able to **discriminate** between items that are eligible for protection by copyright, trademark, and patent.
- Learners will be able to **label** items as copyrightable or not copyrightable.
- Learners will be able to **name** the six exclusive rights of the copyright owner.
- Learners will be able to **state** the purpose of copyright protection using their own words.

Materials/Resources/Suggested Reading(s)

Reading(s)

	Simpson and Wolf (2021)	**Crews (2020)**	**Russell (2023)**	**Butler (2004)**
Copyright Basics	Chapter 1: 1–40	Part I: pp. 3–50 for a broad treatment of the basics of the law	Chapters 1 and 2 (pp. 1–38)	p. 7
Public Domain	Chapter 2: pp. 41–44	Chapter 5: pp. 39–50 for focused treatment of Public Domain	Broadly, Chapter 2 (pp. 15–38)	
Rights of Copyright Owners	pp. 2–8	Chapter 8: pp. 73–82	pp. 18–19	

Resources

- Example of how choreography is written: https://dance.mandigould.com/choreography/

Materials

- Teachers will need to collect images of a variety of items that represent copyrightable and non-copyrightable materials.

  Images of copyrightable items include:

  - Literary, musical, and dramatic works:

    Books, text, musical scores, play scripts, movie scripts ("near hits"), software code snippets, database-held data ("far hits"), etc.

  - Pantomimes and choreographic works:

    Images of mimes (indirect representation of pantomimes), images of well-known ballet performances such as *The Nutcracker*, *Swan Lake*, etc. (See linked article in "Resources" for an example of how choreography is recorded in written format.)

  - Pictorial, graphic, and sculptural works:

    Images of well-known artwork, examples of well-known photographs, examples of recognizable graphic work, including murals, and images of sculptures. Be sure to collect both well-known and novel (unique, unknown) examples as pertains to the students in your class.

  - Motion pictures and other audiovisual works:

    Images of movie posters, links to online displays of movie trailers, images of multimedia presentations such as presentations from your own teaching (near hits), images or links to student-created multimedia projects (far hit).

  - Sound recordings:

    Links to "records" of songs, images of songs recorded by artists well known to your students, images of "record" covers, or "CD" covers of concerts.

  - Architectural works:

    Images of famous buildings, images of architectural drawings (a.k.a., blueprints).

  Images of non-copyrightable items include:

  - Commonly known items that would be recognized as "inventions":

    Cars, gadgets, medicines, etc. (near hits for "non-copyrightable" works).

  - Representations of algorithms:

    Netflix/YouTube recommendations, images containing text such as "you might also like," etc.

  - Factual information:

    Black line outline maps of states/countries, lists of simple facts such as states/capitals, multiplication tables, etc.

  - Logos

- Common phrases:

  "Happy Birthday," "Get up and go!", "Just Do It!", etc.

- Symbols:

  @, ©, &, etc.

- Everyday objects:

  Furniture, clothing, items found in nature, etc.

- Something not created by a human

Procedures/Activity

Activity Summary

Using a matched example/non-example strategy (see below for details), teachers lead students to recognize items that are eligible for copyright protection. The goal of this guided activity is for students to be able to differentiate between copyrighted and non-copyrighted items. Non-copyrighted items might still be protected by other forms of intellectual property such as trademark or patent.

Next, students will participate in a discussion concerning the six exclusive rights of the copyright owner. This discussion will use previously identified item images of copyrighted materials to describe the types of uses of their created materials that copyright owners would want or need to control.

Finally, students will derive the purpose of copyright protection in their own words as a part of small group discussions. Alternatively, students will describe how the stated purpose of copyright protection is a benefit to members of a community or society.

Activity Preparation

Students

No special preparation by students is necessary. This is an introductory lesson, so students need not do any special reading, especially younger students. Teachers of older, more advanced students might find assigning introductory reading to be useful in order to jumpstart the exploratory and guided activities.

Teacher

- Locate images representing different types of copyrighted and non-copyrighted materials. See "Materials" for examples of types of images that would be appropriate to use.
- If desired, mount images on card stock to create flashcards or similar items.
- If desired, import images into electronic media such as interactive display board presentations or other electronic presentations.

Environment

No special environmental preparation is needed beyond a teacher's normal arrangement for presentations and small group activities.

Activity Procedures

Matched Example/Non-Example Procedures

1. Begin lesson by telling students that you are going to show them examples of a mystery type of "thing" or "object" or "item."
2. Display three to five copyrightable items that you've collected, allowing enough time for students to thoroughly examine the image or item. Precede display of each item by saying, "This IS an example of the mystery type," or something similar. If students have questions about what the image represents, provide answers, but do not reveal that it's copyrightable.
3. After each item is displayed, place it in a location where students will be able to keep seeing it, such as another part of a magnetic board, or, if using an interactive display board, in a separate section of the display.
4. Display two or three non-copyrightable items that you've collected, allowing enough time for students to thoroughly examine the image or item. Precede the display of these items by saying, "This is NOT an example of the mystery type," or something similar. If students have questions about what the image represents, provide answers, but do not reveal that it's not copyrightable.
5. Display a new image and ask students whether they think the item IS or is NOT an example of the mystery type. Confirm or correct their guess.
6. Repeat step 5 two or three times. If you find that students are consistently accurate in their guesses, prompt them to tell how they are making their decisions. Guide students to realize that all examples of the mystery type are creative in nature and have an author or creator that is a person/human.
7. If you find that students are consistently inaccurate in their guesses, guide them in describing the similarities that members of the mystery type have, such as being creative works and having an author/creator that is a person. Also, have students compare the set of non-examples with examples so that they can recognize the absence of creativity, creation by a person. Also, non-examples might have very different similarities within the group, such as being a process or invention (patent protected) or representing a particular commercial product (trademark protected), or being neither of these (useful objects, nature items).
8. Repeat step 5 until students are consistently able to place new objects into the appropriate category at least four times in a row.

9. Give students time to brainstorm possible names for the mystery type. Share the names with the group. If any are close to the idea/name of "copyrighted," identify it as being the name of the mystery type. If none of the ideas are close to the idea/word "copyrighted," introduce "copyrighted" as the name of the mystery type and draw connections between that term and the terms provided by students.

Six Exclusive Rights of the Copyright Holder

1. Decide whether your students will respond more effectively to a hypothetical situation prompting their responses or to a straightforward statement that they will use to guide their discussions.
2. If using the hypothetical situation, introduce the following hypothetical to your students: "Imagine that you've written a book, painted a painting, composed a song [whichever would be most important to your students]. What would you be concerned about other people doing with that item? What would you want to prevent people from being able to do with your item in order to maintain your ability to keep creating other things like it? If you intend to make money from your item, do the types of things that other people can do with your item change from what you've already said?"
3. Moderate a group discussion around these questions. Alternatively, divide the class into smaller groups for each group to discuss them.
4. If using the straightforward statement, begin your discussion with the following: "When creative people write, compose, paint, draw, or engage in other types of creation for copyrightable works, they are invested in the work that they've done. They've spent time and energy and likely given up significant personal time to complete their creations. It's not unreasonable for them to want to be sure that their works are protected from certain types of uses. They might need to protect them to make money. They might need to protect them for entirely personal reasons."
5. Regardless of the approach, guide the discussion to eliciting the six types of actions/rights that copyright holders would want to protect:
    - Reproduction (copying)
    - Distribution ("passing around" or "giving out")
    - Adaptation (changing or altering)
    - Public Display (applies to static items, showing them off in public)
    - Public Performance (applies to things that happen over time such as singing, moving, etc., performing them in public)
    - Public Performance via Digital Audio Transmission (applies to digital versions of things that happen over time, such as songs, movies, audio books, etc., playing/showing them in public)

6. Teachers should be aware that the first three rights are usually fairly quickly identified by students. They are the easiest to understand.
7. The last three, the ones that begin with the word "public," tend to be a little trickier for some students to grasp. Key distinctions between them include the concepts of "public", "display," and "performance." Legal definitions for these terms can be found in the law; or a lay-person-friendly version can be found in the glossary at the end of this book.
8. Some teachers may find it more efficient to provide the names of the rights and guide students in their understanding of what they each mean.
9. Some students may benefit from creating their own icons to represent the six rights to aid in their memory of the names and what they signify. Teachers should use their judgement in deciding whether to implement the "create your own icon" or the provision of the names first strategy.

Purpose of Copyright

A note to teachers: The purpose of copyright law and protection is frequently misunderstood by members of the public. The stated purpose of copyright protection is written into the law itself, as to "promote the progress of science and useful arts, . . ." (The Heritage Foundation, 2024, Article 1, Section 8). For such a short phrase, the impact is huge. Because copyright's purpose is so frequently misunderstood, using a pro/con or advantage/disadvantage identification strategy works well to help students understand the purpose.

1. Establish a state of disequilibrium for your students by posing the following question: "If many people view copyright as a set of things that 'keeps us' or 'prevents us' from doing something, how is it that the stated purpose of it can be to 'promote the progress of science and useful arts'?"
2. Moderate a class discussion surrounding answers to the question you just posed. It is likely that the conversation will be slow to start, as students may be significantly confounded. Allow them plenty of time to think.
3. As students begin to respond, record their answers so that the whole class can see them. Paraphrase where necessary. Verify any paraphrasing with the contributor who made the original statement.
4. As the conversation progresses, guide students to shift their thinking in order to see the following connections:
    a. Progress can't be made when innovators and creators also can't count on their work being protected from misappropriation or abuse.

b. Protecting creative works provides a safe environment in which creators can express themselves, increasing the chances of innovation in the creative process.

c. Having protections spelled out in the law provides creative content creators with avenues to recoup damages if their work is used improperly.

5. Take care that if the conversation begins to include concepts such as "fairness" or "what if no one knows . . .?" (in relation to use of copyrighted materials), you point out that the purpose of the conversation is to understand the intended purpose of copyright and that discussion about exceptions to (students would say, "yeah, but what about when . . .") copyright law will be addressed in a different lesson. The lesson on fair use is a good next step if you find that your students' comments are trending in this direction.

Assessment and Evaluation Suggestions

Identifying copyrighted vs. non-copyrighted materials

First option: Select objective items from the Test Bank for use on a formal written test/quiz.
Second option: Create sorting activity that students complete. Possible formats for the sorting activity include:

- Mount images on card stock and have students physically sort into two piles, copyrighted/non-copyrighted.
- Create worksheet including images and have students write yes/no, copyrighted/not copyrighted as appropriate next to each image.
- Display images and have students hold up yes/no, red/green cards to indicate appropriate classification.

Third option: Provide several short scenarios to students describing the use of intellectual property. Have students underline/circle the copyrighted materials in the scenarios. Be sure that some scenarios include non-copyrighted materials. Students should correctly avoid marking non-copyrighted materials in the scenarios.

Six Exclusive Rights of the Copyright Owner

First option: Select objective items from Test Bank for use on a formal written test/quiz.
Second option: Select scenarios from Test Bank and have students mark (circle/underline) the action that represents one of the six exclusive rights, and then name the right that was marked.
Third option: Have students write examples of their personal uses of copyrighted materials that represent the six exclusive rights.
Fourth option: Have students write scenarios similar to those in the Test Bank that include a situation where one or more of the six rights is a part of the scenario.

Stating the purpose of copyright in learners' own words

Ask students to write the purpose of copyright using their own words; words that a younger sibling would understand; words that a classmate would understand; words that a parent or another adult would understand.

Suggested Scoring Criteria

The original stated purpose of copyright is:

> . . . to promote the Progress of Science and useful Arts, by securing for limited times to authors and inventors the exclusive right to their respective writings and discoveries (U.S. Const. art I, §8).

Answers might include phrases such as:

. . . encourage people to write (or paint or create . . .)

. . . help science discover things

. . . protect people's art (or writing or creations . . .)

. . . give protection for short period of time

And similar phrases.

Answers should NOT include suggestions that copyright protects any sort of financial gain, or description of punishment or consequences of any sort.

Topic: What Is Fair Use?

Lesson 3: Do I Always Have to Get Permission to Borrow Someone Else's "Stuff"? (Understanding the Basics of Fair Use)

Approximate Length of Lesson/Topic

60–90 minutes

Intended Audience

Learners of all levels. The lesson can be adapted for more or less experienced learners by altering the scenarios that are used for the instruction and practice activities.

Learning Goals

- Learners will be able to **explain** the purpose of fair use.
- Learners will be able to **describe** fair use using their own words.
- Learners will be able to **name** the four tests of fair use.
- Learners will be able to **label** specific examples of copyrighted works being used as "fair" or "not fair" use.
- Learners will be able to apply the four tests of fair use within authentic scenarios.

Materials/Resources/Suggested Reading(s)

Reading(s)

	Simpson and Wolf (2021)	**Crews (2020)**	**Russell (2023)**	**Other**
Fair Use (general and K–12 perspective)	Chapter 4, pp. 55–70	Chapters 10–12, pp. 95–126	Chapter 3, pp. 39–56	Butler (2004): Chapter 2, pp. 15–20
Fair Use (particularly from higher education perspective)				Butler (2014): Chapter 2, pp. 13–18

Resources

- Copyright Card Game Scenario cards (https://copyrightliteracy.org/resources/copyright-the-card-game/) —Scroll to find the links to the US version of the game. An online version is also available, limited to UK copyright law, however.
- Scenarios from the Scenario Bank
- Gallery Walk Copyright Analysis Scaffold found in Appendix A
- Starter Slides—Fair Use
- Fair use informational website from University of Minnesota https://www.lib.umn.edu/copyright/fairuse
- Fair use evaluator tool(s):
  - Fair use evaluator from ALA—https://librarycopyright.net/resources/fairuse/index.php
  - Fair use checklist from Wayne State University—http://copyright.wayne.edu/checklist.php

Materials

- "Sticky" chart paper (if desired)
- Erasable markers (if desired)
- Magnet or sticky icons to indicate "yes," "no," "maybe" (if desired)

Procedures/Activity

Activity Summary

In this lesson, students will learn about the most widely applicable exception to the six exclusive rights of the copyright owner. They will understand and be able to describe, using their own words, the four conditions that must be met in order for the use of copyrighted materials to be considered "fair use."

Teachers will use the first part of the lesson to provide direct instruction to students regarding the purpose of fair use, as well as the four factors of fair use. The second part of the lesson serves as a practice venue in which students practice their ability to apply the four factors of fair use to authentic scenarios. Teachers may choose to use both options of practice, or only one, depending on the learning needs of their students and the time available to them in their classroom.

Part two of the lesson is a gallery walk activity in which students document their analysis efforts in order to gain feedback from the teacher as well as class peers. Using the Analysis Scaffold (available in Appendix A) gives students support while they conduct their initial analysis of scenarios.

Activity Preparation

Students

- Complete readings as directed by the teacher.
- Be able to name and identify the six exclusive rights of a copyright holder within scenario based examples.

Teacher

- Download, revise, and print Copyright the Card Game scenario cards if desired.
- Select, collate, and reproduce selected scenarios from the text Scenario Bank if desired.
- Download, reproduce, and distribute Analysis Scaffold from Appendix A if desired.
- Enlarge and reproduce Analysis Scaffold for use as documentation that the entire group/ class can see if desired.
- Download and customize Fair Use starter slides if desired.

Environment

- Gather and distribute appropriate gallery walk materials, if using. These include dry erase markers, chart paper, erasable surfaces for walls or desks, and similar items.
- No other special environmental preparations are required beyond the normal ones that teachers implement in their classrooms.

Activity Procedures

Direct Instruction

1. Review the six exclusive rights with students, emphasizing that ONLY the copyright owner is permitted to "do" those things or give permission to do the actions described by the exclusive rights.
2. If desired, have students identify the exclusive rights that are being performed in two or three authentic scenarios that you create or have chosen from the Scenario Bank.
3. Explain to students that the people who wrote the copyright law realized that there should be certain circumstances where copyright owners could not prevent others from using their works.
4. Guide students to understand that the reason for these EXCEPTIONS was to "promote the progress of science and useful arts" (from the previous lesson, "What Is Copyright?").
5. Encourage students to realize that because only certain circumstances permit users of copyrighted materials to use them without getting permission, having a set of rules in place to describe those circumstances is important.

6. Explain to students that the types of use that are permitted in these circumstances are collectively called "fair use."
7. Deliver presentation you've customized from the fair use starter slides.

Practice: Gallery Walk

Gallery walks are an effective strategy that instructors can use as practice activities or as formative assessment activities when they would like to encourage student engagement (Facing History & Ourselves, 2017). Typically, gallery walks comprise small groups of students working together to create informal records of their reactions and thoughts surrounding a concept, exhibit, or other type of evidence of their thinking.

Instructors should also remember that analyzing scenarios is a high-level cognitive demand skill that may require significant support or scaffolding in order for students to experience success. Exposing students to situations where they can apply their analysis skills with the support of peers and the teacher positions them for success in a risk-free environment.

The Gallery Walk activity has four portions. First, teachers should model the scenario analysis process, using a think-aloud process and documenting the results of their thinking using the Fair Use Analysis Scaffold from Appendix E.

1. Display (or distribute) a scenario that you've chosen. Try to choose one that is relatively straightforward in terms of the fair use issues described.
2. Using a pace that is appropriate for your learners, complete the Fair Use Analysis Scaffold for the sample scenario. Be sure to speak aloud as you consider the items on the scaffold, as you decide between multiple choices, and as you make final decisions for each of the decision points on the scaffold.
3. As you progress through your documentation, you may wish to elicit student hypotheses about the information that should be entered for the various fields in the scaffold.
4. When you've completed the entire scaffold, be sure to summarize the rationale you used to make each of the fair use determinations at the end of the scaffold.

Second, in small groups, students will practice their analysis skills in a structured fashion, rotating to a new scenario at each step of the analysis process, using the Gallery Walk organizational structure.

1. Divide the group/class into small groups. Group sizes of five or fewer tend to be the most productive, but teachers should use their professional judgement in making group size decisions.
2. Distribute one scenario to each group.
3. Distribute Fair Use Analysis Scaffolds to each group. Depending on the specific learning environment that you are using, you may find that electronic display boards, erasable

surfaces such as white/glass boards or tables, or "sticky" chart paper are effective ways to display the scenarios and scaffolds for each group.

4. Direct students to read their scenario as a group, using whatever highlighting/annotating strategy they prefer to mark important elements in the scenario.
5. Then, have each group complete the first two sections of the scaffold. Encourage them to annotate their scenarios in meaningful ways so that they have evidence for their decision, especially for the "Factor 1" portion of the scaffold.
6. Next, have each group rotate to a different scenario in the room. Allow time for the groups to read the new scenarios as well as to revise the top portion of the scaffold if they feel it is warranted.
7. Direct students to complete the "Factor 2" portion of the scaffold. Encourage them to annotate the scenarios so that there is evidence for their decision.
8. Repeat the "rotate, read/revise, complete scaffold" for the "Factor 3" and "Factor 4" sections of the Scaffold.
9. Direct students to return to their original scaffold. Allow enough time for them to re-read the scenario as well as review the work of their peers during the rotation portion of the activity.
10. Direct students to complete the final section of the Scaffold. Remind them that they should be prepared to share their conclusions and the rationale for each conclusion with their peers.
11. Allow time for each group to report back to the large group with the results of their final conclusions. Guide the discussion so that students are aware of misconceptions, accurate thinking, and other refinements that are needed in order to solidify their analysis efforts.

Third, in small groups, students will apply their analysis skills to scenarios, one scenario per group, documenting the results of their thinking using the Fair Use Analysis Scaffold.

1. Distribute new scenarios and new copies of the Fair Use Analysis Scaffold (if needed) to students in small groups.
2. Direct each small group to complete a fair use analysis from start to finish, using the same scenario for all steps, no rotating.
3. Allow sufficient time for all groups to complete their analysis.
4. Remind students to document their decision making using the Fair Use Analysis Scaffold.

Lastly, students will provide feedback to their peers' analyses on a rotating basis, using the Gallery Walk organizational structure.

1. Ensure that each of the small groups has documented their analysis efforts and final decisions for their scenarios.

2. Direct students to rotate to another group's documentation of their analysis.
3. Each group should read the scenario at the new location. Then, they should review the analysis on display. Using the marking system of your choice (magnets/colored markers/etc.), the group should come to consensus as to the accuracy of the analysis on display. Accuracy levels can be binary (agree/disagree) or can be multi-leveled (yes/maybe/no or similar). Tell each group to be sure that they document the rationale they use for their review decision.
4. Repeat the rotate/review process at least two more times.
5. Once each group has had the opportunity to review three or more of their classmates' analyses, bring the class together as a whole and have each group summarize the findings of their original scenarios.
6. Be sure to guide the discussion to clarify points of confusion or incorrect assumptions, as well as to highlight accurate thinking and decision making.

Assessment and Evaluation Suggestions

Objectively scored assessment items

Create a test or quiz using selected items from the Test Bank.

Subjectively scored assessment items

Create a test or quiz using selected scenarios from the Scenario Bank. Have students complete short-answer questions corresponding to each scenario. Sample short-answer questions could be:

- Is the use described in the scenario fair use?
- Which of the four fair use factors is violated in the scenario? How do you know?
- Is [the main character] correct in their conclusion? (Teachers could name any character in the scenario for this question.)

Suggested Scoring Criteria

For objectively scored tests/quizzes, create an answer key based on the question answer key from the Test Bank. Depending on the age and skill level of the learners, scores between 75 and 85 percent can be minimum required scores for mastery.

Using the annotations in the Scenario Banks, create an answer key for short-answer items. If you have included prompts for students to explain their rationale, evaluate their responses on the accuracy of their rationale with respect to the four fair use factors. Answers that make erroneous assumptions about facts not in evidence of the scenarios should result in lower scores. Answers in which students are able to document assumptions that they used in making their determinations, and those assumptions are reasonable, should result in higher scores.

Sample Rubric for Subjectively Scored Short-Answer Items

Every teacher uses rubrics in a manner that works best for them in any one given situation. The rubric presented here is ONE way that subjectively scored items can be scored. The descriptors of quality in each cell are intentionally broad, to allow teachers room to customize them for their use with their own classes. If teachers choose to customize the cells, the information provided here can be used to guide their work, helping them keep the critical aspects in mind as they revise the rubric so that it is most workable for their own teaching practice. The column headers are also provided as a suggestion and should be revised to be most meaningful for individual teachers and their students. See the beginning of Chapter 2 for more detailed information regarding how I typically use rubrics.

	Excellent	**Good**	**Poor**	**Missing**
Accuracy	Student conclusions and rationales match those presented in the scenario annotation/key of the text.	Student conclusions closely match those presented in the scenario annotation/key of the text. Conclusions may be correct, but rationale may be mismatched.	Student conclusions and rationales do not match, or nearly match, those presented in the scenario annotation/key of the text.	Student fails to provide a final conclusion. Statement indicated as final conclusion is not actually a conclusion.
Completeness	Student rationales address all relevant aspects of the four fair use factors.	Student rationales have one or more of the four factors missing, but the missing items do not affect the accuracy of the student conclusion.	Student rationales have one or more of the four factors missing, and the missing items affect the accuracy of the student conclusion.	Students fail to provide a rationale based on the four factors. Student provides a rationale based on irrelevant information.
Assumptions	Student responses include reasonable assumptions that were appropriately considered in the rationale/decision presented.	Student responses include assumptions that were considered in the rationale/decision presented. These assumptions may be incomplete, non-impactful, or irrelevant in terms of the final decision.	Student responses include assumptions that are unreasonable or not feasible given the details of the scenario.	Student responses are lacking appropriate assumptions. Note: this cell should be formatted in consideration of directions provided to students as well as the age/level of the learners.
Insight	Student responses include questions requesting further clarification, or other indicators of particular insight that demonstrate a full and complete understanding of the nuances of the four tests of fair use that is developmentally appropriate.	Student responses include questions requesting further clarification, or other indicators that the student recognizes gaps in the information provided in the scenario.	Student responses indicate partial understanding of the four tests of fair use. No requests for further information are made. Note: most scenarios are incomplete in terms of the information provided, so some level of information gap can be assumed.	Student responses indicate complete misunderstanding of the four tests of fair use.

Topic: How Do Licenses Influence How I Am Permitted to Use Copyrighted Materials?

Lesson 4: What Do You Mean I'm Not Really Allowed to Borrow Someone Else's "Stuff"?! (Understanding How Licenses Influence the Use of Copyrighted Materials)

Approximate Length of Lesson/Topic

45–60 minutes

Intended Audience

Intermediate learners (over the age of thirteen)—with teacher curation of licensing information as handouts. Intermediate learners may not find searching for and locating online sources of licenses to be an efficient use of their time.

Advanced learners (post high school graduation)—advanced learners should be able to efficiently locate the license or terms of service document for online resources.

Learning Goals

- Learners will be able to **define** "license" in their own words as it pertains to the use of copyrighted works.
- Learners will be able to **explain** the relationship between license restrictions and fair use as they pertain to the use of copyrighted works.
- Learners will be able to **name** common licenses that control the use of copyrighted works.

Materials/Resources/Suggested Reading(s)

Reading(s)

	Simpson and Wolf (2021)	**Crews (2020)**	**Russell (2023)**	**Other**
Licensed material (general)	Chapter 3 (pp. 45–54)	Chapter 24 (pp. 251–260)		
Licensing in specific situations	Video (pp. 106–109); Music (pp. 145–146); Internet (p. 180); Software (p. 214); Permissions (pp. 251–253)	pp. 201–202 (films)	Non-negotiated licenses: (pp. 89–90); School performances (pp. 127–129); Music (pp. 94–95); Online materials (p. 114); Public Performances (pp. 81–82); TEACH Act scenarios (p. 85)	

Resources

Note: The links to the terms of use listed here represent commonly accessed sites that teachers and learners encounter during the school day as well as in their daily lives. The list is not intended to be exhaustive. The links here were accurate as of the time of publication, but the author cannot guarantee that they will remain active over a period of time. Should you discover that one of the links is no longer working, you can search for that service's terms of service by using "[name of service] terms of service" as your search terms in your favorite online search engine. I've organized the list according to the type of service represented.

Streaming video services

- Netflix Terms of Use—https://help.netflix.com/legal/termsofuse
- Disney+ Terms of Service—https://www.disneyplus.com/legal/subscriber-agreement
- Amazon Prime Video Terms of Service—https://www.primevideo.com/help/ref=atv_hp_nd_nav?nodeId=G202095490

Streaming music services

- Pandora Terms of Use—https://www.pandora.com/legal
- Spotify Terms of Service—https://www.spotify.com/us/legal/end-user-agreement/

Learning management or other academic content management systems

- Pearson Publishing Terms of Use—https://loginstatic.pearson.com/html/PearsonEULA.html and https://loginstatic.pearson.com/html/AcceptableUsePolicy.html
- Wiley Publishing Terms of Use—https://www.wiley.com/en-us/terms-of-use
- PowerSchool (Schoology) Terms of Use—https://www.powerschool.com/terms/
- Canvas Terms of Use—https://www.instructure.com/policies/terms-of-use
- Moodle Terms of Service—https://apps.moodle.com/admin/tool/policy/view.php?versionid=3

Social media

- Instagram Terms of Use—https://help.instagram.com/581066165581870
- TikTok Terms of Use—https://www.tiktok.com/legal/page/us/terms-of-service/en
- Snapchat Terms of Use—https://snap.com/en-US/terms
- X (Formerly Twitter) Terms of Service—https://twitter.com/en/tos
- Pinterest Terms of Service—https://policy.pinterest.com/en/terms-of-service

Cloud storage/computing

- Flickr Terms of Use—https://www.flickr.com/help/terms
- Google Terms of Use—https://policies.google.com/terms
- Microsoft Terms of Use—https://www.microsoft.com/en-us/legal/terms-of-use

Other online services or content

- Open AI Terms of Use—https://openai.com/policies/terms-of-use
- Creative Commons Licenses—https://creativecommons.org/share-your-work/cclicenses/

Materials

- Teachers may wish to find links to local agencies that control licensing for leisure activities such as hunting, fishing, or boating.
- Teachers may wish to find links to local agencies that control the licensing of drivers.
- Teachers may wish to find links to agencies that control professional licensing, such as for medical personnel, teachers, the trades, or other similar agencies as appropriate for the members of their classes.

Procedures/Activity

Activity Summary

This lesson is centered around an important, and frequently misunderstood by non-attorneys, conceptual relationship within the copyright field. The three parts of the lesson are first, a guided discussion to derive a working definition of "license"; second, a direct instruction portion to explain how licenses take precedence over, or "trump," fair use claims; and last, an opportunity to practice analysis of scenarios assuming straight fair use and use under terms of a license.

Depending on the level of experience held by the learners, teachers may wish to move the analysis practice to an additional class session rather than extend the total time of the lesson to an unreasonable length.

Activity Preparation

Students

- Complete readings as assigned by the teacher.
- Be able to access online websites and locate information within online documents.

Teacher

- Create curated web links of sample licenses from the resources list above, if desired.

- Review selected licenses to locate specific sections using language such as:
    - "non-exclusive license"
    - "intellectual property"
    - "non-commercial use"
    - "personal use"
    - "distribute/distribution"
    - "reproduce/reproduction"
    - "display"
    - "adapt/adaptation"
    - age minimum (usually either thirteen or eighteen, or sometimes stated as "age of majority")
    - indications of *permitted* actions
    - indications of *prohibited* actions
- Locate and curate web links for local licensing agencies as indicated in the materials section of the lesson plan, if desired.
- Customize starter slides "Licenses and Fair Use" if desired.
- Locate examples of materials that are and are not controlled by licenses, making sure to record the source so that students will be able to accurately complete the analysis practice activity:
    - Links to media from streaming services
    - Links to items that are licensed by Creative Commons
    - Links or items that are NOT controlled by a license

Environment

- Ensure that display equipment is present and working properly for the direct instruction portion of the lesson.
- If desired, arrange the learning space to accommodate a gallery walk strategy during the analysis portion of the lesson.

Activity Procedures

Guided Discussion

1. Initiate a conversation about licenses from a universal or general point of view.

a) Ask students if they know what a license is (particularly for younger or less experienced learners); OR ask learners to name different licenses that they might possess or have heard named.

b) Typical responses might include hunting, fishing, boating, driving, business (perhaps specific types of business), medical, professional (such as teaching, cosmetology, electrical, etc.).

2. Guide students to identify common characteristics of the types of licenses they've named.

   a) At the conclusion of the discussion, three common characteristics should have been identified (the "3 Ps" of licenses).

   b) Permissions—Examples of permissions that might be described in leisure or professional licenses include:

      i. "Seasons" of permitted activity ("bow season," "duck season," etc.)

      ii. Activities (diagnosis, prescribing, wiring houses, teaching, hunting, fishing, driving boats or cars, etc.)

      iii. Persons—typically, the holder of the license

   c) Prohibitions—Examples of prohibitions that might be described in leisure or professional licenses include:

      i. Ages ("under . . ." thirteen, eighteen, twenty-one, etc. for given activity)

      ii. Limits of permitted behaviors or conditions relative to a specific activity (male vs. female specimens collected in hunting activities; time of day for younger holders of the licenses, especially driving; "scope" of activities, usually within a broader field, especially medicine)

      iii. Geographical prohibitions (particularly in relation to leisure activities such as hunting and boating)

   d) Proficiencies—Examples of proficiencies that might be necessary for leisure or professional licenses include:

      i. Safety courses, especially for those activities that pose a potential risk to the safety of people, such as hunting and driving

      ii. Formal academic preparation, especially for professional licensing such as medicine, law, education, and many trades

      iii. Periodic demonstration of currency of skill, such as continuing education (found frequently in medicine, law, and education)

Direct Instruction

1. Transition to a direct instruction model, using the customized starter slides "Licenses and Fair Use."

2. Teachers should be aware that limiting the determination of whether and how to use a protected item in this way (license vs. fair use) is an incomplete analysis strategy. The lesson

"Is It OK if I. . .?" contains more detailed information about the complete analysis process for the use of copyright-protected materials.

3. Teachers should be aware that some license terms may not be available to users of those materials, such as those for databases that are commonly found through public or school library access (ERIC, PsycINFO, NexiUni, etc.). If users are concerned about their use of materials acquired from these types of databases and have a compelling need to have a detailed understanding of the terms for the database that they are using, they should contact the person in their organization who is in charge of negotiating those vendor contracts as a first step. They can also always choose to fall back on a broad fair use analysis to determine the permissibility of their intended use (G. Stachokas, personal communication, March 6, 2024).
4. Teachers should also be aware that for materials users access through institution-provided database access, *in general*, most common uses of those materials have been negotiated to be permissible within the terms of those licenses. Activities such as downloading, printing, distributing within a restricted area such as a learning management system, and public display or performance are *likely* to be permitted, provided that the item is accessed through a credentialed account (G. Stachokas, personal communication, March 6, 2024).
5. Points 3 and 4 would only need to be included in a lesson in the most detailed of learning situations. For the vast majority of students, these points should NOT be included in a lesson. They are included here to help teachers and instructors contextualize the scope of license influence and provide information for specific questions that might arise during the lesson.

Analysis Practice

1. Distribute selected protected items (including sources) and copies of the License Use Analysis Scaffold—Appendix D (if needed) to students' small groups.
2. Record the name, source, and controlling license (if appropriate) for the item in question. Note: teachers should be sure to provide the source of the ITEM for students throughout the practice activity. The name/type of license should be provided to students, but teachers may elect to have students search for or locate the license themselves (advanced learners), or they may elect to provide the URL/location of the license (novice learners).
3. Model the analysis of a sample item for students. Be sure to speak aloud the thinking process you engage in as you analyze the sample item. For instance,
   a) "I found my image on 'Quality Logo Products' (used as an example), here's the URL of that image . . ."
   b) "I want to use this picture to create a bulletin board." (Note: a bulletin board is likely considered to be a derivative work when using multiple images from sources, especially if that image is altered.)

c) "My use is reproduction, derivative, and public. When I look at the terms of service for quality logo products (https://www.qualitylogoproducts.com/terms-of-use.htm), I see that 'derivative' items are not permitted. I should check 'no' for that type of use being permitted."

d) Based on my answers, it looks like I'm not permitted to use this image for my bulletin board.

4. Model a second analysis that would be permitted. For instance,

a) "What if my image was found at 'clipart.com,' though?"

b) "I would have to check their terms of service, but they are a little tricky to interpret. Wait! I found an FAQ (https://clipart.com/faq.php?keys=&results=40&safe=1) that has information about educational uses."

c) "My use is still the same as before, and when I look at the FAQ, I see that all of my uses are permitted."

d) Based on my answers, it looks like I am permitted to use an image from clipart.com.

Note: Depending on the searching skills and reading level of the learners, finding information in terms of service documents or FAQs can sometimes be a challenge. Refer to the list of targeted language in the "teacher preparation" section of the lesson plan for specific terms that can be used for search purposes. Also, be sure to practice finding this information yourself prior to teaching the lesson, so that you're comfortable guiding students through the process.

5. Distribute new items, or sources of items, to small groups, making sure to use a variety of sources for protected items. See the "Materials" section for a list of possible sources for copyright-protected materials that have licenses or terms of service controlling their access and use.

6. Direct each small group to complete a license use analysis from start to finish, documenting their thinking processes.

7. Allow sufficient time for all groups to complete their analysis, rotating from group to group to ensure they are all making appropriate progress.

8. Remind students to document their decision making using the License Use Analysis Scaffold.

9. If desired, implement a gallery walk strategy as described in the "Do I Always Have to Get Permission . . ." lesson.

Assessment and Evaluation Suggestions

Objectively scored assessment items

Select desired items from objective item Test Bank.

As this is a relatively narrow concept in terms of cognitive knowledge, teachers may want to consider incorporating applicable items in an assessment tool or test that has a broader focus across multiple aspects of copyright.

Subjectively scored assessment items

For subjectively scored assessment, create a test or quiz using selected scenarios from the Scenario Bank. Include links to explicit items from varying different sites that have terms of service to control the use of those items. Due to the complexity of the interpretation of online documentation, allowing learners ample time to complete these items is vital. A "take home" or extended in-class testing period is warranted.

Have students complete short-answer questions corresponding to each scenario and included copyright-protected item. Sample short-answer questions could be:

- Is the use described in the scenario permitted when considering licensing requirements?
- Which specific portion(s) of the license or terms of service did you use to make your use-decision?

Suggested Scoring Criteria

Within a group of objectively scored items, a ratio of approximately 80 percent correct answers is reasonable to demonstrate mastery of this concept.

Sample Rubric for Subjectively Scored Projects

Every teacher uses rubrics in a manner that works best for them in any one given situation. The rubric presented here is ONE way that subjectively scored items can be scored. The descriptors of quality in each cell are intentionally broad, to allow teachers room to customize them for their use with their own classes. If teachers choose to customize the cells, the information provided here can be used to guide their work, helping them keep the critical aspects in mind as they revise the rubric so that it is most workable for their own teaching practice. The column headers are also provided as a suggestion and should be revised to be most meaningful for individual teachers and their students. See the beginning of Chapter 2 for more detailed information regarding how I typically use rubrics.

	Excellent	Good	Poor	Missing
Accuracy	Student conclusions and rationales match those presented in the scenario annotation/key of the text.	Student conclusions closely match those presented in the scenario annotation/key of the text. Conclusions may be correct, but rationale may be mismatched.	Student conclusions and rationales do not match, or nearly match, those presented in the scenario annotation/key of the text.	Student fails to provide a final conclusion. Statement indicated as final conclusion is not actually a conclusion.
Completeness	Student rationales address all relevant aspects of the intended use as well as corresponding portions of the terms of service or licensing documentation.	Student rationales have one or more of the intended uses as well as corresponding portions of the terms of service or licensing documentation. missing, but the missing items do not affect the accuracy of the student conclusion.	Student rationales have one or more the intended use as well as corresponding portions of the terms of service or licensing documentation is missing, and the missing items affect the accuracy of the student conclusion.	Students fail to provide a rationale based on the intended use as well as corresponding portions of the terms of service or licensing documentation. Student provides a rationale based on irrelevant information.
Assumptions	Student responses include reasonable assumptions that were appropriately considered in the rationale/decision presented.	Student responses include assumptions that were considered in the rationale/decision presented. These assumptions may be incomplete, non-impactful, or irrelevant in terms of the final decision	Student responses include assumptions that are unreasonable or not feasible given the details of the scenario.	Student responses lack appropriate assumptions. Note: this cell should be formatted in consideration of directions provided to students as well as the age/level of the learners.
Insight	Student responses include questions requesting further clarification, or other indicators of insight that demonstrate a full and complete understanding of the nuances of the intended use as well as corresponding portions of the terms of service or licensing documentation that is developmentally appropriate.	Student responses include questions requesting further clarification, or other indicators that the student recognizes gaps in the information provided in the scenario.	Student responses indicate partial understanding of the intended use as well as corresponding portions of the terms of service or licensing documentation. No requests for further information are made. Note: most scenarios are incomplete in terms of the information provided, so some level of information gap can be assumed.	Student responses indicate complete misunderstanding of the intended use as well as corresponding portions of the terms of service or licensing documentation.

Topic: How Do Licenses Influence How I Am Permitted to Use Copyrighted Materials?

Lesson 5: How Does Creative Commons Help Me? (Understanding Creative Commons)

Approximate Length of Lesson/Topic

45–60 minutes

Intended Audience

Intermediate or advanced learners

Learning Goals

- Learners will be able to **describe** how Creative Commons came into existence in their own words.
- Learners will be able to **identify** the type of Creative Commons license that is attached to specific items.
- Learners will be able to **name** the six different Creative Commons licenses.
- Learners will be able to **match** the license icon with the corresponding name of the Creative Commons license.
- Learners will be able to **locate** Creative Commons licensed materials.
- Learners will **choose** to use Creative Commons licensed materials.

Materials/Resources/Suggested Reading(s)

Reading(s)

	Simpson and Wolf (2021)	Crews (2020)	Russell (2023)	Other
Creative Commons—citation	p. 165			
Creative Commons—general discussion	pp. 46–51	pp. 69, 252–253	pp. 27–29	Creative Commons (2020)
Creative Commons—history, elements, and locating materials				See items in resources section, below.

Resources

History

- Creative Commons: A History—https://scholarworks.boisestate.edu/sw_pubs/37/ (for older learners)
- The Story of Creative Commons—https://certificates.creativecommons.org/cccertedu/chapter/1-1-the-story-of-creative-commons/ (for older learners)
- Why Was Creative Commons Created?—https://www.youtube.com/watch?v=tft3zNhzQHs
- A brief history of Creative Commons (interactive timeline)—https://creativecommons.org/timeline/
- A Creative Commons for Kids—https://www.youtube.com/watch?v=xcrtq7jsS8s
- History of CC story

Licenses

- Creative Commons Licenses—https://creativecommons.org/share-your-work/cclicenses/
- What Are Creative Commons Licenses?—https://www.youtube.com/watch?v=srVPLrmlBJY (Intermediate grades and above)
- Creative Commons Licenses Explained—https://www.youtube.com/watch?v=2dw9MtyTunU

Locating CC Items

- Using Creative Commons content—https://www.youtube.com/watch?v=1OULrgm4iW4&t=1s (Intermediate grades and above)
- Finding CC licensed materials from Eastern Michigan—https://guides.emich.edu/creativecommons/locating
- OER lab on finding CC licensed materials—https://oercommons.org/courseware/lesson/97649/overview
- List of sources of CC licensed materials—https://smartcopying.edu.au/how-to-find-creative-commons-licensed-materials/
- CC search portal—https://search.creativecommons.org/

Materials

- Teachers may wish to locate specific examples of CC licensed content or items.
- Teachers may wish to select, duplicate, and prepare Concentration game cards.

Procedures/Activity

Activity Summary

The first part of this lesson is an extension of the previous lesson on the characteristics of licenses as well as the effects that license terms have on the ability to use copyrighted materials. Learners will learn how a special set of licenses, Creative Commons licenses, came into being, and the benefits they get from using CC licensed materials.

In the second part of this lesson, learners acquire the ability to describe the six different CC licenses as well as to locate CC licensed materials online.

Practice opportunities within this lesson include:

- a Concentration game that younger learners will likely find particularly useful.
- a scavenger hunt for CC licensed materials that can be adapted for use with learners of all ability levels.

Activity Preparation

Students

1. If assigned by the teacher, complete reading or viewing before the class.
2. Be able to describe the purpose of licenses in general: "To control the behavior of people through specific permissions, prohibitions, and proficiency requirements." Alternatively, licenses "tell us what we are allowed to do, what we aren't allowed to do, and any special qualifications we need in order to hold the license."
3. Be able to describe how the terms of licenses have precedence over our use of copyrighted material, even though fair use might otherwise permit that use.

Teacher

1. Select appropriate readings for your students from the resources list above. A variety of options are provided. Some are text; others are video or other media. The intended audience for the items varies from elementary students to more sophisticated adult learners. A short annotation for each of the resources can be found in Chapter 4, which you may find useful in choosing which item you'd like to use with your students. Depending on the level of your students, you may wish to assign reading to your learners to complete prior to the commencement of this lesson.
2. Locate, print, and label CC licensed images, video screen shots, webpages, and other creative content possessing CC licenses.
3. Create (or print), reproduce, duplicate (as appropriate), and cut apart Concentration game cards.
4. Create scavenger hunt clues/lists. Possible scavenger hunts can be:
   a) Find one CC licensed item for each of the different CC license types. Teachers can permit students to use different search terms or limit them to using the same search term or concept for all of their items.
   b) Find a CC licensed item for each of the following conditions (e.g., CC BY—apple; CC BY NC—happiness; CC 0—fun).
   c) Customize the lists in terms of complexity as appropriate to the needs of your students.
   d) Be sure to have students provide the URLs for the items that they locate. You will use those URLs to evaluate the accuracy of their results.

Environment

1. Ensure that presentation equipment is working properly.
2. Arrange students in pairs or small groups, as desired, to facilitate the role-playing and Concentration game activities.
3. Ensure that students have access to the internet for the scavenger hunt activity.

Activity Procedures

Direct Instruction

1. Explain to students that there are six main types of Creative Commons licenses, plus an extra for items that are put directly into the public domain.
2. Display the different icons for each element of the licenses (circular icons) and explain their meanings.
3. Display the different icons for each of the different licenses (rectangular icons) and explain their meanings.
4. Transition to instruction on how to locate CC licensed materials.
5. Customize the Creative Commons starter slides presentation to illustrate the process for locating CC licensed materials in a variety of sources (e.g., Google images, YouTube, various repositories).
6. Model the process for locating different types of media (images, video, text). Use a think-aloud protocol to help students be aware of the decisions and navigation needed in order to locate CC licensed materials.
7. Model the process of locating the specific CC license attached to the item(s) you find. Make sure to demonstrate to students the various places on an item where the license might be found.
8. Transition to the practice activity of your choice (Concentration game or scavenger hunt).

Concentration game practice activity

1. Distribute Concentration game cards to pairs or small groups of students, depending on the number of cards that you've distributed, ensuring that you've given each group at least four or five pairs. Fewer pairs (four or five in total) should be used with student pairs or trios, and more pairs (up to ten pairs) can be used with groups of four or five students.
2. Remind students that the purpose of the game is for them to practice their memory about the key concepts related to Creative Commons.

3. Review the rules for the game with students:
    a) Shuffle the cards so that the pairs are mixed up.
    b) Lay the game cards out in an array, face down.
    c) Choose the person who will take the first turn.
    d) The first player turns over two cards. If the two cards form a conceptual pair, that player keeps them. If the cards do not form a conceptual pair, turn the cards back over to the face-down position.
    e) The turn passes to the next player.
    f) That player turns over two cards. If a pair is formed, the player keeps the pair. If a pair is not formed, the cards are returned to their face-down position.
    g) Repeat steps e and f until all pairs are found.
    h) The player with the most pairs in their possession "wins".
    i) Teachers can choose to award actual prizes or not, as appropriate for their students.

Scavenger hunt practice activity

1. Begin the activity in a whole-class organization.
2. Direct all students to locate any CC licensed item using a simple/concrete search concept such as "apple," "house," or "book."
3. Ask students to share the item they found, and identify the specific license attached to the item they found. Reinforce accurate identification of licenses. Make corrections to student results as needed.
4. Direct students to locate a different CC licensed item using the same search concept as the first time, but with a different CC license than they first found.
5. Ask students to share the item they found and identify the specific license attached to the item they found. Reinforce accurate identification of licenses. Make corrections to student results as needed.
6. Repeat steps 2–5 with a more abstract concept, such as "teaching," "friendship," or "love."
7. Depending on the sophistication of learners, steps 2–6 can be completed in pairs or trios, as needed.
8. Gradually expand the abstraction of concepts used for search terms, having students suggest sample ones to include them in the process.
9. Once students are comfortable locating CC licensed items with teacher support and scaffolding, distribute scavenger hunt lists and allow students sufficient time in class or outside of class as homework or projects to complete the hunt.

Assessment and Evaluation Suggestions

Suggested Scoring Criteria

Concentration game

Since Concentration is a game, I don't recommend attaching formal points to the outcome. However, teachers may elect to distribute prizes if it would be incentivizing for their students.

Scavenger hunt

When evaluating student submissions for the scavenger hunt, you will need to make a judgement call to determine whether the given concept and the item located by the student are aligned properly.

Verify the accuracy of the stated license by accessing the URLs indicated by the students.

Each item could have a two-part aspect for grading purposes: concept alignment and accuracy of license identification.

A percentage of 75–80 percent as a floor is a reasonable threshold for mastery, depending on the number of items that students must locate in the scavenger hunt. Teachers may also choose to treat the scavenger hunt as a practice activity, which would not yield a formal scoring process.

Topic: What Exceptions to the Copyright Law Affect My Teaching/Learning?

Lesson 6: "Yeah, . . . But! . . ." (Understanding Common Exceptions to Copyright Protections)

Note: Teachers are strongly encouraged to verify whether their students have a foundational understanding of the general concept of fair use before embarking on this lesson.

If you determine that your students do NOT have a foundational understanding of fair use, and your students are experienced learners, you may find that folding the fair use lesson into this one is beneficial. Doing so will increase the length of this lesson but may be worth the extra time to ensure a complete understanding by your students.

It is also important to note that the information contained in this lesson is not comprehensive with respect to the requirements in the stated exceptions. The provisions described in this lesson are intended to provide guidance for informed users, not as comprehensive interpretation of the law.

Approximate Length of Lesson/Topic

45–60 minutes (lecture portion)
45–60 minutes (scaffolded analysis portion)
30–45 minutes (bingo portion)

Intended Audience

Experienced learners, suggested ages: high school and older

Learning Goals

- Learners will be able to **name** common exceptions to copyright protections.
- Learners will be able to **describe** common exceptions to copyright protections.
- Learners will be able to **match** authentic scenarios with the appropriate exception to copyright protections that governs the use described in the scenario.

Materials/Resources/Suggested Reading(s)

Reading(s)

Note: The exceptions listed here are the most commonly encountered in school- and instruction-based settings. There are other exceptions listed within the law that can be explored at Chapter 1 of the copyright law: https://www.copyright.gov/title17/92chap1.html

	Simpson and Wolf (2021)	Crews (2020)	Russell (2023)	Other
Exceptions—general discussion		Chapter 9 (pp. 83–94)	Chapter 4 (pp. 57–76)	
Fair Use	Chapter 4 (pp. 55–72)	Part III (pp. 95–150)	Chapter 3 (pp. 39–56)	US copyright law, §107
Library Exceptions	Chapter 12 (pp. 223–238)	Chapter 18 (pp. 183–194)	pp. 57–68	US copyright law, §108
First Sale	Throughout the text, in a variety of locations. Particularly in Chapters 1, 6, and 14	pp. 85–86	pp. 70–72	US copyright law, §109
Classroom performances; TEACH Act	Chapter 9 (pp. 170–173)	Chapter 16 (pp. 159–168)	pp. 84–85	US copyright law, §110
Reproductions for the Blind and Disabled	Chapter 13 (pp. 239–244)	p. 89	pp. 115–120	US copyright law, §121 and §121A

Resources

- US copyright law, Title 17—https://www.copyright.gov/title17/92chap1.html

Materials

- Starter slides—Exceptions
- Selected scenarios

Procedures/Activity

Activity Summary

In this lecture-based lesson, instructors organize and deliver the content in the manner that best fits their own instructional philosophy and style.

Instructors also guide students as they analyze scenarios that illustrate circumstances where various exceptions to copyright protections would apply.

An optional practice activity of Copyright Exceptions Bingo is included for those instructors who find it useful.

Activity Preparation

Students

- Be able to describe the purpose of fair use in their own terms.
- Be able to apply the four tests of fair use to authentic scenarios.

Teacher

Lecture Portion

- Customize electronic presentation, using Exceptions starter slides as a starting point.
- Select appropriate scenarios to use in the analysis portion of the lesson.

Bingo Option

- No special physical environmental preparation is needed.
- Distribute blank bingo cards to learners. Less expert learners may find more success in completing cards as a pair, rather than as an individual.
- Reproduce call list as appropriate.

Activity Procedures

1. Provide a review of the following concepts to ensure that learners are prepared to learn:
    a) Exclusive rights of the copyright owner
    b) Fair use
2. Deliver instruction using slide starters as basis of displayed lecture slides.
3. Refer to procedures in "Comprehensive Lecture" lesson to increase interactivity of lecture for students.

Scaffolded Analysis

1. Divide learners into groups of desired size, or direct learners to complete the activity independently.
2. Distribute supplies as desired for students to document their work (e.g., erasable white board markers, poster paper, pens, paper, etc.).
3. Distribute desired number of scenarios to each learner or group. Use scenarios from this text or those from the Copyright Card Game referenced in the materials section.
    a) Teachers may choose to have learners/groups complete this activity one scenario at a time.
    b) Teachers may choose to have learners/groups complete a set number of scenarios, generally at least three for groups and no more than three for individual students.
    c) If possible, ensure that the general characteristics of the scenarios are varied within a group or individual student so that their analysis efforts are appropriately distributed across all aspects of using copyrighted materials.
4. Provide the following guidance to learners in the completion of their analysis:
    a) The Exceptions Analysis Scaffold provides a place for them to document their thinking.
    b) Unless otherwise directed, feel free to use bullets or keywords to complete the scaffold.

c) Some scenarios will describe situations that might be incomplete in terms of the information provided. In these cases, use the question areas to write any questions that learners might need to have answered in order to come to a complete resolution of the analysis.

d) Students working in groups should strive to come to consensus on each aspect of the analysis.

5. Model the analysis of a scenario for students, making sure to use a think-aloud protocol so that they can be aware of the portions of the scenario that you use to make your final decision regarding the permissibility of the activity described.

6. Allow students adequate time to analyze their scenarios (I've found that a minimum of 15 minutes per scenario is needed for students working in groups to come to consensus. However, younger students may need additional time. Remember, you know your students best; allow the time that you know is appropriate for your students).

7. Be sure that the scenarios you've chosen represent situations where exceptions would apply. Encourage students to identify the correlation between the types of users described, the environment in which the item is being used, and the types of use being described in the scenarios.

8. Modify the conditions under which students analyze the scenarios using the following suggestions:

    a) To make the activity more challenging, reduce the amount of time to work OR increase the number of scenarios to complete.

    b) Changing the scale used to determine riskiness can increase or decrease the challenge level, especially if you also require students to justify their rating. A three-level risk assessment is less challenging than a ten-level one.

    c) Permitting or disallowing reference sources can alter the level of difficulty of the task.

    d) Requiring specific citations for the basis of decisions made can increase the difficulty of the task.

    e) Your own established group-work requirements, such as group member roles or other controls, should be used as appropriate.

    f) Add another layer of complexity to the task by having students rewrite scenarios so that the general intent of the scenario is met, but with a risk level as low as possible or with a fair use determination that is unequivocally "fair."

Bingo

The classic bingo format permits individuals or teams to identify relevant concepts that describe cases. An alternative version permits learners to identify concepts illustrated in specific court cases. Teachers need to create their own bingo cards, depending on their preferences. Online bingo card creators are available that support the creation of randomly generated cards, automatic creation of the call list, and the importing of user owned graphics, such as Bingo Baker—https://bingobaker.com/.

Directions to Students

1. Complete your bingo card by finding a complete row, column, or diagonal line (corner to corner) and covering the spaces with a token.
2. Each space you cover should match the clue read by your teacher in terms of the court case described, the finding described, or the concept described.
3. Once you've completed your card, shout "BINGO."
4. Verify your card with the teacher and claim your prize.

Game Modifications

1. To make the game more challenging:
   a) Create a call list that has multiple possible spaces to be marked (e.g., calling "distance education" could yield spaces containing "Classroom Exceptions," "Section 110," or "TEACH Act." If the student has the "TEACH Act" space and marks it, they won't then be able to use it again when "Performance exceptions" is called).
   b) Increase the speed with which the clues are called.
   c) Increase the number of clues called that have multiple matching spaces available to be marked.
2. To make the game less challenging:
   a) Permit the class to determine the speed with which the clues are called.
   b) Permit students to work in pairs or small teams.
   c) Ensure that clues called match to one and only one possible resulting space.

Assessment and Evaluation Suggestions

Two methods are recommended as being the best fit in order to determine learner mastery of the learning goals. Instructors should select the one that best meets their teaching philosophy and instructional needs.

Objectively scored test items

1. Construct test using accompanying Test Bank of questions.
2. Insert additional questions as desired.

Subjectively scored test items

1. Construct test using accompanying Test Bank of questions, modifying them to take a "fill-in" or "short-answer" format as desired.
2. Insert additional questions as desired.
3. Select appropriate scenarios from the Scenario Bank, or write your own, to use for essay format analysis questions.
4. When creating a scoring key, ensure that items where "answers may vary" have key concepts noted so that scoring is able to be efficient and consistent.

Suggested Scoring Criteria

Unless learners are part of a law school course about copyright, 100 percent accuracy or knowledge is not necessary in order for instructors to be confident that learners have satisfactorily mastered the learning goals.

Recommended passing thresholds for the following levels of learners are:

- Advanced learners (adults: librarians, school administrators, teachers): 75–85 percent or equivalent in "points out of" format.
- Mid-level learners (teens, adults: secondary students, undergraduate, graduate students): 70–85 percent or equivalent in "points out of" format.
- Entry-level learners (teens, adults: advanced middle school, lay-people): 65–75 percent or equivalent in "points out of" format.

These thresholds should be considered recommendations and not hard and fast limits. Instructors should always use their best discretion in determining final mastery thresholds for their learners.

Sample Rubric for Subjectively Scored Projects

	Excellent	Good	Poor	Missing
Accuracy of Exception Identification	Correct exception identified; multiple exceptions as appropriate identified.	Correct exception identified; multiple exceptions not recognized if appropriate.	Exception identified, but incorrect.	No exception identified.
Reasonableness of Risk Assessment	Risk assessment accurate and nuanced. Assessment based on appropriate and reasonable additional information provided after student questioning.	Risk assessment accurate. No evidence of basis for assessment.	Risk assessment unreasonably harsh or lenient.	No risk assessment provided, or drastically inaccurate.
Reasonableness of Fair Use Assessment	Fair use assessment accurate and nuanced. Assessment based on appropriate and reasonable additional information provided after student questioning.	Fair use assessment accurate. Minimal or no evidence for the basis for assessment.	Fair use assessment unreasonably harsh (e.g., using a "just don't use it . . ." sort of assessment); basis for assessment is inappropriate for information provided within the scenario.	Fair use assessment not provided or drastically inaccurate.

You should feel free to modify the rubric as best fits your needs, especially if you've chosen to include a justification as a part of your requirements of student work. See Chapter 2 for more information regarding operational definitions that I use for the quality descriptors of "Excellent," "Good," "Poor," and "Missing."

Topic: How Do I Determine Whether What I Want to Do/ Use Is Permissible? (Five Questions from Kevin Smith—CC Licensed)

Lesson 7: Is It OK If I . . .? (Analyzing Scenarios for Permissibility of the Use of Copyrighted Materials)

Approximate Length of Lesson/Topic

Variable, but to be especially effective, allow at least 60 minutes if working as a group activity in an in-class setting. May also be implemented as an individual effort in a "homework" type assignment/setting.

Intended Audience

All ages—this lesson is particularly adaptable by changing the threshold used to determine the accuracy of student responses.

Learning Goals

- Learners will be able to **identify** exclusive rights of the copyright holder applicable to a given authentic scenario.
- Learners will be able to **identify** copyrightable works affected by a given authentic scenario.
- Learners will be able to **name** appropriate licenses that affect the nature of use of copyrighted material in a given authentic scenario.
- Learners will be able to **annotate** authentic scenarios according to the four factors of Fair Use, Creative Commons licensing, and appropriate licensing influences.
- Learners will be able to **rate** authentic scenarios according to the level of riskiness in terms of use of copyrighted materials.
- Learners will be able to **label** the actions described in authentic scenarios as "Fair Use" or "Not Fair Use."
- Learners will be able to **write** questions that would need to be answered in order to make authentic scenarios more explicit in terms of use of copyrighted materials.

Materials/Resources/Suggested Reading(s)

Reading(s)

<table>
<tr><th></th><th>Simpson and Wolf (2021)</th><th>Crews (2020)</th><th>Russell (2023)</th><th>Other</th></tr>
<tr><td>Fair Use</td><td>Chapter 4 (pp. 55–72)</td><td>Part III (pp. 95–150)</td><td>pp. 39–56</td><td>Smith, K. and Macklin, L. (2014)</td></tr>
<tr><td>Library Exceptions</td><td>Chapter 12 (pp. 223–238)</td><td>Chapter 17 (pp. 169–182)</td><td>Broadly, Chapter 4 (pp. 57–76)</td><td></td></tr>
<tr><td>First Sale</td><td>Throughout the text, in a variety of locations. Particularly in Chapters 1, 6, and 14</td><td>pp. 85–86</td><td>pp. 70–72</td><td></td></tr>
<tr><td>Classroom performances; TEACH Act</td><td>Chapter 9 (pp. 170–173)</td><td>Chapter 16 (pp. 159–168)</td><td>p. 85</td><td></td></tr>
<tr><td>Reproductions for the Blind</td><td>Chapter 13 (pp. 239–244)</td><td>p. 89</td><td>pp. 115–120</td><td></td></tr>
<tr><td>Print Guidelines</td><td>Chapter 5 (pp. 73–96)</td><td rowspan="4">Chapter 13 (pp. 127–136)</td><td>CONFU: Appendix A (pp. 141–144) and Appendix E (pp. 161–165)</td><td></td></tr>
<tr><td>Audiovisual Guidelines</td><td>Chapter 6 (pp. 97–136)</td><td></td><td></td></tr>
<tr><td>Music Guidelines</td><td>Chapter 7 (pp. 137–152)</td><td>Appendix B (pp. 145–146)</td><td></td></tr>
<tr><td>Multimedia Guidelines</td><td>Chapter 8 (pp. 153–168)</td><td></td><td></td></tr>
<tr><td>Creative Commons</td><td>p. 165 (Citations); pp. 46–51 (general discussion)</td><td>pp. 69, 252–253</td><td>pp. 27–29</td><td>Creative Commons (2020)</td></tr>
</table>

Resources

- Scaffolds found in Appendices A, B, C, D, E, F. (Teachers may wish to duplicate and distribute these as appropriate for their students' needs.)

Materials

- Copyright Card Game (https://paulbond.info/blog/copyright-the-card-game-u-s-version/). Note: If you're interested in international versions of the game, you can find them at: https://copyrightliteracy.org/resources/copyright-the-card-game/.

Procedures/Activity

Activity Summary

This lesson is designed to be a *practice* level assignment in that it assumes a base level of understanding of copyright concepts. The activity is very flexible in that it can be customized to work in nearly any instructional setting, including small group, partner, or individual work.

To complete this activity, students will analyze authentic scenarios that describe various uses of copyrighted materials. They will document their analysis by completing an Analysis Scaffold. The Analysis Scaffold (Appendix A) is based on the work of Kavin Smith, Lisa Macklin, and Anne Gilliland (Smith & Macklin, 2014 2014). As possible extensions to the activity, students will rewrite the scenarios according to criteria that change the explicitness of their descriptions or the level of riskiness described.

Activity Preparation

Students

- Students should be able to name and describe the four fair use considerations.
- Students should be able to describe the relationship between licenses and fair use considerations.
- Students should be able to name and identify the six exclusive rights of copyright holders.
- Students should understand the common exceptions to copyright protections.

Teacher

1. Complete direct instruction lesson(s) covering:
    - **a)** Identifying six exclusive rights of copyright holders
    - **b)** Identifying copyrighted works
    - **c)** Understanding common exceptions to copyright protections
    - **d)** Applying appropriate licensing requirements to the use of copyrighted materials
    - **e)** Applying the four tests of fair use to copyrighted materials
2. Gather desired number and variety of authentic scenarios.
3. Reproduce *Analysis Scaffold* in appropriate quantity for class enrollment.
4. Arrange classroom or learning environment as desired.

Environment

Group-work option: This activity can be completed in a small group arrangement by using chart paper, markers and display board (chalk, white, etc.), or even large posters.

Partner option: This activity can be completed in pairs or threes using commonly sized paper, small erasable whiteboards, or other appropriately organized methods of displaying student work.

Individual option: This activity can be completed using reproduced *Analysis Scaffold* or student-created assignment submissions.

Activity Procedures

Copyright Card Game

1. Divide learners into groups of four to six learners.
2. Distribute Copyright Card Game card sets to each group.
3. Review the game directions with the class. Directions are located at the link in the resources section of this lesson plan.
4. Allow learners adequate time to play the game for at least four different scenarios (approximately 45–60 minutes, depending on the sophistication of the learners).
5. Rotate between the groups as play progresses to provide feedback regarding the accuracy of student conclusions.

Scenario Analysis

1. Divide learners into groups of desired size, or direct learners to complete the activity independently.
2. Distribute supplies as desired for students to document their work (e.g., erasable white board markers, poster paper, pens, paper, etc.).
3. Distribute desired number of scenarios to each learner or group. Use scenarios from this text or those from the Copyright Card Game referenced in the materials section.
   a) Teachers may choose to have learners/groups complete this activity one scenario at a time.
   b) Teachers may choose to have learners/groups complete a set number of scenarios, generally at least three for groups and no more than three for individual students.
   c) If possible, ensure that the general characteristics of the scenarios are varied within a group or individual student so that their analysis efforts are appropriately distributed across all aspects of using copyrighted materials.

4. Provide the following guidance to learners in the completion of their analysis:
   a) The Analysis Scaffold provides a place for them to document their thinking.
   b) Unless otherwise directed, feel free to use bullets or keywords to complete the scaffold.
   c) Some scenarios will describe situations that might be incomplete in terms of the information provided. In these cases, use the question areas to write any questions that learners might need to have answered in order to come to a complete resolution of the analysis.
   d) Students working in groups should strive to come to consensus on each aspect of the analysis.
5. Allow students adequate time to analyze their scenarios (I've found that at least 15 minutes per scenario is needed for students working in groups to come to consensus. However, you know your students best; allow the time that you know is appropriate for your students).
6. Modify the conditions under which students analyze the scenarios using the following suggestions:
   a) Making the activity more challenging by reducing the amount of time to work OR increasing the number of scenarios to complete.
   b) Changing the scale used to determine riskiness can increase or decrease the challenge level, especially if you also require students to justify their rating. A three-level risk assessment is less challenging than a ten-level one.
   c) Permitting or disallowing reference sources can alter the level of difficulty of the task.
   d) Requiring specific citations for the basis of decisions made can increase the difficulty of the task.
   e) Your own established group-work requirements, such as group member roles or other controls, should be used as appropriate.
   f) Adding another layer of complexity to the task by having students rewrite scenarios so that the general intent of the scenario is met, but with a risk level as low as possible or with a fair use determination that is unequivocally "fair."

Assessment and Evaluation Suggestions

Evaluating the quality of student responses to this activity is more complex than matching their answers to an answer key. Rather, the teacher must determine the reasonableness of student responses. The criteria suggested here should guide you in establishing your own scoring procedures and criteria.

Suggested Scoring Criteria

The Copyright Card Game is not intended to be used as a high-stakes activity. Rather, it functions as "risk-free practice" for students. Teachers may elect to award prizes if needed to encourage engagement by the students.

Several portions of the *Analysis Scaffold* can be evaluated for correctness. They are Rights, Works, Licenses, and Exceptions. Teachers should use their discretion when deciding whether to accept synonymous responses for the exclusive rights, the types of copyrighted works, the license names, and the names of the exceptions to the exclusive rights.

The risk factor and fair use determination are a bit more subjective. For scenarios that are located in this text, a general risk assessment is included in the Scenario Bank. Use that as a basis for your evaluation. If you've modified the scenarios, be aware that the risk factor may also need to be modified.

Remember that there are no hard-and-fast rules about whether a particular action IS fair use. There are a few hard-and-fast rules about what might NOT be considered fair use. Where a hard-and-fast determination is indicated in scenarios within the Scenario Bank, an indication is made.

As a reference, though, the following is made available for you here:

Six Exclusive Rights of a Copyright Holder

1. Reproduction
2. Distribution
3. Adaptation
4. Public Display
5. Public Performance
6. Public Performance through Digital Audio Transmission

Types of Copyrightable Works

1. Literary Works
2. Musical Works, including words
3. Dramatic Works, including music
4. Pantomimes and Choreographic Works
5. Pictorial, Graphic, and Sculptural Works
6. Motion Pictures and Other Audiovisual Works
7. Sound Recordings
8. Architectural Works

Common Exceptions to Exclusive Rights of a Copyright Holder

Note: The exceptions listed here are the most commonly encountered in school- and instruction-based settings. There are other exceptions listed within the law that can be explored at: https://www.copyright.gov/title17/92chap1.html.

1. Fair Use (section 107)
2. Library Exceptions (section 108)

3. First Sale Doctrine (section 109)
4. Classroom Performances, TEACH Act (section 110)
5. Reproductions for the Blind (section 121)
6. Other exceptions in sections 111, 112, 117, 119, and 122 of the law (URL listed above)

Common Licenses that Control the Use of Copyrighted Materials

1. Creative Commons licensing
2. End User/Terms of Service Licenses (typically associated with online products and services)
3. Purchasing licenses

Sample Rubric for Subjectively Scored Projects

	Excellent	Good	Poor	Missing
Accuracy of Exclusive Rights Identification (number and name)	All appropriate exclusive rights identified; no incorrect exclusive rights identified.	All appropriate exclusive rights identified; rights identified that may be incorrect.	Rights identified that are not affected within scenario; rights that are identified are incorrect.	No rights identified; named rights are not actually the names of rights.
Accuracy of Type of Copyrighted Work Identification (number and name)	All appropriate types of copyrighted work identified; no incorrect works identified.	All appropriate types of copyrighted work identified; some rights identified but may be incorrect.	Appropriate copyrighted works identified, but some are missing; some rights identified but may be incorrect.	Works identified are incorrect or misnamed; no copyrighted works identified.
Accuracy of License Identification	Correct license identified; more than one possible applicable license identified; no incorrect licenses identified.	Correct license identified; missing additional applicable licenses identified.	License identified but is incorrect; multiple licenses identified—also incorrect.	No licenses identified; identification provided but not even a license.
Accuracy of Exception Identification	Correct exception identified; multiple exceptions as appropriate identified.	Correct exception identified; multiple exceptions not recognized if appropriate.	Exception identified, but incorrect.	No exception identified.

	Excellent	Good	Poor	Missing
Reasonableness of Risk Assessment	Risk assessment accurate and nuanced. Assessment based on appropriate and reasonable additional information provided after student questioning.	Risk assessment accurate; no evidence of basis for assessment.	Risk assessment unreasonably harsh or lenient.	No risk assessment provided, or drastically inaccurate.
Reasonableness of Fair Use Assessment	Fair use assessment accurate and nuanced; assessment based on appropriate and reasonable additional information provided after student questioning.	Fair use assessment accurate; minimal or no evidence for the basis for assessment.	Fair use assessment unreasonably harsh (e.g., using a "just don't use it . . ." sort of assessment); basis for assessment is inappropriate for information provided within the scenario.	Fair use assessment not provided or drastically inaccurate.

You should feel free to modify the rubric as best fits your needs, especially if you've chosen to include a justification as a part of your requirements of student work. See Chapter 2 for more information regarding operational definitions that I use for the quality descriptors of "Excellent," "Good," "Poor," and "Missing."

Topic: What Are the Important Laws and Guidelines That Affect My Use of Copyrighted Materials?

Lesson 8: What Am I Allowed to Use in My Projects? (Understanding Multimedia Guidelines for K–12 Students)

Approximate Length of Lesson/Topic

45–60 minutes

Intended Audience

K–12 students

Learning Goals

- Students will be able to **describe** the quantity limits for the use of copyrighted materials in the multimedia guidelines.
- Students will be able to **create** multimedia projects containing copyrighted materials in alignment with the multimedia guidelines.

Materials/Resources/Suggested Reading(s)

Reading(s)

	Simpson and Wolf (2021)	Crews (2020)	Russell (2023)	Other
Multimedia Guidelines	Chapter 8 (pp. 153–168)	Chapter 13 (pp. 127–136)		Multimedia guidelines: http://files.eric.ed.gov/fulltext/ED402920.pdf (for secondary students of sophisticated reading levels)

Resources

- Appendix K Laws and Guidelines Quick Reference
- Starter slides: Guidelines
- Multimedia Guidelines Cheat Sheet

Materials

- Sample multimedia projects (teacher created)
- Descriptions of multimedia projects (teacher created)

Procedures/Activity

Activity Summary

From the perspective of those who will be using copyrighted works, the source and inception of the various guidelines that are highlighted in this lesson is not needed. Knowing the "broad strokes" of what the guidelines say, though, is needed. Therefore, minute details about the guidelines are not a part of this lesson.

It is important to note that most of the guidelines provide guidance to teachers alone, and not to students. The multimedia guidelines are the only set of guidelines that provide guidance to student use of copyrighted work.

Therefore, adult learners will find the details of the guidelines most useful, while younger learners, those in K–12 grades, will likely only need to know the limits associated with the multimedia guidelines.

Guided discovery of guidelines as being a result of compromise between rights holders and stakeholders.

Practice—Concentration game.

Practice—Scaffolded and independent analysis of scenarios.

Assessment—Revising projects to be within guideline limitations.

Activity Preparation

Students

Intermediate students—No special preparation needed.
Secondary students—Complete reading of texts as assigned by the teacher. Note: the text of the multimedia fair use guidelines (linked in the readings section of this lesson plan) is a primary source document and may require sophisticated reading levels in order to comprehend.

Teacher

- Create requirements for subjectively scored project, if desired.
- Customize scoring rubric for subjectively scored project, if desired.
- Customize starter slides "Guidelines" as desired.

- Concentration
  - Reproduce and duplicate Concentration cards as needed.
  - Teacher should decide how the pairs will be organized, using the conceptual pairs list in Appendix I as a guide.
- Scaffolded Analysis
  - Create sample "mini" projects for analysis practice. Be sure to include examples of appropriate and inappropriate use of copyrighted materials.

Environment

- Ensure all projection and display equipment is functioning properly.
- No special grouping of students is needed for the direct instruction portion of the lesson.

Concentration

- Arrange tables/desks or other seating to permit the Concentration boards to be laid out with adequate room.
- Concentration gameboards for younger or less expert learners should be limited to 4×4 (8 total pairs) or 6×6 (18 total pairs) cards in size. Gameboards must have an even number of cards in rows and columns in order for there to be no cards left over once all pairs are identified.
- More expert learners can handle gameboards up to 8×8 (32 total pairs) or even 10×10 (50 total pairs) cards.
- Divide learners into appropriately sized teams of play (two or three learners per gameboard, depending on size of gameboard).

Scaffolded Analysis

- Arrange students in pairs, trios, or small groups as desired and useful to provide them with peer support for their initial analysis practice.

Activity Procedures

1. Deliver instruction using slide starters as basis of displayed lecture slides.
2. Refer to procedures in "Comprehensive Lecture" lesson to increase interactivity of lecture for students.

Concentration

Directions to students:

1. Shuffle your pile of cards so that they are thoroughly mixed.
2. Lay your cards face down in a grid of 4×4, 6×6, 8×8, or 10×10 cards. Make sure that each row and column has the same number of cards.
3. Choose one student to take the first turn (use established classroom procedures to do so, as appropriate).
4. When it's your turn, flip two cards. Determine whether they match according to:
    - **a)** Title/Outcome
    - **b)** Title/Key Concept
    - **c)** Related issue or concept
5. If they match, that player keeps the cards (optional: permit one additional turn).
6. If they do not match, flip the cards back over so that they rest face down.
7. Play progresses to the LEFT of the current player.
8. Repeat steps 4–7 until all matches have been located, or time of play expires (as set by the teacher).
9. Players waiting their turn to flip cards should pay attention to those cards being flipped, as they can use that information on their turn to locate matches.

Game modifications:

1. To make the game more challenging:
    - **a)** Increase the size of the gameboard
    - **b)** Decrease the time of play (turn it into "speed" Concentration)
    - **c)** Use secondary concepts as the "match" for case title/key concept style of play
2. To make the game less challenging:
    - **a)** Reduce the size of the gameboard
    - **b)** Increase the time of play
    - **c)** Permit the use of reference sources in determining matches
    - **d)** Permit learners to work in teams
3. To increase competition/interest:
    - **a)** Conduct a "Concentration tournament"
    - **b)** Establish a set time each week or month (as desired) to play copyright Concentration

c) Record winners during each game session, maintaining a cumulative score for each student or team

d) At the conclusion of the tournament, declare the overall winner based on total matches, shortest time to clear gameboards, or other metric chosen by the teacher or class

Scaffolded Analysis

1. Model analyzing a multimedia project using a think-aloud protocol.
    a) Begin analysis by determining whether the appropriate notification is placed at the beginning of the project.
    b) Next, determine whether there are appropriate citations or attributions for all copyrighted material within the project.
    c) Continue modeling the analysis by proceeding through each type of media that could be included in the project, determining whether the amount used meets the limits within the guidelines.
        i. Motion media
        ii. Text
        iii. Music, lyrics, and music video
        iv. Illustrations, cartoons, and photographs
        v. Numerical data sets
2. Transition to having students complete analysis in pairs, trios, or small groups as appropriate.
3. Conclude with students completing analysis independently.
4. Rotate between groups and independent students, providing formative feedback on the accuracy of their work.

Assessment and Evaluation Suggestions

Objectively scored assessment

1. Construct test using accompanying Test Bank of questions.
2. Insert additional questions as desired.

Subjectively scored assessment

Two possible methods are appropriate to determine mastery of the "create" learning objective, in particular.

First, as items on a written test, students can be asked to describe copyrighted material to include in a portion of a multimedia project. Their responses can be evaluated against the quantity limits of the multimedia guidelines.

Second, students can be directed to create multimedia projects. These projects can then be evaluated against the quantity limits as well as additional requirements of the multimedia guidelines. Younger learners may benefit from using the multimedia cheat sheet (Appendix J). The cheat sheet can also be made available to older learners as a resource for their own self-evaluation processes.

A sample rubric for the marking of these projects can be found on the next page.

Suggested Scoring Criteria

For a traditional objectively scored test, an acceptable score to demonstrate mastery is between 70 and 85 percent, depending on the sophistication of the learners. Younger students' mastery levels should be adjusted to allow for their mathematical skills, as some limits are based on percentages. Not all younger students are able to calculate percentages yet. Therefore, the items chosen for younger students should be reflective of their cognitive abilities and mathematical skills. Chosen items should be revised to be understandable by younger students.

Sample Rubric for Subjectively Scored Projects

Note: When making decisions about the contents of a scoring rubric, you should be sure to include any criteria that you've included in your specific assignment. You should also decide how you will handle those items that are appropriately missing from the project, such as numerical data sets. Those aren't the type of copyrighted material that is commonly included in K–12 multimedia projects. Options include assigning the highest value on the rubric or having an "N/A" option included.

	Excellent	Good	Poor	Missing
Appropriate notification for the use of copyrighted material	Notification present.			Notification not present (this is a binary criterion).
Attribution for copyrighted works included in project	All copyrighted works appropriately cited in project. Formatting of citations expertly reflects formatting of chosen style manual (APA, MLA, Chicago, etc.).	All works included in citation list, but not appropriately cited in some cases; small number of items may be missing; formatting may align with a style manual, but also may not.	Several works missing from citation list; citation formats do not adhere to any recognizable style manual.	Copyrighted works not cited; many items are missing.
Text used within guideline limits	Text used within appropriate guidelines; where use exceeds limits, text use is in alignment with fair use.	Text used within appropriate guidelines; a fair use assessment not made if use exceeds guideline limits.	Text use exceeds guideline limits; fair use justification is tenuous at best.	Text use does not conform with guidelines or fair use.
Motion media used with guideline limits	Motion media used within appropriate guidelines; where use exceeds limits, text use is in alignment with fair use.	Motion media used within appropriate guidelines; a fair use assessment not made if use exceeds guideline limits.	Motion media use exceeds guideline limits; fair use justification is tenuous at best.	Motion media used does not conform with guidelines or fair use.
Music and related items used within guideline limits	Music and related items used within appropriate guidelines; where use exceeds limits, text use is in alignment with fair use.	Music and related items used within appropriate guidelines; a fair use assessment not made if use exceeds guidelines limits.	Music and related items use exceeds guideline limits; fair use justification is tenuous at best.	Music and related items used do not conform with guidelines or fair use.
Illustrations/images used within guideline limits	Illustrations/images and related items used within appropriate guidelines; where use exceeds limits, text use is in alignment with fair use.	Illustrations/images used within appropriate guidelines; a fair use assessment not made if use exceeds guideline limits.	Illustrations/images use exceeds guideline limits; fair use justification is tenuous at best.	Illustrations/images used do not conform with guidelines or fair use.
Numerical data used within guideline limits	Numerical data sets used within appropriate guidelines; where use exceeds limits, text use is in alignment with fair use.	Numerical data sets used within appropriate guidelines; a fair use assessment not made if use exceeds guidelines limits.	Numerical data sets use exceeds guideline limits; fair use justification is tenuous at best.	Numerical data sets used do not conform with guidelines or fair use.
Additional teacher required criteria, as desired				

Topic: What Are the Important Laws and Guidelines That Affect My Use of Copyrighted Materials?

Lesson 9: What's the Safest Way to Use Copyrighted Materials? (Understanding Guidelines That Affect the Use of Copyrighted Materials for Teachers)

Approximate Length of Lesson/Topic

60–90 minutes

Intended Audience

Post secondary learners; adults; pre-service teachers, librarians, and school administrators; practicing teachers, librarians, and administrators.

Learning Goals

- Learners will be able to **match** the type of copyrighted work that is affected by specific use guidelines.
- Learners will be able to **describe** the limits for specific types of copyrighted works.
- Learners will be able to **match** authentic scenarios to the appropriate set of guidelines that would govern the use described in the scenario.
- Learners will be able to **create** instructional materials that include copyrighted materials within the limits of the appropriate set of guidelines.

Materials/Resources/Suggested Reading(s)

Reading(s)

	Simpson and Wolf (2021)	**Crews (2020)**	**Russell (2023)**	**Other?**
Print Guidelines	Chapter 5 (pp. 73–96)	Chapter 13 (pp. 127–136)	CONFU: Appendix A (pp. 141–144) and Appendix F (pp. 161–165)	Circular 21—Reproduction of Copyrighted Works by Educators and Librarians (https://www.copyright.gov/circs/circ21.pdf)
Audiovisual Guidelines	Chapter 6 (pp. 97–136)			Section 110 of US copyright law

	Simpson and Wolf (2021)	Crews (2020)	Russell (2023)	Other?
Music Guidelines	Chapter 7 (pp. 137–152)		pp. 94–95	US copyright Law: A Guide for Music Educators (https://nafme.org/resource/united-states-copyright-law-a-guide-for-music-educators/)
Multimedia Guidelines	Chapter 8 (pp. 153–168)			Multimedia Guidelines http://files.eric.ed.gov/fulltext/ED402920.pdf (for secondary students of sophisticated reading levels)

Resources

- Appendix K Laws and Guidelines Quick Reference
- Starter slides: Guidelines

Materials

- Select scenarios from Scenario Bank.

Procedures/Activity

Activity Summary

From the perspective of those who will be using copyrighted works, the source and inception of the various guidelines that are highlighted in this lesson is not needed. Knowing the "broad strokes" of what the guidelines say, though, is needed. Therefore, minute details about the guidelines are not a part of this lesson.

It is important to note that most of the guidelines provide guidance to teachers alone, and not to students. The multimedia guidelines are the only set of guidelines that provide guidance to student use of copyrighted work.

Therefore, adult learners will find the details of the guidelines most useful.

Direct instruction of guidelines as being a result of compromise between rights holders and stakeholders as well as the limits associated with each set of guidelines.

Practice—Matching scenario to appropriate guideline to use.

Practice—Scaffolded and independent analysis of scenarios.

Assessment—Revising projects to be within guideline limitations.

Activity Preparation

Students

- Complete reading of texts as assigned by the teacher. Note: the text of the multimedia fair use guidelines (linked in the readings section of this lesson plan) is a primary source document and may require sophisticated reading levels in order to comprehend.
- Be able to define fair use in their own words.

Teacher

- Create requirements for subjectively scored project, if desired.
- Customize scoring rubric for subjectively scored project, if desired.
- Customize starter slides "Guidelines" as desired.
- Select appropriate brief scenarios to represent situations where various guidelines would control the use described.

Scaffolded Analysis

Create sample "mini" projects for analysis practice. Be sure to include examples of appropriate and inappropriate use of copyrighted materials.

Environment

- Ensure projection and display equipment is functioning properly.
- Arrange students in pairs or trios, or provide peer support for their initial analysis practice.

Activity Procedures

1. Deliver instruction using slide starters as basis of displayed lecture slides.
2. Refer to procedures in "Comprehensive Lecture" lesson to increase interactivity of lecture for students.

Practice—Scenario Matching

This practice has students match scenarios to the set of guidelines that best covers the uses of copyrighted materials described within them. It does not ask students to determine the permissibility of the use described.

1. Distribute sets of brief scenarios to pairs/trios/small groups of students.
2. Direct students to annotate the scenarios to indicate the evidence that supports the use of copyrighted materials in alignment with specific sets of guidelines. For example:

a) Color A: Teacher or Student use

b) Color B: Type of copyrighted work

c) Color C: Type of use

3. Direct students to label each scenario with the appropriate set of guidelines that apply to the use described.
4. Encourage students to use Appendix K "Guidelines and Laws Quick Reference" to aid in their analysis.

Practice—Scaffolded Analysis

This practice activity has students extend their work with various guidelines to being able to interpret guidelines in order to determine the permissibility of the use of copyrighted material.

1. Distribute sets of extended scenarios to pairs/trios/small groups of students. Using the extended scenarios provides students with additional details they can use to inform their decision regarding the permissibility of the actions described.
2. Model, using a think-aloud protocol, the analysis of a scenario based on the requirements of specific fair use guidelines. Demonstrate the use of the Guideline Analysis Scaffold, Appendix E.
3. Allow students adequate time to practice analyzing scenarios using the Guideline Analysis Scaffold as needed.
4. Monitor student work as desired, making sure to provide formative feedback on the accuracy of their work.
5. Use a gallery walk strategy, if desired, to encourage student engagement and opportunities for peer feedback.

Assessment and Evaluation Suggestions

Objectively scored assessment tool

Select appropriate items from the Test Bank to create a test or quiz.

Subjectively scored assessment tool(s)

Select scenarios from the Scenario Bank representing a variety of situations where copyrighted materials are being used. Have students respond in short-answer or essay format regarding the permissibility of the actions described.

Have students create projects that are appropriate to the requirements of your class or course. Be sure to have requirements in the project regarding the use of copyrighted materials.

Suggested Scoring Criteria

Objectively scored assessment

As the recommended learners for this lesson are adults, a reasonable mastery score on an objectively scored assessment is 80–85 percent.

Subjectively scored assessment

Many subjectively scored assessments for the ability to use copyrighted materials within the limits of specific fair use guidelines are subsets of the requirements of authentic projects that students complete. Therefore, scores on the project should not be used as the metric by which to determine student mastery. Instead, teachers may want to use a sub-score threshold of 80–85 percent for the use of copyrighted materials portion as acceptable evidence that students are able to use copyrighted materials in appropriate manners.

Sample Rubric for Subjectively Scored Projects

This rubric is easily used as a yes/no or binary set of measures.

	Excellent	Good	Poor	Missing
Copyrighted material use is in line with quantity limits	Yes			No
Copyrighted material use is in line with brevity limits	Yes			No
Copyrighted material use is in line with cumulative effect limits	Yes			No
***Copyrighted material is in line with print guidelines**	Yes			No
***Copyrighted material is in line with audiovisual guidelines**	Yes			No
***Copyrighted material is in line with multimedia guidelines**	Yes			No
***Copyrighted material is in line with music guidelines**	Yes			No
Teacher specified criteria, as desired				

*These rows can be evaluated as N/A if the project doesn't contain material covered by the indicated set of guidelines.

Topic: What Are the Important Laws and Guidelines That Affect My Use of Copyrighted Materials?

Lesson 10: How Can I Legally Use Copyrighted Materials? (Understanding Laws That Affect the Use of Copyrighted Materials for Teachers)

Approximate Length of Lesson/Topic

30–45 minutes

Intended Audience

Adult learners

Note: While the information in this lesson provides details and insight for adults as to the particular laws that have changed the nature of copyright law, seldom do users get "quizzed" on the details of these laws. However, it is not unheard of for people to wonder why a rule, limit, condition, or type of right is in place. The details of the law answer those questions.

Learning Goals

- Learners will be able to **name** the laws that govern the use of copyrighted materials.
- Learners will be able to **match** the type of copyrighted work that is affected by specific laws regarding that use.
- Learners will be able to **describe** the requirements for specific laws that govern the use of copyrighted materials.

Materials/Resources/Suggested Reading(s)

Reading(s)

	Simpson and Wolf (2021)	Crews (2020)	Russell (2023)	Other
VARA	pp. 8–9, 21	pp. 78–79, 267–268		
DMCA	pp. 22–24	p. 80	pp. 67–68, 71, 86–87	
MTIA	p. 27	pp. 28–29, 89–90, 276–277	pp. 118–119	
MMA	pp. 25–26	pp. 208–216	pp. 94–95	
CTEA	p. 24	pp. 54–55	p. 21	
TEACH	p. 25, Chapter 9	p. 87, Chapter 16 (pp. 200–201)	p. 85	Section 110 of US copyright law

Resources

- Appendix K Laws and Guidelines Quick Reference
- Starter Slides: Laws

Materials

- Typical materials such as projectors or other display equipment may be useful.
- No other special materials are required.

Procedures/Activity

Activity Summary

This lesson begins with a traditionally delivered lecture, followed by an activity in which students revise scenarios so that they are in compliance with copyright laws and guidelines.

Activity Preparation

Students

- Complete readings as assigned by teacher.

Teacher

- Customize starter slides "Laws" as desired.
- Bingo Option—Create and reproduce bingo cards (using online tools such as Bingo Baker: http://bingobaker.com) as needed.

Environment

- Ensure projection and display equipment is working properly.

Bingo Option

- No special physical environmental preparation is needed.
- Distribute blank bingo cards to learners. Less expert learners may find more success in completing cards as a pair, rather than as an individual.
- Reproduce call list as appropriate.

Activity Procedures

1. Deliver instruction using slide starters as basis of displayed lecture slides.
2. Refer to procedures in "Comprehensive Lecture" lesson to increase interactivity of lecture for students.
3. Optional practice activity: Court Case Bingo.

The classic bingo format permits individuals or teams to identify relevant concepts that describe cases. An alternative version permits learners to identify concepts illustrated in specific court cases. Teachers need to create their own bingo cards, depending on their preferences. Online bingo card creators are available that support the creation of randomly generated cards, automatic creation of the call list, and the importing of user owned graphics, such as Bingo Baker: https://bingobaker.com/.

Bingo

Directions to Students

1. Complete your bingo card by finding a complete row, column, or diagonal line (corner-to-corner) and covering the spaces with a token.
2. Each space you cover should match the clue read by your teacher in terms of the court case described, the finding described, or the concept described.
3. Once you've completed your card, shout "BINGO."
4. Verify your card with the teacher and claim your prize.

Game Modifications

1. To make the game more challenging:
   - **a)** Create a call list that has multiple possible spaces to be marked (e.g., calling "CTEA" could yield spaces containing "Sonny Bono," "length of protection now life of author +70 years").
   - **b)** Increase the speed with which the clues are called.
   - **c)** Increase the number of clues called that have multiple matching spaces available to be marked.
2. To make the game less challenging:
   - **a)** Permit the class to determine the speed with which the clues are called.
   - **b)** Permit students to work in pairs or small teams.
   - **c)** Ensure that clues called match to one and only one possible resulting space.

Practice—Scenario Revision

1. Distribute selected scenarios to individual or small groups.
2. Model the revision of a sample scenario for students. Be sure to narrate the thinking process you engage in as you revise the sample item. For instance,
   - **a)** "As I read this scenario, I notice that the environment is online education. So, I'll want to check the TEACH Act requirements."

b) "I don't have enough information about how the institution in the scenario is operating, so I'll want to make a note that I need that additional information."

c) "I see that the scenario is using music items, so the MMA may need to be consulted."

d) "Based on what I read, the teacher is using the images properly, but the use of the music needs to be changed."

e) "I would change what the teacher does by finding a different musical work, as well as the amount of the work that's being used."

3. Model a second or third revision as desired.

Note: Depending on the experience held by the students in your class, revisions may exhibit more or less sophistication. It is not uncommon for students to revise scenarios by simply eliminating the use of copyrighted work or works. Frequently, students see NOT using something as being the most "for sure" way of being safe. Be sure to encourage students to create revisions that describe the original intent, rather than drastically altering the situation described. In other words, avoidance is not an informed method to use copyrighted materials.

4. Distribute new scenarios, as needed.
5. Direct students to complete scenario revisions until you and they are confident about their revision skills.
6. Allow sufficient time for all groups to complete their revisions, rotating from group to group to ensure they are all making appropriate progress.
7. Remind students to document their decision making in the manner that works best for them.
8. If desired, implement a gallery walk strategy as described in the "Do I Always Have to Get Permission . . ." lesson.

Assessment and Evaluation Suggestions

Suggested Scoring Criteria

Objectively scored assessment

It is likely that cognitive items measuring knowledge of the laws affecting copyright would be a sub-set of questions on a test or quiz examining knowledge about copyright on a broad level. Therefore, establishing a threshold of 75–80 percent of correct answers for this sub-section is appropriate for adult learners to demonstrate their mastery of the content.

Bingo game

As bingo is a game, formal points as a part of a grade are not necessarily appropriate. Teachers may want to award prizes for winners, but I discourage you from attaching grades to the bingo game.

Scenario revision

Revising scenarios is decidedly a case where "answers may vary" applies to the nature of the responses that students provide. Therefore, using a rubric to evaluate the quality of student responses is most useful. A well-written rubric permits the teacher to efficiently mark student responses, and students to receive feedback on a more detailed level, than otherwise would be available using a more holistic scale.

Sample Rubric for Subjectively Scored Projects

	Excellent	**Good**	**Poor**	**Missing**
Identification of portion of scenario needing revision	All elements needing revision are identified. No elements NOT needing revision are marked.	Most or all elements, regardless of obviousness, needing revision are identified. Few, if any, elements NOT needing revision are marked.	Only obvious elements needing revision are marked, not enough to demonstrate awareness of the need for revision. Some are missing. Several items not needing revisions are also marked.	Items marked do NOT require revision. Obvious elements needing revision are not marked.
Application of appropriate copyright-related law in revision	Laws used to support revision are accurately chosen. Details of laws are appropriately applied.	Laws chosen to support revision are correct, but details may be incorrectly applied.	Laws chosen are incorrect; details of laws may be correctly applied within the law, but improperly for the situation.	Improper or no laws are used to support revision decision.
Reasonableness of revision	Revision is insightful and demonstrates creativity in resolving the situation described.	Revision is accurate and reasonable in light of the intent of the scenario.	Revision is inappropriately harsh or lenient. Revision causes further infringements or conflicts with copyright law.	Revision relies on a "just don't use the item" type of response. No required revision is made.
Teacher required criteria, as desired				

Topic: What Significant Court Cases Have Influenced Copyright Law?

Lesson 11: Who Says . . .? (Lecture-based)

Approximate Length of Lesson/Topic

60–120 minutes, depending on the level of customization

Intended Audience

Advanced learners—high school students and older learners—would benefit most from this lesson. Librarians, school administrators, and teachers will find this lesson to be particularly useful.

If limiting the lesson to landmark cases, learners as young as middle school would benefit from this lesson, provided they are able to handle the reading level of the primary documents and have a baseline understanding of the six exclusive rights of a copyright owner and the concept of fair use.

Learning Goals

- Learners will be able to **list** the landmark court cases that established important precedents regarding the application of US copyright law.
- Learners will be able to **describe** the major findings of specific court cases that inform the application of US copyright law.
- Learners will be able to **cite** appropriate court cases in support of their analysis of authentic scenarios regarding the use of copyrighted materials.
- Learners will be able to **name** the plaintiff and defendant in specific court cases that inform the application of US copyright law.
- Learners will be able to **match** the title of specific court cases that inform the application of US copyright law with the concepts of copyright law that are influenced by them.
- Learners will be able to **discriminate** between landmark and non-landmark court cases that inform the application of US copyright law.

Materials/Resources/Suggested Reading(s)

Reading(s)

Publicly available primary and secondary documents for each of the key court cases are linked in Appendix G. Instructors who wish to have learners read those documents should access them from the appendix. There are too many to reasonably list here in the readings section of the lesson.

	Simpson and Wolf (2021)	Crews (2020)	Russell (2023)	Other
Court Cases	Concordance (pp. 325–339)			Appendix G Key Court Cases

Resources

- Appendix G: Key Court Cases

Materials

- Starter Slides: Who Says . . .?

Procedures/Activity

Activity Summary

In this lecture-based lesson, instructors organize and deliver the content in the manner that best fits their own instructional philosophy and style.

An optional practice activity of Court Case Bingo is included for those instructors who find it useful.

Activity Preparation

Students

- Minimal preparation is required.
- Students should review case-information as assigned by their teacher/instructor.
- Students should be able to name and define the six exclusive rights of a copyright owner; be able to explain the concept of fair use; be able to list the four fair use factors; and understand the relationship between licenses and copyright protection.

Teacher

- Review case information as needed.
- Download (if desired) and customize "Who Says . . .?" presentation as appropriate, using the following considerations as guidelines for customization:
  - Delete non-landmark cases to simplify the lecture.
  - Organize cases according to broad copyright concepts to aid in encoding of content.
  - Organize cases by jurisdiction if desired.
  - Organize cases by level (trial, appeal, SCOTUS, etc.) if desired.
- Intersperse formative assessment slides as appropriate for individual learner groups.

- Bingo Option—Create and reproduce bingo cards (using online tools such as Bingo Baker: http://bingobaker.com) as needed.

Environment

- No special learning environment required.
- Computer and display equipment should be arranged as appropriate.

Bingo Option

- No special physical environmental preparation is needed.
- Distribute blank bingo cards to learners. Less expert learners may find more success in completing cards as a pair, rather than as an individual.
- Reproduce call list as appropriate.

Activity Procedures

1. Provide a review of the following concepts to ensure that learners are prepared to learn:
   a) Exclusive rights of the copyright owner
   b) Fair use
2. Deliver instruction using slide starters as basis of displayed lecture slides.
3. Refer to procedures in "Comprehensive Lecture" lesson to increase interactivity of lecture for students.
4. Optional practice activity: Court Case Bingo.

The classic bingo format permits individuals or teams to identify relevant concepts that describe cases. An alternative version permits learners to identify concepts illustrated in specific court cases. Teachers need to create their own bingo cards, depending on their preferences. Online bingo card creators are available that support the creation of randomly generated cards, automatic creation of the call list, and the importing of user owned graphics, such as Bingo Baker: https://bingobaker.com/.

Bingo
Directions to Students

1. Complete your bingo card by finding a complete row, column, or diagonal line (corner-to-corner) and covering the spaces with a token.
2. Each space you cover should match the clue read by your teacher in terms of the court case described, the finding described, or the concept described.
3. Once you've completed your card, shout "BINGO."
4. Verify your card with the teacher and claim your prize.

Game Modifications

1. To make the game more challenging:
   a) Create a call list that has multiple possible spaces to be marked (e.g., calling "*Harper & Row v. Nation Enterprises*" could yield spaces containing "transformative use," "using unpublished work is NOT fair use," or "four fair use factors aren't only things to use in determining fair use." If the student has the "transformative use" space and marks it, they won't then be able to use it again when "*Author's Guild v. Google Inc.*" is called).
   b) Increase the speed with which the clues are called.
   c) Increase the number of clues called that have multiple matching spaces available to be marked.
2. To make the game less challenging:
   a) Permit the class to determine the speed with which the clues are called.
   b) Permit students to work in pairs or small teams.
   c) Ensure that clues called match to one and only one possible resulting space.

Assessment and Evaluation Suggestions

Two methods are recommended as being the best fit in order to determine learner mastery of the learning goals. Instructors should select the one that best meets their teaching philosophy and instructional needs.

Objectively scored test

- Construct test using accompanying Test Bank of questions.
- Insert additional questions as desired.

Subjectively scored test

- Construct test using accompanying Test Bank of questions, modifying them to take a "fill-in" or "short-answer" format as desired.
- Insert additional questions as desired.
- When creating a scoring key, ensure that items where "answers may vary" have key concepts noted so that scoring is able to be efficient and consistent.

Suggested Scoring Criteria

Unless learners are part of a university course about school or business law (including copyright), 100 percent accuracy or knowledge is not necessary in order for instructors to be confident that learners have satisfactorily mastered the learning goals.

Recommended passing thresholds for the following levels of learners are:

- Advanced learners (adults: librarians, school administrators, teachers): 75–85 percent or equivalent in "points out of" format.
- Mid-level learners (teens, adults: secondary students, undergraduate, graduate students): 70–85 percent or equivalent in "points out of" format.
- Entry-level learners (teens, adults: advanced middle school, lay-people): 65–75 percent or equivalent in "points out of" format.

These thresholds should be considered recommendations and not hard and fast limits. Instructors should always use their best discretion in determining final mastery thresholds for their learners.

Topic: What Significant Court Cases Have Influenced Copyright Law?

Lesson 12: Who Says . . .? (Learner-centered, Exploratory)

Approximate Length of Lesson/Topic

60–90 minutes

Intended Audience

This lesson is most appropriate for advanced learners. High school students and older would benefit most from this lesson.

Librarians, school administrators, and teachers will find this lesson to be particularly useful.

Learning Goals

- Learners will be able to **list** the landmark court cases that established important precedents regarding the application of US copyright law.
- Learners will be able to **describe** the major findings of specific court cases that inform the application of US copyright law.
- Learners will be able to **cite** appropriate court cases in support of their analysis of authentic scenarios regarding the use of copyrighted materials.
- Learners will be able to **name** the plaintiff and defendant in specific court cases that inform the application of US copyright law.
- Learners will be able to **match** the title of specific court cases that inform the application of US copyright law with the concepts of copyright law that are influenced by them.
- Learners will be able to **discriminate** between landmark and non-landmark court cases that inform the application of US copyright law.

Materials/Resources/Suggested Reading(s)

Reading(s)

Publicly available primary and secondary documents for each of the key court cases are linked in Appendix G. Instructors who wish to have learners read those documents should access them from the appendix. There are too many to reasonably list here in the readings section of the lesson.

	Simpson and Wolf (2021)	Crews (2020)	Russell (2023)	Other
Court Cases	Concordance (pp. 325–339)			Appendix G Key Court Cases

Resources

- Appendix G: Key Court Cases
- Online timeline creator applications
- Online Flash Card creator applications
- Reproducible Concentration game cards
- Reproducible scavenger hunt clue sheets
- Bingo card concept list

Materials

- Starter Slides: Who Says . . .?

Procedures/Activity

Activity Summary

Due to the exploratory nature of this lesson, younger students may find it challenging to manage, since the basis of the activities is primary sources of court cases. The vocabulary and sentence structure in legal documents may be more complex than younger students can manage. Teachers should be sure to adapt materials and procedures to ensure that learners are able to manage the tasks of the lesson without undue frustration.

Alternatively, this lesson can be used as a practice activity that is completed after the lecture-based lesson is delivered.

Concentration Game

A variation on the classic game of Concentration that sees players flip cards to find matches. The player with the most matches "wins."

Scavenger Hunt Activity

Learners explore primary and secondary resources to find citations and references relating to copyright concepts. Teams or individuals may complete the activity. Incentives for speed, variety, and accuracy may be awarded at the teacher's discretion.

Copyright Bingo

The classic bingo format permits individuals or teams to identify relevant concepts that describe cases. An alternative version permits learners to identify concepts illustrated in specific court cases. Teachers need to create their own bingo cards, depending on their preferences. Online bingo card creators are available that support the creation of randomly generated cards, automatic creation of the call list, and the importing of user owned graphics, such as Bingo Baker: https://bingobaker.com/.

Activity Preparation

Students

- Minimal preparation is required.
- Students should review case-information as assigned by their teacher/instructor.
- Students should be able to name and define the six exclusive rights of a copyright owner; be able to explain the concept of fair use; and be able to list the four fair use factors.

Teacher

- Depending on the age/grade level of the learners, duplicate and provide appropriate reference materials for students to reference during the activity, such as:
    - Online flashcard practice set
    - Curated list of court cases in online or written format, as desired
- Concentration
    - Reproduce and duplicate Concentration cards as needed.
    - Teacher should decide whether the pairs will be organized by major ruling/case title (e.g., *Feist Publications v. Rural Telephone Services* / A minimal amount of creativity must be present for a work to be eligible for copyright protection); key concepts/case title (*Author's Guild v. Google Inc.* / Transformative Use); or in a more complex organization, cases related to one another (*Campbell v. Acuff-Rose Music, Inc.* / *Berlin v. E.C Pubs., Inc.*—both dealt with key concept of parody being an example of fair use).
- Scavenger Hunt
    - Create/reproduce scavenger hunt lists as appropriate (see Appendix H for one example; others are available in the online resource repository).
    - Create hidden/coded message if desired (can serve as the "answer key").
    - Create "prize cards"—cards that have on one side the answer to the clues (either cases or concepts) and on the other, a letter and a number. The letter is in the hidden message, and the number is the number of those letters. For instance, if the hidden message is "Free Homework Pass," a letter prize might be the "e" and the number 3, indicating that there are three letter "e"s in the puzzle.
- Bingo
    - Create and reproduce bingo cards (using online tools such as Bingo Baker: http://bingobaker.com) as needed.

Concentration

- Arrange tables/desks or other seating to permit the Concentration boards to be laid out with adequate room.

- Concentration gameboards for younger or less expert learners should be limited to 4×4 (8 total pairs) or 6×6 (18 total pairs) cards in size. Gameboards must have an even number of cards in rows and columns in order for there to be no cards left over once all pairs are identified.
- More expert learners can handle gameboards up to 8×8 (32 total pairs) or even 10×10 (50 total pairs) cards.
- Divide learners into appropriately sized teams of play (two or three learners per gameboard, depending on size of gameboard).

Scavenger Hunt

- No special physical environmental preparation is needed.
- Curated information about court cases can be made available online in the form of Path Finders, "Outliners" on the curational tool Diigo, or other similar formats.
- Write the hidden message on the board in "Wheel of Fortune" or "Hangman" style (e.g., _ _ _ _   _   _ _ _ _ _   _ _ _ "Have a good day").

Bingo

- No special physical environmental preparation is needed.
- Distribute blank bingo cards to learners. Less expert learners may find more success in completing cards as a pair, rather than as an individual.
- Reproduce call list as appropriate.

Activity Procedures

Concentration

Directions to students:

1. Shuffle your pile of cards so that they are thoroughly mixed.
2. Lay your cards face down in a grid of 4×4, 6×6, 8×8, or 10×10 cards. Make sure that each row and column has the same number of cards.
3. Choose one student to take the first turn (use established classroom procedures to do so, as appropriate).
4. When it's your turn, flip two cards. Determine whether they match according to:
   a) Title/Outcome
   b) Title/Key Concept
   c) Related issue or concept

5. If they match, that player keeps the cards (optional: permit one additional turn).
6. If they do not match, flip the cards back over so that they rest face down.
7. Play progresses to the LEFT of the current player.
8. Repeat steps 4–7 until all matches have been located, or time of play expires (as set by the teacher).
9. Players waiting their turn to flip cards should pay attention to those cards being flipped, as they can use that information on their turn to locate matches.

Game modifications

1. To make the game more challenging:
   a) Increate the size of the gameboard.
   b) Decrease the time of play (turn it into "speed" Concentration).
   c) Use secondary concepts as the "match" for case title/ key concept style of play.
2. To make the game less challenging:
   a) Reduce the size of the gameboard.
   b) Increase the time of play.
   c) Permit the use of reference sources in determining matches.
   d) Permit learners to work in teams.
3. To increase competition/interest:
   a) Conduct a "Concentration tournament."
   b) Establish a set time each week or month (as desired) to play copyright Concentration.
   c) Record winners during each game session, maintaining a cumulative score for each student or team.
   d) At the conclusion of the tournament, declare the overall winner based on total matches, shortest time to clear gameboards, or other metric chosen by the teacher or class.

Scavenger Hunt

Directions to Students

1. Use the clues on your clue sheet to locate copyright-related court cases or concepts that will correspond to the letters in the hidden message on the board.
2. When you have solved your clue, and have a court case or concept, show the teacher, who will give you your letter prize.
3. Collect your letter prizes to solve the hidden message.

Game Modifications

1. To make the game more challenging:
   - **a)** Increase the length or complexity of the hidden message.
   - **b)** Decrease the amount of time permitted to solve the puzzle.
   - **c)** Restrict access to reference resources only to those available in the classroom, in print, or in non-full text searchable formats.
   - **d)** Restrict students to working as individuals.
2. To make the game less challenging:
   - **a)** Decrease the length or complexity of the hidden message.
   - **b)** Increase the amount of time permitted to solve the puzzle.
   - **c)** Permit students to access searchable reference resources online.
   - **d)** Permit students to work in pairs or teams.

Bingo
Directions to Students

1. Complete your bingo card by finding a complete row, column, or diagonal line and covering the spaces with a token.
2. Each space you cover should match the clue read by your teacher in terms of the court case described, the finding described, or the concept described.
3. Once you've completed your card, shout "BINGO."
4. Verify your card with the teacher and claim your prize.

Game Modifications

1. To make the game more challenging:
   - **a)** Create a call list that has multiple possible spaces to be marked (e.g., calling "*Harper & Row v. Nation Enterprises*" could yield spaces containing "transformative use," "using unpublished work is NOT fair use," or "four fair use factors aren't the only things to use in determining fair use." If the student has the "transformative use" space and marks it, they won't then be able to use it again when "*Author's Guild v. Google Inc.*" is called).
   - **b)** Increase the speed with which the clues are called.
   - **c)** Increase the number of clues called that have multiple matching spaces available to be marked.

2. To make the game less challenging:

   a) Permit the class to determine the speed with which the clues are called.

   b) Permit students to work in pairs or small teams.

   c) Ensure that clues called match to one and only one possible resulting space.

Assessment and Evaluation Suggestions

Suggested Scoring Criteria

Concentration

The following options are available for determining the "winner" of the game. Teachers should use their discretion in awarding prizes to the winners.

- The player with the highest number of matches from a single gameboard is declared the winner.
- The team with the highest number of matches in the class is declared the winning team.
- The player or team in the class that clears the board in the shortest amount of time is declared the class winner.
- If a tournament structure is used, cumulative points, cumulative time to clear the board, or other similar cumulative metric can be used to determine the overall winner.

Scavenger Hunt

The scavenger hunt is scored as a binary correct/incorrect for each item. It would not be appropriate to use the activity as a measure of mastery, however. It is intended to be a practice activity for students to complete prior to a more formal assessment of their mastery. If you wish, you may choose to use it as a participation score if that is appropriate for your class.

Bingo

As bingo is a game, formal points as a part of a grade are not necessarily appropriate. Teachers may want to award prizes for winners, but I discourage you from attaching grades to the bingo game.

Topic: What Happens When Copyright Is Infringed?

Lesson 13: Who's Really Responsible When There's Been a Copyright Infringement?

Approximate Length of Lesson/Topic

60 minutes

Intended Audience

Learners of all ages and levels

Learning Goals

- Learners will be able to **define** the four types of infringement: innocent, willful, vicarious, and contributory.
- Learners will be able to **name** specific roles in the workplace that illustrate the four types of infringement.
- Learners will be able to **identify** examples of the four types of infringement in authentic scenarios.
- Learners will be able to **differentiate** between copyright infringement and plagiarism.

Materials/Resources/Suggested Reading(s)

Reading(s)

	Simpson and Wolf (2021)	**Crews (2020)**	**Russell (2023)**	**Other**
Types of infringements	pp. 27–30			Butler (2004) pp. 54–57
Liability	p. 30	Chapter 18 (pp. 183–204)		

Resources

- Scenarios from the Scenario Bank
- Starter Slides: "Types of Infringement"

Materials

- Highlighters or pens of at least four different colors

Procedures/Activity

Activity Summary

This activity begins with a brief direct instruction section in which teachers may elect to use the starter slides, "Types of Infringement." Then, small groups or individual students complete a practice activity of coding authentic scenarios according to the type of infringement illustrated. Finally, teachers guide students in a "mini debate" style discussion. Learners work together to make decisions regarding whether an infringement of copyright is described as well as the relative severity of any infringement of multiple characters in authentic scenarios.

Activity Preparation

Students

- Be able to name and identify instances of the six exclusive rights of the copyright holder.

Teacher

- Write a set of scenarios if not using scenarios from the Scenario Bank.
- Create or reproduce an "answer key" of the infringement types for the scenarios used in the practice activity. For scenarios from the Scenario Bank, the types of infringement are already marked.

Environment

- Ensure that display equipment is present and operating properly.
- Ensure if using small groups for the practice activity that students have sufficient room to consult with one another and document the results of their work.

Activity Procedures

Direct Instruction

1 Begin with a direct instruction model and deliver the customization of starter slides, "Types of Infringement."

2 Be sure to help learners differentiate between the four types of infringement that all users can demonstrate:

a) Innocent: believing that what you're doing is truly alright to do, but in the end, being wrong about that

b) Standard: straightforward misuse of one of the six exclusive rights

c) Willful: blatant misuse of the six exclusive rights; especially after requesting permission and not receiving it, or failure to pay licensing fees

d) Vicarious: knowing about an infringement and being able to benefit from while having also having supervisory control over the infringer, but failing to prevent the infringement. Benefit could be saving money or avoid paying money.

3 Help learners make the connection of vicarious infringement the avoidance of paying money or striving to save money, as well as the supervisory knowledge of an infringement but failure to prevent it.

4 Help learners understand the term "vicarious" as meaning "assistance" when applied to copyright infringements.

5 Help learners understand that plagiarism is an ethical violation where one person claims authorship for the work of another. Copyright infringement is limited to violating one of the six exclusive rights.

6 Use plagiarism vs. copyright Venn diagram (available from the companion website) to illustrate relationship between copyright infringement and plagiarism. Sometimes, users can both infringe copyright and plagiarize, but not always.

Practice: Coding Scenarios

1. Organize the class as desired. Pairs, trios, small groups, or individuals will work equally effectively. Keep in mind that younger, less experienced learners will benefit from having peers with whom to practice.
2. Distribute three to five scenarios to each student or group.
3. Direct students to color-code the scenarios in terms of the type of infringement that is present in the scenario.
   a) Color A: innocent infringement
   b) Color B: willful infringement
   c) Color C: vicarious infringement
   d) Color D: contributory infringement
4. Use your desired method to provide feedback regarding the accuracy of learner practice.
5. Alternatives to this practice organization:
   a) Gallery walk strategy: Post scenarios using chart paper or individual electronic display options. Have students complete the coding, and then rotate to provide peer feedback to one another. This is particularly useful for small group work and when using scenarios that require a significant number of assumptions or additional information in order to adequately analyze them.
   b) Use a "homework" strategy as practice. Collect student work and mark for applicable "credit" within a class.

Mini Debate Discussion

1. Transition to a debate format.
2. Distribute scenarios describing various levels of using copyrighted materials. Some scenarios should be obvious, others moderately so, and others very murky. Additionally, some scenarios should illustrate permissible behaviors in addition to those that illustrate infringements.
3. Have students in the groupings of your choice (whole class, small groups, pairs, etc.) determine answers to the following questions:
   - **a)** Is there an infringement of copyright in this scenario?
   - **b)** For each character in the scenario, what type (if any) of infringement do they portray?
   - **c)** Which of the scenarios that you were given portrays the most extreme, or worst, example of copyright infringement?
   - **d)** Which portrays the least extreme, or most lenient, example of copyright infringement?
   - **e)** Which character in the scenario is the most/least responsible for the violation described?
   - **f)** Support each of your answers with specific evidence from the scenario, class readings, or the law.

Assessment and Evaluation Suggestions

Objectively scored assessment tools
Select appropriate items from the Test Bank and include as a sub-section within a written test or quiz.

Subjectively scored assessment tool
Using scenarios as the basis for each item, have students complete short-answer items that are similar to the coding exercise in the lesson or the debate questions in the lesson.

Using scenarios as the basis for each item, have students rewrite the scenario to eliminate a specific type of infringement.

Suggested Scoring Criteria for Objectively Scored Assessment Tool

A minimum of 80–85 percent correct answers for the sub-section within a longer written test or quiz is reasonable evidence that the learner has mastered the learning objectives.

Sample Rubric for Subjectively Scored Assessment Tool

	Excellent	Good	Poor	Missing
Accuracy	Response/revision is accurate in both the identification of the issue as well as the evidentiary support used to justify the conclusion. The response also includes subtle aspects and details that add to the accuracy of the response.	Response/revision is accurate regarding the evidentiary support used, but the identification of the issue may not be complete. The high-level and obvious aspects of the scenario are addressed.	Response/revision is inaccurate regarding the evidentiary support used. The rewritten response describes additional infringements or fails to completely correct the issues described in the scenario.	Response/revision does not change the actions described in all practical ways. No evidentiary support is provided.
Reasonableness of response or revision	Response/revision is insightful and demonstrates creativity in resolving the situation described.	Response/revision is accurate and reasonable in light of the intent of the scenario.	Response/revision is inappropriately harsh or lenient. Revision causes further infringements or conflicts with copyright law.	Response/revision relies on a "just don't use the item" type of response. No required revision is made.
Completeness of evidentiary support	Student evidentiary support addresses all relevant aspects of the intended use as well as supplies evidence from both primary (the law) and secondary (readings) sources or from multiple secondary sources.	Student evidentiary support addresses most relevant aspects of the intended use as well as supplies evidence from either primary (the law) or secondary (readings) sources.	Student evidentiary support addresses relevant aspects of the intended use and includes irrelevant aspects of the use or irrelevant information from the scenario. Supplied evidence of support does not conceptually align with the aspects of the use/scenario that are identified.	Students fail to provide evidentiary support for their conclusions. Where citations are included, the sources are not appropriate primary or secondary sources.

Topic: What Happens When Copyright Is Infringed?

Lesson 14: What Really Happens When Copyright Is Infringed?

Approximate Length of Lesson/Topic

60 minutes

Intended Audience

Learners of all ages and levels

Learning Goals

- Learners will be able to **define** "cease-and-desist letter."
- Learners will be able to **define** actual and statutory damages.
- Learners will be able to **differentiate** between actual and potential damages.
- Learners will be able to **name** the types of consequences (sanctions) that result from copyright violation.
- Learners will be able to **describe** the effect of copyright violation on employment status (adult learners only).

Materials/Resources/Suggested Reading(s)

Reading(s)

	Simpson and Wolf (2021)	Crews (2020)	Russell (2023)	Other
Consequences, particularly for schools	pp. 34–37			
Sample cease-and-desist letter	p. 35 (Figure 1.2)			
General coverage of consequences		Chapter 18 (pp. 183–191)	pp. 31–38	Butler (2004) pp. 54–57, 79–80, 98–101, 119–121, 134–138, 154–157, 195–196

Resources

- Stranger Things funny cease-and-desist letter: https://sharongivoni.com.au/netflix-cease-desist-letter-copyright/
- Activision lawyers send Spyro fan game cease-and-desist: https://www.eurogamer.net/spyro-myths-awaken-fan-game-sent-cease-and-desist
- Dr. Seuss goes after photographer after Grinch-themed photo shoot: https://petapixel.com/2019/10/02/dr-seuss-goes-after-photographer-over-grinch-themed-photo-shoot/

Materials

- Starter slides "Consequences of Infringement"

Procedures/Activity

Activity Summary

This lesson begins with a brief direct instruction using starter slides as foundation. Then, teachers facilitate small group analysis of scenarios where students identify the infringing characters in scenarios. Then, they describe the type of infringement within the scenario. Finally, they determine the most likely consequence of the infringement, followed by the most extreme consequence of the infringement.

Activity Preparation

Students

- Be able to define the different types of infringement (standard, willful, vicarious, contributory).
- Be able to identify examples of the different types of infringement.

Teacher

- Customize starter slides to use in the direct instruction portion of the lesson.
- Select appropriate scenarios to use in the analysis activity.

Environment

- No special environmental arrangements need to be made other than those needed for presentation display.

Activity Procedures

Direct Instruction

1. Begin with a direct instruction model and deliver the customization of starter slides, "Consequences of Infringement."
2. If needed, review the four types of infringement from the previous lesson. Ensure that students are able to accurately discriminate between all of the types.
3. Ensure that students understand the difference between statutory and actual damages.
4. Ensure that students understand the purpose of a cease-and-desist letter.
5. Use sample cease-and-desist letters in the resources section of the lesson plan to illustrate the common sections and contents found in that type of letter.
6. Ensure that students understand the consequential difference between infringing copyright law and violating workplace policy.
7. Ensure that students understand the purpose of an injunction.
8. Remind students about the situations in which copyright infringement and plagiarism can occur, and the different types of consequences of each.

Scenario Analysis

1. Organize the class as desired. Pairs, trios, small groups, or individuals will work equally effectively. Keep in mind that younger, less experienced learners will benefit from having peers with whom to practice.
2. Distribute three to five scenarios to each student or group.
3. Direct students to work together in order to determine the most likely FIRST consequence for infringements described in each scenario.
4. Once students have identified the first response, likely a cease-and-desist letter or employment action, for the scenarios, have them trade scenarios and letters. Then, create new portions to the scenarios where some or all elements of the cease-and-desist letters are or are not followed.
5. Have students create the next most likely response to the new scenario situations.
6. Debrief student analyses and letters to ensure that they have accurately applied an appropriate level of response for the infringement described in each scenario.

Assessment and Evaluation Suggestions

Objectively scored assessment tool (test/quiz)

Select appropriate items from the objective item Test Bank. Use as a sub-section of a longer test or quiz.

Written responses to scenario infringements

Suggested Scoring Criteria for Objectively Scored Items

Students scoring at least 80 percent (of the items in this sub-section of a larger test/quiz) can be considered to have sufficiently mastered the objectives of this lesson.

Sample Rubric for Subjectively Scored Projects

The activity in this lesson is intended to function as formative assessment rather than a formal assessment in a subjectively scored fashion. Therefore, the debriefing recommended in the procedures section should be used to determine whether students are making appropriate progress toward mastery of the learning goals for the lesson.

Key elements to focus on when determining student progress include:

- If writing cease-and-desist letters, do they include the appropriate information as described in the scenario?
    - Authority to write on behalf of copyright owner
    - Specific description of the infringement
    - Requested action to be ceased
    - Actions that will result from non-compliance
- Is the cease-and-desist letter written using an appropriate tone and voice?
- Are the actions being requested reasonable?
- For responses to the follow-on scenarios where the cease-and-desist letters are not followed, are the actions recommended in alignment with those described in the original cease-and-desist letter?

For more formal projects, teachers are encouraged to create rubrics that are most useful to them and in alignment with project requirements that they create. There are many possible rubric criteria that might be created, so the writing of them is left up to the teacher.

3 Assessment Items

Test Bank

Throughout this book, I've given recommendations for measuring student understanding and mastery of the learning objectives within each lesson. In order to help teachers streamline the process of creating traditional quizzes and tests, I've created 231 questions that can be used to measure the copyright concepts covered in this book. The questions have been created to represent a variety of Bloom's Taxonomy levels, as indicated in the concordance. Each of the objectively scored items is provided here as a stem, without accompanying distractors. Some questions can be customized to measure a variety of related concepts. Those questions are annotated using square brackets that include italicized directions for appropriate forms of customization. For example, question 3.17 reads:

> 17. Which of the following types of licenses would control or govern the use of material found at [*insert web location here*]?

Teachers could choose whichever website is most appropriate for their students and learning context. They could also repeat the question using more than one website, thereby increasing the usefulness of each item.

Question 5.10 reads:

> 10. Imagine that your classmate does not understand how to determine whether they are permitted to use [*insert specific video here*] during one of their [*insert subject area*] classes. Write an explanation of the factors of video fair use that your classmate would be able to understand.

Teachers could specify the URL of a video or use a description of a video that is located in the library. It would be appropriate to use the subject area that best describes the class in which the students are enrolled or that the teachers are teaching.

For readers who wish to have more structured information about the test items and how to customize them, an annotated set of the test items is included on the website for this book. Annotations will include information such as the appropriate considerations that should be taken when creating distractor sets, ways to revise questions to increase or decrease the complexity levels, and other important information that teachers need when deciding whether or not to include a particular question in a test that they are writing. Two examples of annotated items can be found below. A formatted version of these questions is also available on the website that includes distractors and correct answers. The formatted version can easily be imported to commonly used learning management systems such as Schoology, Canvas, and Moodle.

Which of the following items are protected by copyright? (Check all that apply)

- ☐ The class notes that Sally took during her biology class.
- ☐ The dance routine that the cheer squad performed at the basketball game.
- ☐ The Google Doodle contest entry that the 3rd grade class completed as an art assignment.
- ☐ The idea for a book that the superintendent of schools told his assistant he wanted to write.
- ☐ The lesson plans that the Math department faculty wrote during their common planning period were comprehensive and detailed.
- ☐ The school's logo.
- ☐ The term paper that all HS seniors are required to write.

Notes about this question:

1. Note that the distractors for this item are incorrect for the following reasons:
   - Dance routine (not in tangible format). If the dance routine *choreography* were mentioned, the choreography would be copyrighted; likewise, if the dance routine were filmed as a part of a performance, the resulting video would be copyrighted.
   - Book idea (ideas can't be copyrighted). If the book idea were in a written proposal form, it would be copyrighted.
   - School logo (logos are typically trademarked, not copyrighted, although the artwork that is used to create logos might be protected by copyright).
2. This question can be customized by replacing the characters and situations with ones that are appropriate to your intended audience (higher education, teachers, students, etc.).
3. This question can be made more challenging by including a greater number of distractors that have higher levels of similarities: for instance, using a well-known item such as the "Happy Meal" from McDonald's vs. an advertisement about Happy Meals vs. the recipe for the special sauce on a Big Mac as distractors. In this example, only the advertisement is copyrighted; the other elements are either trademarked or considered to be trade secrets. Also include items that have fallen into the Public Domain, are Works Made for Hire, are governed by a specific license, or have had copyright protection expire.
4. This question can be made simpler by limiting the number of distractors to four or five and making them obvious or verbatim from the lists of items that are provided in the law.

A public school 6th grade teacher chooses to show a movie that she borrowed from the school library in class and invites the students to bring their parents to see the video on parent's day. Then, the students and parents complete an in-class activity that analyzes the information from the video. Which of the five criteria for classroom video use has the teacher infringed?

- ☐ Non-profit use
- ☐ Location: classroom or similar space
- ☐ Viewers/Presenters: instructors or pupils of the class
- ☐ Activity: face-to-face teaching
- ☐ Source of video: lawfully obtained copy

Notes about this question:

1. Note that the distractors for this item are incorrect for the following reasons:
    - The location is a non-profit public school.
    - The film is being shown in the classroom.
    - There is an accompanying instructional activity.
    - The film was borrowed from the library, so it is safe to assume that the copy was lawfully obtained.
2. This question can be customized by replacing the characters and situations with ones that are appropriate to your intended audience (higher education, teachers, students, etc.).
3. This question can be made more challenging by including less obvious references to the five criteria of classroom use of video. For instance, statements such as the "Little Red Schoolhouse preschool teacher" imply that the setting is a for-profit preschool rather than a public school.
4. This question can be made simpler by formatting it as a T/F or Y/N question, with the final question of the scenario being something similar to: "Is the teacher's use of the video permissible under the classroom use exceptions of copyright law?"

Numbering Convention

Test items are numbered sequentially within each of the eight broad copyright-related topics. The list of topics is:

1. What is copyright?
2. What is fair use?
3. How do licenses influence how I am permitted to use copyrighted material?

4. What exceptions to the copyright law affect my teaching/learning?
5. How do I determine whether what I want to do is permissible?
6. What are the important laws and guidelines that affect my use of copyrighted materials?
7. What significant court cases and laws have influenced copyright law?
8. What happens when copyright is violated?

The concordance in Chapter 5 uses this numbering convention to refer to individual questions. As you use the concordance to select question items for each lesson, you should refer to this test item bank for the complete text of the question. For example, question 1.19 reads, "Which of the following items is able to be copyrighted?" while question 6.2 reads, "Which type of copyrighted work does the [*insert law name here*] law control or govern in terms of its use?"

1. What Is Copyright?

Students will state the six exclusive rights of a copyright holder.

1. Which of the following items is NOT one of the exclusive rights of a copyright holder?
2. What are the exclusive rights of a copyright holder? (Check all that apply)

Students will define the six exclusive rights of a copyright holder.

3. Match the exclusive right on the left with its definition on the right. Not all definitions will be used.
4. Which of the following descriptions best describes the exclusive right of [*fill in name of exclusive right here*]?

Students will state the definition of Public Domain.

5. "Public Domain" describes creative items that are: . . .
6. Which of the following characteristics is TRUE for items in the public domain?

Students will identify items that are protected by copyright.

7. Match the item on the left with the type of intellectual property on the right that protects it.
8. Which of the following symbols is required to indicate that an item is protected by copyright?

Students will list the types of items that can be protected by copyright.

9. Which of the following items are protected by copyright?
10. Write the names of X specific items that are protected by copyright.

Students will define patent, trademark, and copyright in their own (age-appropriate) language.

11. Write the definition for each term provided.
12. For each type of intellectual property law on the left, demonstrate your ability to define them by matching the term with the proper definition on the right. Not all definitions will be used.

Students will define plagiarism in their own (age-appropriate) language.

13. Write the definition of plagiarism.
14. Which of the following statements BEST describes what plagiarism is?

Learners will be able to state the purpose of copyright protection in their own words.

15. Which of the following best describes the purpose of copyright protection?
16. Imagine that one of your classmates asks you why copyright protection is important. How would you reply to that classmate in language that they would easily understand?

Learners will be able to label items as copyrightable or not copyrightable.

17. Write "copyrightable" or "not copyrightable" on the line next to each of the items listed here.
18. Sort each of the following images of items into the appropriate group, either "copyrightable" or "not copyrightable."
19. Which of the following items is able to be copyrighted?
20. Which of the following items is unable to be copyrighted?

Learners will be able to describe the types of works that are eligible for copyright protection.

21. Using language that your classmates would understand, describe the types of items that are eligible for copyright protection.
22. For each of the items pictured here, write how you know that it is eligible for copyright protection.
23. For each of the items pictured here, write how you know that it is ineligible for copyright protection.

Students will identify the exclusive right of a copyright owner that is affected in specific scenarios.

24. Match the actions on the left with the exclusive right of copyright holders on the right that it best illustrates. Not all actions will have a matching exclusive right. Some exclusive rights may be matched with more than one action.
25. Which exclusive right of copyright owners is affected by the scenario provided?

Students will determine which type of intellectual property law governs specific scenarios.

26. Match the type of intellectual property law on the left with the scenario in which it's used on the right. If NO intellectual property law is used in a scenario, choose "none."
27. Which type of intellectual property law would govern the scenario provided?

Students will discriminate between works protected by patent, trademark, and copyright.

28. Which of the following items are eligible for copyright protection under the current copyright law? Write a "yes" on the line in front of those items that are eligible for protection and a "no" on the line in front of those items that are not eligible for protection.
29. What is the difference between copyright and trademark?
30. What is the difference between copyright and patent?

Students will compare/contrast copyright infringement and plagiarism.

31. For each of the statements below, describe their relationship to the concepts of copyright infringement and plagiarism by writing "copyright," "plagiarism," "both," or "neither," as appropriate. (Can also format as a four-choice multiple choice.)
32. Write a specific example that illustrates copyright infringement.
33. Write a specific example that illustrates plagiarism.
34. Write a specific example that illustrates the intersection of copyright infringement and plagiarism.

Students will explain the difference between copyright infringement and plagiarism.

35. The concepts of copyright infringement and plagiarism have the ability to overlap in certain situations. However, they have distinct differences that separate them as well. Write X significant differences between the two concepts.
36. Write how you would explain the difference between copyright infringement and plagiarism to students in [*insert grade level here*] grade/level of education.

Students will differentiate between commonly confusing concepts (transformative use/derivative use; copyright/plagiarism; copyright/trademark/patent).

37. Demonstrate your ability to differentiate between [*insert concepts here*] by choosing the appropriate label that best describes the scenario.

38. Which of the following concepts best describes the situation presented? (Multiple choice format; be sure to include pairs of commonly confused concepts as at least two of the distractors.)

Students will determine whether a specific item falls into the public domain.

39. If a book is published in [*insert year here*], in what year will it fall into the public domain?

   a. Given that it is written by a single author.
   b. Given that it is written by the staff writer for State University as a part of her job.
   c. Given that it is written by two professors within the same department.
   d. Given that it is written by a political critic under an assumed name.
   e. Given that it is written in [*insert year here*] but has not yet been published as of this year.

Students will annotate scenarios according to the six rights of a copyright holder.

40. For each of the scenarios provided, write the appropriate exclusive rights of a copyright holder that are affected in the blank(s) provided. If none of the rights are affected, write "none" in the blank provided.
41. For each of the scenarios provided, circle/underline the text that provides evidence of a specific exclusive right of copyright holders being affected/violated. Write the name of the exclusive right that is affected in the blank provided.

Students will create instructional activities that use public domain materials.

42. For each of the scenarios provided, replace the copyrighted materials that are used with materials from the public domain. Provide the URL of the location for your replacement materials as well as evidence that supports the conclusion that your material is in the public domain.
43. For each of the scenarios provided, create/develop one original appropriate teaching aid that uses components (text, images, etc.) from the public domain. Indicate how you know that your item is in the public domain.

---

2. What Is Fair Use?

Students will state the four tests of fair use.

1. Which of the following statements constitute the four tests of fair use? (Check all that apply)
2. Which of the following statements is NOT one of the four tests of fair use?

Students will explain what fair use means in their own words.

3. Which of the following statements best describes [*specific fair use factor*]?
4. Imagine that a classmate is having trouble understanding the four tests of fair use. Write how you'd explain EACH of the tests so that your classmate can understand them.

Students will apply the four tests of fair use to specific scenarios.

5. For each of the scenarios provided, determine whether the actions described comply or do not comply with each of the fair use factors.
6. For each of the scenarios provided, indicate which of the four fair use factors would be most influential in determining the fair use status of the scenario.

Students will analyze instructional scenarios in terms of fair use.

7. For each of the scenarios provided, indicate whether the use meets the four fair use factors by writing "pass" or "fail" in the blank provided.
8. For each of the scenarios provided, describe why it can be considered fair use or not, making sure to reference the specific factors of fair use that apply.

Students will annotate scenarios according to the four fair use factors.

9. For each of the scenarios provided, write the names of the fair use factors that are FAILED, as well as your evidence for your decision.
10. For each of the scenarios provided, write the names of the fair use factors that are PASSED, as well as your evidence for your decision.
11. For each of the scenarios provided, circle/underline the text that provides evidence appropriate to apply to the specific fair use factor indicated.

Learners will be able to annotate authentic scenarios according to Creative Commons licensing.

12. For each of the scenarios provided, write the names of the items that are Creative Commons licensed.
13. For each of the scenarios provided, circle/underline the text that provides evidence of Creative Commons licensing being used.
14. For each of the scenarios provided, circle/underline the specific actions taken that adhere to the Creative Commons license indicated.
15. For each of the scenarios provided, circle/underline the specific actions taken that are in violation of the Creative Commons license indicated.

Learners will be able to annotate authentic scenarios according to appropriate licensing influences.

16. For each of the scenarios provided, write the type of license that governs/controls the use of the highlighted work.
17. For each of the scenarios provided, circle/underline the specific actions taken that adhere to the license indicated.
18. For each of the scenarios provided, circle/underline the specific actions taken that are in violation of the license indicated.

Learners will be able to label the actions described in authentic scenarios as "Fair Use" or "Not Fair Use."

19. For each of the scenarios listed, write "fair use" or "not fair use" above the appropriate text describing a use of copyrighted material.

Learners will be able to rate authentic scenarios according to the level of riskiness in terms of the use of copyrighted materials.
Students will arrange scenarios in order from the safest to the least safe activities in terms of fair use.

20. For each group of scenarios provided, demonstrate your ability to evaluate the safety of each scenario by putting them in order from "safest" to "least safe" by writing the appropriate number in the blank provided. 1 = safest to 4 = least safe.
21. For each group of scenarios provided, demonstrate your ability to evaluate the safety of each scenario by circling the SAFEST one.
22. For each group of scenarios provided, demonstrate your ability to evaluate the safety of each scenario by circling the LEAST SAFE or RISKIEST one.

Students will rewrite scenarios so that the activities described are within the fair use guidelines.

23. For each of the scenarios provided, demonstrate your understanding of fair use by rewriting them so that the actions described are within fair use. Your rewritten scenario should achieve the same overall goal as the original scenario and should provide clear evidence of the fair use factors being met.
24. For each teaching scenario provided, demonstrate your understanding of fair use by writing how you would assist the teacher in their instructional efforts. Your assistance should provide clear evidence that you've considered the four fair use factors and that your use is within the fair use guidelines.

Students will create instructional activities that use copyrighted materials according to the fair use guidelines.

25. Select a topic to teach to a specific target learning audience. Develop an instructional activity that uses copyrighted materials in accordance with fair use. Be sure to explain how your use of copyrighted materials is in accordance with the four fair use factors. (Instructors: Be sure to create a set of directions that guides learners in the form and formatting of their final product to meet your requirements.)

Learners will be able to write questions that need to be answered in order to make authentic scenarios more explicit in terms of the use of copyrighted materials.

26. For each of the scenarios below, some information is missing that would permit you to make a more confident decision regarding whether the use of materials described is fair use or not. Write the question(s) you would need to ask in order to have enough information to make a confident fair use decision regarding how copyrighted materials are used in the scenario.

---

3. How Do Licenses Influence How I Am Permitted to Use Copyrighted Materials?

Learners will be able to identify the type of Creative Commons license attached to specific items.

1. Use the information provided in each example to determine the type of Creative Commons license attached to it. Write the name of the Creative Commons License attached to the item on the line provided.
2. Which of the following licenses is attached to the sample creative work shown?

Learners will be able to name the six different Creative Commons licenses.

3. Which of the following is one of the Creative Commons licenses?
4. Which of the following is NOT one of the Creative Commons licenses?
5. The list of Creative Commons licenses shown here has at least one error. Correct the error or errors so that the list of Creative Commons license names is accurate.

Learners will be able to match the license icon with the corresponding name of the Creative Commons license.

6. Which of the following icons represents the [*insert Creative Commons license name here*]?
7. For each of the Creative Commons license icons shown, write the name of the Creative Commons license it represents.

Learners will be able to name common licenses that control the use of copyrighted works.

8. Which of the following is a type of license that controls the use of copyrighted material?
9. Which of the following is NOT a type of license that controls the use of copyrighted material?
10. Which of the following types of licenses most likely controls the use of the copyrighted material shown?

Learners will be able to locate Creative Commons licensed materials.

11. For each of the Creative Commons licenses indicated, locate a creative item that has that license attached to it. Write the Title, Author, Source/URL in the space provided.
12. Locate a [*insert media type here*] that has the indicated Creative Commons license attached to it. Write the title, author, and source/URL in the space provided.

Learners will be able to describe how Creative Commons came into existence in their own words.

13. Which of the following statements best describes how the Creative Commons came into existence?
14. Which of the following statements is NOT a part of the Creative Commons origin story?
15. Write how you would describe to one of your classmates how the Creative Commons came into existence.

Learners will be able to define "license" in their own words as it pertains to the use of copyrighted works.

16. Which of the following best describes what a license is when the use of copyrighted works is happening?
17. Write how you would describe to one of your classmates what a license is as applied to the use of copyrighted works.

Learners will be able to explain the relationship between license restrictions and fair use as they pertain to the use of copyrighted works.

18. Which of the following best describes the relationship between licenses and fair use assessments as they pertain to the use of copyrighted works?

19. Write how you would describe to one of your classmates how licenses and fair use assessments are related to each other as they pertain to the use of copyrighted works.

Students will differentiate between transformative use and derivative use.

20. For each of the uses provided, indicate whether the use is transformative or derivative by writing the appropriate label in the blank provided.

21. Which of the following statements best describes the difference between transformative use and derivative use?

22. Which type of license would govern the use of the copyrighted material indicated in the scenario below?

Students will differentiate between Creative Commons, public domain, and general knowledge.

23. For each of the examples on the left, choose the proper description on the right that it represents. Descriptions may be used more than once.

24. Which of the following statements best describes items in the Creative Commons?

25. Which of the following statements best describes items in the public domain?

26. Which of the following statements best describes items that can be considered general knowledge?

Students will identify lawfully acquired copyright-protected resources.

27. For each of the sources of copyright-protected materials below, indicate whether they are lawfully acquired. For those that are lawfully acquired, write "yes" in the blank provided; for those that are not lawfully acquired, write "no" in the blank provided.

28. For each scenario provided, indicate whether the teacher/instructor acquired the copyright-protected materials in a legal fashion.

No specific goal.

29. Which of the following Creative Commons licenses would best be attached to an item that the creator wished to have used in any way except for commercial purposes? [*Adapt as needed for different license requirements*]

30. Given the following "Terms of Use" document, circle the text that tells users whether children under thirteen may use the resources from that site.
31. Given the following "Terms of Use" document, circle the text that tells users whether the following use of copyrighted material is permitted.
32. Write "PERMITTED" or "NOT PERMITTED" in the blank next to each scenario that describes the use of copyrighted materials, using the indicated license or "Terms of Use" to guide your decision making.
33. Rewrite the following scenario so that the use of copyrighted materials complies with the appropriate Terms of Service or other license agreements.
34. Which of the following statements best describes the relationship between licenses and fair use in the use of copyrighted materials?
35. For each of the scenarios provided, indicate whether a license governs how the copyrighted materials are permitted to be used by writing "yes" or "no" in the blank provided.
36. For each of the scenarios provided, indicate whether fair use or a license governs the use of the copyrighted materials in question by writing "fair use" or "license" in the blank provided.
37. Which of the following licenses gives users a set of agreed-upon rules that can be attached to a creative work by the creator of that work?
38. Which of the following types of licenses would control or govern the use of material found at [*insert web location here*]?

---

4. What Exceptions to the Copyright Law Affect My Teaching/Learning?

Students will name the exceptions to copyright law that affect teaching/learning.

1. Which section of the copyright law permits libraries to provide electronic copies of periodical items to other libraries—sometimes referred to as inter-library loan?
2. Which section of the copyright law permits bookstores to sell used copies of books?
3. Which section of the copyright law permits people to use copyrighted materials without getting explicit permission from the copyright owner?
4. Which section of the copyright law permits teachers to show movies in their classes that relate to the unit of instruction at hand?

Students will state the five factors of video fair use.

5. Which of the following questions does NOT need to be considered when deciding about showing a video in a class?
6. Which of the following statements best describe the questions that need to be considered when showing a video in a class? (Check all that apply)
7. Which of the following statements constitutes the five factors of video fair use? (Check all that apply)
8. Which of the following statements is NOT one of the five factors of video fair use?

Students will explain the five tests of video fair use using age-appropriate language.

9. Which of the following explanations is the most accurate?
10. Imagine that your classmate does not understand how to determine whether they are permitted to use [*insert specific video here*] during one of their [*insert subject area*] classes. Write an explanation of the factors of video fair use that your classmate would be able to understand.

Students will describe the exceptions to the six exclusive rights of a copyright holder that affect teaching and learning, teachers, and students.

11. Which of the following best describes the [*insert exception here*] exception to the six exclusive rights of a copyright holder?
12. For each of the exceptions to the six exclusive rights of a copyright holder, demonstrate your understanding of the exception by writing how you would explain it to students in [*insert grade level here*] grade/educational level.

Students will differentiate between public and private use/showing.

13. Which of the following sets of conditions describe a "PUBLIC" space in the context of determining whether a performance can be a public performance?
14. For each description of a performance, indicate whether it is public or private.

Students will match scenarios to the appropriate exception that affects their copyright interpretation.

15. Demonstrate your understanding of the exceptions to the exclusive rights of the copyright owner by matching the descriptive scenario on the left with the exception controlling it on the right. Some exceptions will be used more than once. Not all exceptions will be used.

16. Which of the following exceptions to the six exclusive rights of the copyright holder governs the scenario provided?

Students will apply the five tests of video fair use to specific scenarios.

17. For each of the scenarios provided, write the status of the use according to each of the five tests of video fair use.
18. Based on the five tests of video fair use, indicate whether the scenario described could meet the classroom performance exceptions for audiovisual works.

Students will annotate scenarios according to the five video fair use factors.

19. For each scenario provided, write the name of the video fair use factors that are PASSED.
20. For each scenario provided, write the name of the video fair use factors that are FAILED.
21. For each scenario provided, circle/underline the text that provides evidence of influencing each of the five factors of video fair use.
22. Determine whether the use of copyrighted material described in each scenario is FAIR or NOT FAIR, using appropriate exceptions to the exclusive rights of a copyright owner to guide your decision making.

Students will create instructional activities that use copyrighted materials according to the video fair use guidelines.

23. For each of the scenarios provided, demonstrate your understanding of video fair use by rewriting them so that the actions described are within fair use. Your rewritten scenario should achieve the same overall goal as the original scenario and should provide clear evidence of the five factors of video fair use tests being met.
24. For each teaching scenario provided, demonstrate your understanding of video fair use by writing how you would assist the teacher in their instructional efforts. Your assistance should provide clear evidence that you've considered the five factors of video fair use and that your use is within the video fair use guidelines.

---

5. How Do I Determine Whether What I Want to Do/ Use Is Permissible?

1. Which of the following statements represents an allowable way for people to determine the permissibility of a specific use of copyrighted materials?

2. For each of the following statements, indicate whether it is an appropriate method to determine the permissibility of a particular use of copyrighted materials by writing "yes" in the blank provided for those statements that are appropriate and "no" in the blank in front of those statements that are not appropriate.
3. In order to request permission from a copyright owner to use his or her work beyond fair use, what information should be included in the request letter?
4. Which of the following items is an orphan work?
5. Which of the following descriptions best describes what an "orphan work" is?
6. For each work described, indicate whether it is considered an "orphan work." (true/false)

Students will interpret copyright scenarios to determine the permissibility/non-permissibility of the activity described in each one.

7. For each scenario provided, write "permitted" if the activity is permissible and "not" if the activity is not permissible. Consider all aspects of copyright law in making your decision, including fair use, other applicable exceptions, etc.
8. For each scenario provided, determine whether you would act in the same way as the teacher/instructor/student/material user. Base your decision on the permissibility/non-permissibility of the activity.
9. For each set of scenarios provided, rank them according to their level of permissibility. Low ranks are more permissible; high numbers are less permissible.

Students will modify activities in copyright-related scenarios so that they are safer vs. riskier in terms of fair use.

10. Each of the following scenarios describes an activity that is either risky or not permitted with regard to US copyright law.
    a. For each of the alternative activities provided after each scenario, choose the LEAST risky.
    b. Rewrite the activity described so that it is safer in terms of fair use.

Students will analyze instructional scenarios in terms of fair use.

11. Determine whether each of the following scenarios represents the fair use of copyrighted materials. For those that are fair use, write "fair" in the blank provided; for those that are not fair use, write "not fair" in the blank provided (can format as two-option multiple choice as well).

12. Determine which of the four fair use factors are met, or not, in each of the scenarios provided. Put a checkmark in the blank next to each fair use factor that is met and leave blank the lines in front of the fair use factors that are not met.

Students will explain why a particular scenario is permissible or not permissible.

13. Determine whether each of the following scenarios is permissible or not permissible according to fair use. Write your decision and your reasoning in a well-formatted paragraph. Be sure to explain your reasons according to the four factors of fair use in your paragraph.
14. For each of the following scenarios, imagine that your colleague is the main character. Explain to your colleague why their actions are permitted/not permitted as appropriate in relation to the question you are asked by them.

Students will select the safest alternative from a list of alternatives to apply to a copyright infringement scenario.

15. Which of the following actions is the SAFEST action to take when making a decision regarding providing copies of readings to students?
16. Which of the following actions would you recommend to a colleague of yours who is extremely concerned about violating copyright law and is looking for the safest option to pursue?

Students will create instructional activities that use copyrighted materials according to the multimedia guidelines.

17. Select a topic to teach to a specific target learning audience. Develop an instructional activity that uses multimedia materials in accordance with the multimedia guidelines. Be sure to explain how your use of multimedia materials is in accordance with the multimedia guidelines. (Instructors: Be sure to create a set of directions that guides learners in the form and formatting of their final product to meet your requirements.)
18. For each of the scenarios provided, demonstrate your understanding of the multimedia guidelines by rewriting them so that the actions described comply with the guidelines. Your rewritten scenario should achieve the same overall goal as the original scenario and should provide clear evidence of the guidelines being applied.
19. For each teaching scenario provided, demonstrate your understanding of the use of the multimedia guidelines by writing how you would assist the teacher in their instructional efforts. Your assistance should provide clear evidence that you've considered the multimedia guidelines and that your use is within the multimedia guidelines.

6. What Are the Important Laws and Guidelines That Affect My Use of Copyrighted Materials?

Learners will be able to match the type of copyrighted work that is affected by specific laws regarding its use.

1. For each type of copyrighted work shown, match the law that tells how its use is permitted or limited. Write the name of the law in the line next to the copyrighted work.
2. Which type of copyrighted work does the [*insert law name here*] law control or govern in terms of its use?

Students will match the names of important copyright laws with the major outcomes within each law that affect teachers or students.

3. Which of the following laws addresses [*insert various major findings/implications*] as its main component?
4. For each court case on the left, match it with its major outcome on the right by writing the letter of the outcome in the blank provided in front of each case. Not all outcomes will be used.

Students will name important laws that affect copyright for teaching and learning, teachers, and students.

5. Which of the following is the name of a landmark copyright-related law or legal case?
6. Which of the following landmark copyright-related cases found that:
7. Demonstrate your ability to name important laws that affect copyright for teaching and learning by writing "yes" in the blank for those laws that DO affect copyright for teaching and learning, and "no" in the blank for those laws that DO NOT affect copyright for teaching and learning.

Learners will be able to describe the quantity limits for the use of specific types of copyrighted works.

8. According to the [*insert law name here*], how much or how many [*insert type of copyrighted work here*] would a teacher be able to use in a lesson presented to their class?
9. According to the [*insert law name here*], how much or how many [*insert type of copyrighted work here*] would a student be able to use in a science fair presentation?
10. According to the [*insert law name here*], how much or how many [*insert type of copyrighted work here*] would an administrator be able to use during a professional development session they were conducting?

Students will be able to describe the quantity limits for the use of copyrighted materials in the multimedia guidelines.

11. According to the multimedia guidelines, which of the following is the greatest number of minutes of music that teachers are advised to use in lessons that they present to their classes?
12. According to the multimedia guidelines, which of the following is the highest number of images that a student is advised to use in a report they are delivering to their class?
13. Write how you would respond to a classmate if they were to ask you, "I want to include a bunch of interesting embellishments to this project that I'm working on for my class. Is it okay if I just put in whatever I want, like images, videos, or even music clips?" Use the recommendations presented in the multimedia guidelines to structure your answer.

Students will summarize the key points of important copyright-related laws.

14. Which of the following copyright-related laws is best summarized as:
15. Which of the following summaries best describes the key points of:

Learners will be able to match authentic scenarios to the appropriate set of guidelines that would govern the use described in the scenario.

16. For each scenario shown, indicate the appropriate set of guidelines that users should consult in order to determine whether the use of copyrighted materials described could be considered acceptable. Write the name of the guidelines in the space provided.
17. For each scenario shown, indicate the appropriate set of guidelines that users should consult in order to determine whether the use of copyrighted materials described could be considered acceptable by choosing the name of the guidelines from the list provided.

Students will annotate scenarios according to the applicable laws that affect the scenario.

18. In each scenario provided, underline the evidence you use to determine whether the use is FAIR or NOT FAIR. For each underlined sentence or phrase, write the name of the applicable law that is represented.

Students will decide which of the important copyright laws is the best one to support a particular activity within specific scenarios.

19. Which copyright-related law is the best one to use to determine whether the use is FAIR or UNFAIR?
20. For each scenario provided, determine whether the use of copyrighted material is FAIR or UNFAIR, using copyright-related laws to guide your decision making.

Learners will be able to create instructional materials that include copyrighted materials within the limits of the appropriate set of guidelines.

21. Which of the following sets of copyrighted materials is appropriate to use within the project described below? Base your decision on an appropriate set of use guidelines.

Students will be able to create multimedia projects containing copyrighted materials in alignment with the multimedia guidelines.

22. Which of the following sets of copyrighted materials is appropriate to use within the project described below? Base your decision on the multimedia guidelines.

Students will create instructional activities that use copyrighted materials according to the TEACH Act.

23. Select a topic to teach to a specific target learning audience. Develop an instructional activity that uses copyrighted materials in accordance with the TEACH Act. Be sure to explain how your use of copyrighted materials is in accordance with the TEACH Act. (Instructors: Be sure to create a set of directions that guides learners in the form and formatting of their final product to meet your requirements.)

24. For each of the scenarios provided, demonstrate your understanding of the TEACH Act by rewriting them so that the actions described are within the act. Your rewritten scenario should achieve the same overall goal as the original scenario and should provide clear evidence of the TEACH Act being applied.

25. For each teaching scenario provided, demonstrate your understanding of the TEACH Act by writing how you would assist the teacher in their instructional efforts. Your assistance should provide clear evidence that you've considered the TEACH Act and that your use is within its requirements.

---

7. What Significant Court Cases and Laws Have Influenced Copyright Law?

Learners will be able to list the landmark court cases that established important precedents regarding the application of US copyright law.

1. Which of the following is a landmark copyright court case?
2. Which of the following is NOT a landmark copyright court case?
3. Match the title of the landmark case on the left with its major finding on the right. Not all findings will be used.

Learners will be able to name the plaintiff and defendant in specific court cases that inform the application of US copyright law.

4. For each of the court cases listed, write the name of the plaintiff in the space provided.
5. For each of the court cases listed, write the name of the defendant in the space provided.
6. Which of the following is the defendant for the [*insert court case name here*] case?
7. Which of the following is the plaintiff for the [*insert court case name here*] case?

Learners will be able to match the titles of specific court cases that inform the application of US copyright law with the concepts of copyright law that are influenced by them.

8. Match the title of the court case on the left with its major findings on the right. Not all findings will be used.
9. Which of the following court cases found [*insert major finding here*]?

Learners will be able to describe the major findings of specific court cases that inform the application of US copyright law.

10. Write a description of the finding(s) for the [*insert case name here*] case using language that your classmates would understand.
11. Which of the following best describes the findings of the [*insert case name here*] case?

Learners will be able to discriminate between landmark and non-landmark court cases that inform the application of US copyright law.

12. Write "landmark" on the line next to the cases that are considered to be landmark cases. Leave lines next to non-landmark cases blank.
13. Sort the following cases into "landmark" and "non-landmark" groups by selecting the appropriate label from the list provided.
14. Which of the following court cases best supports the permissibility of the use described in this scenario?
15. Write the name of the court case that best supports the permissibility of the use described in this scenario.

Learners will be able to cite appropriate court cases in support of their analysis of authentic scenarios regarding the use of copyrighted materials.

16. Organize the court cases here into groups that have similar characteristics. Write two to four sentences for each group that describe how the cases in that group are similar to one another.

17. Which of the following court cases is different from the others in terms of the issues that were examined?

18. Which of the following court cases is different from the others in terms of its findings?

19. For each scenario provided, determine whether the actions described are permissible or impermissible. Support your determination with appropriate citations to applicable court cases.

20. Which of the following court cases best supports the use of copyrighted materials that are described in this scenario?

21. Put yourself in the position of [*insert character name here*] in the scenario provided. Write a response to your supervisor/boss that explains how your use of copyrighted material is supported by court case(s). Be sure to give the name of appropriate case(s) in your response.

No specific goal

22. Which of the following statements is one notable result of the United States becoming a signatory to the Berne Convention Treaty of 1988?

---

8. What Happens When Copyright Is Violated?

Learners will be able to define a "cease-and-desist letter."

1. Which of the following is the best definition of a cease-and-desist letter?
2. Imagine that one of your classmates finds the term "cease-and-desist letter" in a description of the consequences a user received for their use of copyrighted materials but doesn't know what it is. Write how you would define "cease-and-desist letter" using language that your classmate would easily understand.
3. Which of the following statements best describes the purpose of a cease-and-desist letter?

Learners will be able to define actual and potential damages.

4. Which of the following best describes "actual damages"?
5. Which of the following best describes "potential damages"?
6. Write how you would tell a classmate what actual damages are in relation to copyright infringement.
7. Write how you would tell a classmate what potential damages are in relation to copyright infringement.

8. Learners will be able to name the types of consequences (sanctions) that result from copyright infringement. Which of the following is an example of the type of sanction or consequence that might result from a copyright violation?
9. Which of the following is NOT an example of the type of sanction or consequence that might result from a copyright violation?

Learners will be able to define the four types of infringement: innocent, willful, vicarious, and contributory.

10. Which of the following is NOT a type of copyright infringement?
11. Which of the following infringements is demonstrated by supervisors in a workplace?
12. Which of the following is the type of infringement where a user improperly reproduces a copyrighted work?
13. In the scenario provided, which type of infringement does the character [*insert character name here*] demonstrate?
14. Which of the following statements best describes [*insert infringement type here*] infringement?

Learners will be able to name specific roles in the workplace that illustrate the four types of infringement.

15. Which of the following workplace roles would perform [*insert infringement type here*] infringement?
16. In the following scenario, the [*insert workplace role*] is guilty of which of the following types of copyright infringement?

Learners will be able to identify examples of the four types of infringement in authentic scenarios.

17. For each scenario provided, write the type of infringement that is illustrated in the space provided.
18. Which of the following scenarios illustrates [*insert infringement type here*] infringement?

Learners will be able to differentiate between actual and potential damages.

19. Which of the following fictional court rulings best illustrates actual damages?
20. Which of the following fictional court rulings best illustrates potential damages?

21. For each of the types of damages provided, label the type of damage by writing "actual" or "potential" in the space provided.

Learners will be able to describe the effect of copyright violation on employment status (adult learners only).

22. Which of the following best describes how the illustrated copyright violation would affect the employment status of [*insert character name here*]?
23. Suppose a co-worker of yours is concerned about a possible copyright violation that they may have demonstrated. Write what you would tell them if they came to you asking how that violation would impact their employment.

Learners will be able to differentiate between copyright violation and plagiarism.

24. Which of the following is an example of copyright violation?
25. Which of the following is an example of plagiarism?
26. For each scenario provided, write "copyright violation" or "plagiarism" in the space provided to indicate which type of behavior is being illustrated.
27. Organize the following group of scenarios according to the type of behavior being illustrated by choosing the appropriate label from the list provided.
28. For each of the scenarios provided, label the type of consequence that is most likely to result from the infringement described.
29. Based on the information provided in this scenario, which type of infringement is being described by the highlighted text?
30. For each of the characters in the scenario provided, name the type of infringement they demonstrate.
31. In the scenario provided, which character is demonstrating the most severe type of infringement?
32. In the scenario provided, which character is demonstrating the least severe type of infringement?
33. Write a cease-and-desist letter to the appropriate character in the scenario provided that effectively describes the action you wish to have ceased, as well as appropriate consequences of non-compliance.
34. Rewrite the scenario such that the type of infringement is reduced in severity yet still describes infringement.

Scenario Bank

Each of the scenarios below is intended to illustrate common activities regarding the use of copyrighted materials. The names of the characters are drawn from my family, friends, and attendees at the ALA conference (June 2022). While some scenarios are based on situations that I have encountered in the past, all of them are fictionalized and do not represent any actual event. Any relationship found within them to actual events that readers may have experienced is entirely coincidental.

Each of the fifty scenarios below describes different activities that teachers, students, administrators, and parents might perform in the course of using copyrighted material. Most of the scenarios are incomplete in that not every piece of information needed to make a confident analysis or determination of fair use is included. Readers who wish to use more detailed scenarios that contain more complete information, or that can be modified to more strongly indicate a particular concept or issues, should consult the website for the extended scenarios. The extended scenarios contain a short assessment of each scenario, suggested ways to simplify or increase the complexity of the scenario, and suggested questions that might be used to determine student mastery of a variety of copyright-related concepts.

1. Duplicating Videos after Cease-and-Desist

A publisher discovers that a school is making and using copies of videos without permission. The publisher has an attorney send a cease-and-desist letter to the school, directing that the use of the videos should stop immediately. The school continues to use the videos, thinking that the publisher will not find out as the source of the information (a disgruntled parent) has moved away from the district.

2. Background Internet Music

A teacher uses a computer in the classroom to play internet radio stations as background music in the classroom.

3. Historic Speeches

A school hosts a school-wide patriotic speech festival. The participants choose and memorize a speech from a list of competition selections. The choices include Patrick Henry's "Give me liberty or give me death" speech, Franklin Roosevelt's "War Address to Congress," and many more speeches from American history. Rather than print all of these speeches, the teachers decided to make the speeches available online and let the students print the speeches for themselves, thus saving reams of paper for the school.

4. Anthology of Pictures

An art teacher is preparing a lesson on American artists, so the teacher selects twenty pictures from various art books to make a webpage.

5. Scanned Worksheet Online—Severe Weather

A teacher decides to scan (create a PDF) and upload a worksheet from the district-adopted science curriculum to the school's website, which is password-protected. She leaves the worksheet up for one week due to extended school closings for severe weather.

6. CD Duplication

The music teacher brings an audio CD to the library and asks the school librarian to make a cassette tape of the CD because the music teacher does not have a CD player in the classroom.

7. Background Music for Class Assignment Presentation

A student prepares a PowerPoint presentation on her assigned report topic of "Ancient Civilizations: Egypt." She includes as background music for the presentation, "Walk Like an Egyptian" [use any music title that is known to the students].

8. CD Duplication 2

A teacher purchased an audio CD of a class book and wants to lend it to a student. However, she is concerned about the audio CD being lost or damaged. She decides to make a copy of the original audio CD and lend the copy to protect the original CD that she purchased.

9. Vacation Images from the Web

A teacher creates a webpage of original digital photographs that she took while on various vacation trips. She discovers that someone else is using those images on his personal webpage without prior permission.

10. NASA Webpage Copying

A teacher prints, copies, and distributes to her students a webpage from NASA.

11. Music During Graduation

A graduating class wants to play two songs during the graduation ceremony: one when presenting parents with roses and one as the class song. The graduation will take place in the school gymnasium.

12. Scanning Books into Kurzweil

A school purchases a license for a Kurzweil 3000 subscription to be used in its special education classrooms. The teachers have been busy scanning books and uploading those scanned files to the Kurzweil program. The students, using a computer, listen to what has been scanned.

13. Coffee on Standardized Tests

Accidentally, a cup of coffee was overturned on a stack of standardized tests that were being prepared to be administered. Four of the tests were usable, so they were quickly copied to administer them within the specified time frame.

14. Stories Using Favorite Characters

A 5th grade teacher had her class write a story using their favorite character from their favorite book as the main character to help them learn characterization and the nature of writing.

15. Teacher-made Audio Book

A teacher makes an audio recording of J. K. Rowling's *Harry Potter* books for blind students in her classroom.

16. Repeated Installation of Software

At a very poor (financially, not quality) school, the parents (PTA) saved enough supermarket receipts to redeem for six new computers for students to use. However, there are no funds to purchase any software programs, so a parent has decided to donate one software program to the school. The teachers will load this one program onto each computer, one at a time.

17. Digitized Video into Lesson

A science teacher decides to digitize some analog video clips (VHS tape) and insert them into her interactive whiteboard lesson. The video clips are educational and short.

18. Serial Tweeting

Sara-George Ann is the school district reading coach. One of her responsibilities is to offer professional development (PD) sessions for the teachers in the district so that they can more effectively integrate reading instruction into their daily lessons, particularly at the secondary level. Sara-George Ann has found the book *The Literacy Cookbook: A Practical Guide to Effective Reading, Writing, Speaking, and Listening Instruction* and would like to use it as the main source of information for her upcoming PD session. She plans to offer her PD in a distance format. She has selected several chapters of the book to use and plans on "live tweeting" the book by posting passages so that her teachers won't have to purchase the book if they don't want to. She recommends that they purchase it, though, so that their reading will be more meaningful. Sara-George Ann's colleague, the district library supervisor, helped her get her Twitter account set up.

19. Out of Print Book

Norman, a 1st grade teacher, has a student who would benefit from a phonics book that Norman acquired as a doctoral student twenty years ago. The book is out of print, though. Norman decides to photocopy a few pages at a time so that his student can work through the book to improve his decoding skills in reading. The principal found out what Norman did and wrote an official letter of reprimand for his personnel file. The principal said that Norman was being put on notice that further actions that violated copyright law would be grounds for termination.

20. Weather Delay Video

Timothy teaches 2nd grade. The school has been notified that students will be dismissed two hours early due to inclement weather. Since his planned lesson for the afternoon won't be able to be taught, he decides to put the video *Pocahontas* on the classroom monitor for the children to watch after lunch and while they wait for their bus numbers to be called. One of the students in Timothy's class mentioned the movie at the dinner table. The student's mother wrote to the Disney corporation (the producers of the movie) and informed them about what Timothy did. She happened to have been upset that an entire afternoon was spent watching a cartoon movie rather than having some sort of instructional activity taking place.

21. Replacement Pages

Angela is in the middle of teaching her unit on multiplying and dividing fractions at her middle school. As she distributes the textbooks to her students at the beginning of the day, she notices that one of them is soggy from having accidentally been soaked when she watered her plants on her desk earlier in the morning. Four pages of the chapter she'll be teaching are unusable by students. She halts the lesson and uses one of the dry textbooks to make five photocopies of the pages that were wet to use for the five students whose books were damaged. When the school admin assistant sees what Angela is doing, she grabs the copies from Angela and tells her that the photocopying of textbooks is forbidden due to the law.

22. Art Lesson

Bob teaches art at the elementary school. His lesson this week is about using the "Pointillism" style to create pictures. He has created several lab stations where his students can practice the technique. Each station contains a digitally displayed rendition of a well-known painting done in the Pointillist style, directions for using the tools at the station, appropriate tools for creating the exercise images, and directions for completing the activities. The students' resulting exercise images (pictures similar to the ones they use as models) will be hung in the school hallway for the rest of the semester.

23. Oral Reading

Susie teaches 5th grade reading. As a part of each week's lesson, she reads selections from various children's authors' books to her class. While she's reading, her PowerPoint presentation is looping digital images from the book that she's reading. In addition, Susie often plays classical works of music as background or "mood enhancement" while she reads.

24. Gardening

Ralph is a student in Bob's gardening class. Ralph is working in his garden to practice the pruning techniques that he learned last week in class. He photocopied the two pages from his text that have pictures of the proper ways to prune roses and has taken them into the garden with him (he didn't want to get soil on his textbook).

25. Psychology Photocopying

Shelby is teaching a psychology course in which Beth is enrolled. Beth hasn't purchased her textbook yet because her part-time job hasn't yet paid her. Shelby offers to use the office copy machine to create a PDF copy of the readings so that she can email them to Beth. That way, Beth won't have to purchase the text.

26. Film Analysis

Fred is teaching a Film class elective for the HS theater department in a Distance Education format. His students must view several films and analyze them for their use of character development, plot development, and use of music as an additional character. They then present their analyses to the class in the form of recorded presentations that they upload to the course management system. Each presentation must include appropriate clips from the films that they've analyzed.

27. Image Use

Natalie is teaching her first HS class "Calculus for Secondary Students." In order to illustrate the concept of integrals, she's included this image from her mentor's text.

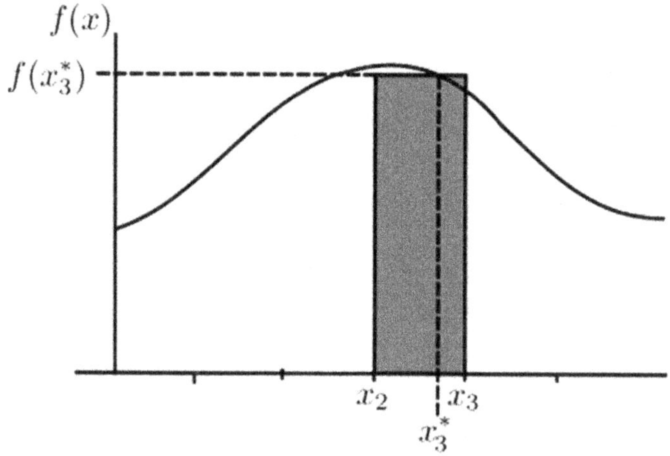

Riemann Integration 2. Source: Juliusross~commonswiki at https://wikimedia.org/wiki/File:Riemann_Integration_2.png. CC BY 2.5 Generic.

She also wants to remind students about trigonometric identities, so she uses this image from her own trigonometry text from high school.

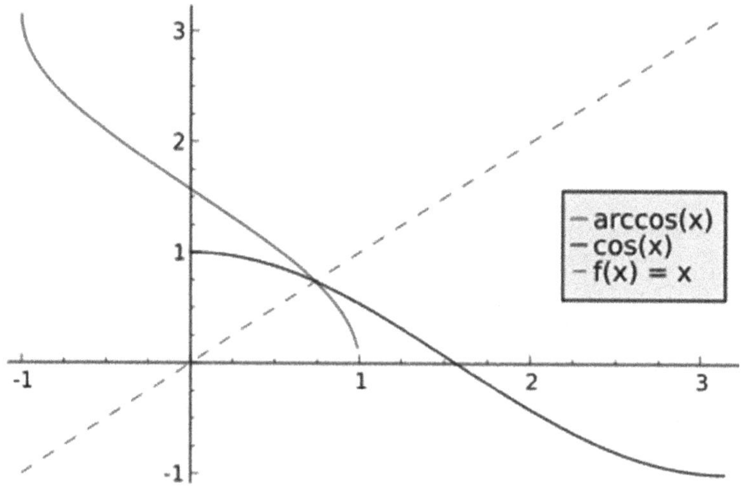

Arccos, Cos, and Identity. Source: Sage Math at https://commons.wikimedia.org/wiki/File:Arccos,_cos,_and_identity.svg. CC0 1.0.

She then realizes that a more recent text she found at Barnes & Noble has better quality images, so she directs the parent volunteer to scan all the images from the text so that she can use them in future presentations.

28. Mrs. Jones Is Worried

One of her students, Matt, has come to school in tears because his younger sister and brother (the twins) got into a fight last night and managed to damage his English textbook. Two entire chapters were cut to shreds when the two of them argued over the "way to use the scissors"! Matt is worried that he's going to get into trouble because his book is damaged and unable to be used. Rather than punish her student, Mrs. Jones decides to slice the damaged pages cleanly out of his book and replace them with photocopies from another student's book. She then asked the textbook chairperson to order a new copy of the text for use next year. This way, Matt can continue to use his book for instructional purposes without losing any time. (She also helped him decide on a special place in his house to store his school books so that his siblings can't find them in the future!)

29. Mrs. Bullock and the Math Class

Mrs. Bullock and her class have worked hard all year on mastering the math content in the 10th grade course of study. As a result, the entire class passed the end-of-year exam with at least an 80 percent grade on the state exam. Mrs. Bullock would like to reward her students for their hard work and decides to show a movie in class as a special treat. Mr. Bannon, the school librarian, helped Mrs. Bullock locate a copy of *MacFarland USA*, since it illustrates the story of hard work paying off. Mr. Bannon and Mrs. Bullock convinced the principal to pay Movie Licensing USA $225 for the copy of the movie (the principal is very impressed with Mrs. Bullock's work) under the condition that she "pass a hat" for students to donate money back as they are able in order to cover the cost.

30. Ms. Smith and a Unit about Explorers

Ms. Smith has been teaching a unit about explorers. As a part of this unit, her students are studying the different exploratory missions that were launched by NASA over the years (Voyager, Mars Rover, etc.). Ms. Smith has made a class set of copies of various online documents that she found at the NASA.gov site. The school library, classroom library, and textbook series have sufficient information for the other aspects of the explorers that are being studied in the unit. She's asked the librarian, Mrs. Clark, to assist her with the copying.

31. Ms. Gibbs, the New Teacher

Ms. Gibbs is a new teacher at her school this year. One of the more experienced and tenured teachers, who has been assigned as her mentor, has given her a copy of the student consumable workbook that was part of last year's reading series. Mrs. Murphy tells Ms. Gibbs that the exercises in last year's book match more closely to the course of study, and she can use it for her reading instruction this year—even though the district has switched textbook companies. "I saved an extra copy for you since I knew you wouldn't have many materials, and this one is better than the new one that they got us. Just ask Janice, the office aide, to make you copies from this book whenever you need to assign them to your students," Mrs. Murphy tells her.

32. Mr. Williams and Alexander the Great

Mr. Williams is teaching a unit on Alexander the Great. He has found a tremendous video on TeacherTube that perfectly describes the "life and times" of Alexander the Great. He has included the link to the video on his teacher page and directed his students to view the video. He is also holding a special lunchtime viewing session for any students who would like to watch the video at school rather than at home.

33. Ms. Wagnon's Field Day Celebration

It's the annual Field Day celebration that Ms. Wagnon holds for her entire elementary school. She has worked for two months to organize each of the activities that the students will complete. As part of the preparatory activities, Ms. Wagnon has challenged the students to complete two-week food diaries that will be used after Field Day is complete to analyze the quality of their diets. She's located a handout in a nutrition text that provides the serving size and calorie count for commonly eaten foods. This handout is five pages of text, and she's requested that the front office parent volunteer reproduce it for every child in the school. The parent is concerned about this copy request and asks the principal for her ruling about whether or not to reproduce the pages. The principal tells Ms. Wagnon that she is not permitting the copying unless Ms. Wagnon can convince her that it isn't an infringement of copyright law.

34. Professional Development Materials

Mr. Burnell is conducting a professional development session for his parent volunteers. He located five different articles that discuss student-centered homework assistance that he wants to use during his session. A week before the scheduled session, he sends an email to all of the parent volunteers telling them that they should bring copies of the articles with them, as they will be using them for an activity during the professional development session.

35. Hallway Bulletin Board

Rex has been assigned the task of designing and assembling a bulletin board to decorate the hallway between the main office and the English department. Being technologically savvy, he decides that he will create an interactive board so that students will engage with it rather than simply view it. As it is October, he chooses a "spooky" theme and decides to display various images, poems, and text excerpts. He creates audio files of different teachers reading the poems and text excerpts in a dramatic fashion. He stores those audio files on the library server at school and creates QR codes that, when scanned, will play the files.

36. Review Materials

Jane paid for a subscription to the "A student's companion to the science curriculum" website. She has fallen in love with the content on the site and wants all of her students to be able to benefit from using it to prepare for the upcoming standardized testing. She modifies her lesson plans to allow 30 minutes per class session during which students may use the site. She asks her principal to pay for subscriptions for her students but is told "no." As the test preparation is high-stakes, she posts her username and password to the website on the wall so that all of her students can see them. The principal thinks this is a good compromise and a fiscally responsible way to acquire the resource. They are able to use it whenever she allows them to work on the website in order to log in.

37. Distance Education Summer School

Superintendent Kaili Clark decides that all students who earned less than a "C" in Algebra I will be enrolled in summer school so that they will be better prepared for their Algebra II class next year. The curriculum for the summer course is delivered via the internet. Students are able to complete the work whenever they choose, as long as they complete all required tasks at least two weeks prior to the start of the next school year. Assignments include text, video, animation, and audio explanations.

38. Graduation

The high school orchestra plays a selection of popular songs to entertain the parents as they arrive and take their seats for the graduation ceremony.

39. Library Display

Every year, John the librarian creates displays on top of the bookshelves highlighting the titles in his collection that have a variety of different themes relevant to the month, season, or current events. The displays consist of book covers, books, and real objects such as models, artifacts, or plushies (animals or dolls). The electronic display also includes a series of slides that direct patrons to different parts of the displays.

40. Copying as Punishment

Jordan, a particularly mean teacher in the eyes of the students, tells Martha that she must transcribe one chapter from the class novel, by hand, for every day that she missed class due to an unsanctioned vacation with her family.

41. School Talent Show

Each spring semester, the senior class puts on a talent show that they perform not just for their school but also for the elementary schools in the district. Students are free to perform any type of talent or act that they choose. This year, the "Sassy Sisters" decide to perform an *a cappella* version of Cyndi Lauper's "Girls just want to have fun," accompanied by images of various practical jokes that students had accomplished throughout their four years in the school.

42. Mural in a Store

A local business owner, whose spouse is the art teacher at the local middle school, commissions the advanced painting class to create a mural on one of the walls inside the store. When they've finished, the business owner donates $3,500 to the art program at the school. The next year, the business owner and the teacher dissolve their marriage in an acrimonious fashion. As a result, the business owner decides to paint over the mural in retaliation, as it is impossible to retrieve the money that was donated.

43. Redacted Book

A local parents' group have taken it upon themselves to audit all of the library books in every school in the district. They've received permission from the administration to enter the buildings to accomplish their efforts. Several members of the group are quite technologically savvy and are tasked with creating replacement pages for those pages that are found to be "offensive" or "inappropriate" by the parents' group. These replacement pages contain the text of the original page but with certain words and phrases omitted and replaced with innocuous ones. The replacement pages are then tipped in to the book after the pages with offensive language have been cut from the book.

44. Redacted Film

A professor with strong beliefs about "what is right and proper" is mandated to show a particular movie in the core class that he teaches. This movie contains brief scenes of nudity, occasional use of vulgarity, and depictions of death that cause the professor great offense. The professor decides to submit his copy of the movie to an online company, "Fresh Films," so that the troublesome portions can be removed. That way, he will still be able to show the movie to his class but not have to sacrifice his own values.

45. The District Math Coach

The district math coach was recently hired from another region of the country and has only been working for the district for a few months. The math curriculum at his previous school system contained ancillary review materials that were specially designed to be attractive to students as well as pedagogically sound in the way that the mathematical concepts were presented. The coach brought a copy of all of these ancillary materials when he moved to the district. Over the summer, before school started, the math coach scanned (cropping off the copyright notices) or retyped (omitting the copyright notices), as needed, the entirety of the set of materials. He planned on using them as resources with the teachers once school started. Once school starts, he loads his electronic version of the ancillary materials on his shared drive space provided by the district. As the year progresses, he provides shared access to the faculty who attend his professional development sessions for the materials that are appropriate for the grades that they teach.

46. Yearbook

Dr. Clark, the yearbook advisor, is at her wits' end. The illustration committee for the yearbook has not yet created appropriate images to illustrate the main sections of the yearbook. The copy is due to the printer tomorrow, though. So, Dr. Clark searches for, downloads, and inserts images that she finds online. Some of these images have CC BY or CC BY ND licenses, while others have CC BY NC or CC 0 licenses.

47. Mandatory Online Posting

While preparing to commence teaching one evening, you overhear a few of your students talking about a situation in another one of their classes. Apparently, the "methods of teaching" professor requires students to create lessons and lesson ideas on a variety of topics. Students are mandated to submit those ideas for grading via a published and publicly accessible website owned and managed by the professor.

48. Book Art

The art teacher spends the summers haunting garage sales and buying books. She uses those books as the source "ingredient," "material," or "supply" for a variety of three-dimensional sculptural projects that her intermediate students complete each year.

49. Tutoring as a Side Gig

The 5th grade math teacher, Dwayne Clark, advertises tutoring services to supplement his income, especially over the summer break. For each student who is tutored, the teacher creates customized practice exercises and learning games. Dwayne has been approached by an independent publisher with an offer to publish the exercises and learning games for the Algebra, Geometry, and Pre-Calculus content. The principal finds out about the teacher's work and forbids it to happen, stating that this work belongs to the school, not to the teacher.

50. Commissioned Song

The superintendent of schools is retiring after forty years of exemplary service to the district. During their tenure, test scores rose, graduation rates soared, and parental complaints diminished to a trickle. This administrator is universally loved and respected. As a tribute to their service, the incoming superintendent (formerly the assistant superintendent) commissions the high school band director and choir director to collaborate to write an orchestrated song, including lyrics that use the theme of servant leadership, devotion, and integrity to laud the superintendent's work. The two directors are paid for their work and sign a contract with the district that describes the scope of the work, the content of the lyrics, and the timeline by which it should be finished. The song will be performed at the retirement ceremony as a surprise to the outgoing administrator.

4 Supplemental Resources

Suggested Readings

Black's Law Dictionary (https://thelawdictionary.org/).

Black's Law Dictionary is one of the most well-known and authoritative sources of legal definitions. Practicing attorneys rely on it on a regular basis. The online version linked here is free to use and so is ideal for teachers, students, and other lay persons needing access to quick definitions related to legal practice.

Butler, R. P. (2004). *Copyright for teachers and librarians.* Neal-Schuman Publishers.

Butler presents copyright concepts aimed at K–12 librarians and teachers. Her work is organized in broad sections, permitting the user to easily choose the chapters that are most useful at any one particular point in time. Included at the end of the book is the text of the copyright law itself.

Butler, R. P. (2014). *Copyright for academic librarians and professionals.* ALA Editions.

Butler presents copyright concepts for college and university librarians, faculty, and students. The same concepts, in the same order, are presented as in Butler's earlier work, so both books can be used as sources of accurate information. The significant differences between the two works are the details of examples included as well as the target reading audience.

Creative Commons. (2020). *Creative Commons for educators and librarians.* ALA Editions.

The print version of the Creative Commons certificate content. The entire work is licensed CC BY 4.0, making it possible to use it however you wish, provided you include an appropriate attribution. The content is also available online at: https://certificates.creativecommons.org/about/certificate-resources-cc-by/, including links to projects from past enrollees.

Crews, K. D. (2020). *Copyright law for librarians and educators: Creative strategies and practical solutions* (4th ed.). ALA Editions.

A text addressing major issues of copyright and related concepts. Aimed at librarians and educators, it is particularly useful for non-K–12 librarians and educators. The title is organized according to broad issues associated with copyright. Several checklists appear as appendices to assist users in making decisions regarding the use of copyrighted materials.

Facing History & Ourselves. (2017). *Gallery walk.* https://www.facinghistory.org/resource library/gallery-walk-0

The Facing History & Ourselves organization's stated mission is to "use lessons of history to challenge teachers and their students to stand up to bigotry and hate." One technique that they recommend to facilitate student engagement is the gallery walk. Their definition is concise and supplemented by video content to explain the power behind them to teachers.

Russell, C. (2023). *Complete copyright for K–12 librarians and educators.* ALA Editions.

Russell's work delivers copyright concepts through an informal scenario approach. She introduces a cast of characters who work their way through various copyright concepts such as fair use, multimedia use, and distance learning. Each of her chapters introduces common activities found in K–12 schools, making this title especially readable for teachers and school librarians.

Simpson, C. & Wolf, S. (2021). *Copyright for schools: A practical guide.* Libraries Unlimited.

The perennial favorite text for school librarians who seek to understand the sometimes-confusing concepts related to copyright in schools. Included in the text are authentic scenarios that illustrate commonly encountered situations in schools. Readers can also find a concept-based concordance that provides the locations within the text for court cases used as the basis for the interpretation of copyright in school settings.

Smith, K. L. & Ellis, E. L. (Eds.). (2020). *Coaching copyright.* ALA Editions.

Smith and Ellis wrote this book to guide those librarians who are asked to help people make decisions about their use of copyrighted materials. Because only licensed attorneys can provide formal legal advice, adopting a "coaching" perspective when answering copyright questions is particularly useful for librarians to adopt. This title expands on the "Five Questions" that help users analyze copyright problems. It's a great companion for preparing school and academic librarians on how to assist patrons as they navigate the copyright landscape.

Subcommittee on Courts and Intellectual Property of the Committee of the Judiciary. (1976). *Fair use guidelines for educational multimedia.* ERIC. http://files.eric.ed.gov/fulltext/ED402920.pdf

Primary source document of the text for the multimedia guidelines. The document begins with content about the inception of the report and the scope of the guidelines. Specific limits on the use of multimedia materials are also described. Explicit statements that apply the guidelines to both teachers and students are present. For those instructors who wish students to read primary documents rather than relying on paraphrases or summaries by various authors, this document is the one to use when studying the multimedia guidelines.

The US Copyright law—Title 17 US Code (https://www.copyright.gov/title17/).

The primary source documents for copyright law. It is the text of the entire law. Chapter 1 of Title 17 is used most often by lay persons as they develop an understanding of copyright law. Chapter 5 of Title 17 describes the penalties associated with violating copyright law, including limitations on those penalties. Chapter 5 is not often read by lay persons and is more often used by law professionals.

Wolf, S. (2018). *Creative Commons: Sharing with the world one creator at a time.* Author. Licensed CC BY NC SA 4.0.

This comic version of how Creative Commons came into existence is written at a 3rd grade reading level. It is particularly useful for younger learners, or older learners who might prefer a lighter treatment of the history of Creative Commons. It is available in the companion website (https://bloomsbury.pub/teaching-copyright) with permission of the author. You are free to reproduce, distribute, adapt, and use it in your teaching activities provided you adhere to the terms of the license on the document.

Suggested Media Resources

A Creative Commons for Kids—https://www.youtube.com/watch?v=xcrtq7jsS8s

A ninety-second video that is aimed at children versus adults. It is not CC licensed itself. Therefore, your use would need to be evaluated against fair use or appropriate guidelines.

Activision lawyers send Spyro fan game cease-and-desist—https://www.eurogamer.net/spyro-myths-awaken-fan-game-sent-cease-and-desist

A seriously worded letter from the gaming community. Users will want to click on the images of the letters in order to enlarge them enough to read. Watermarks are present that may impact some users' enjoyment of the text.

Amazon Prime Video Terms of Service—https://www.primevideo.com/help/ref=atv_hp_nd_nav?nodeId=G202095490

Amazon's video streaming service, Amazon Prime Video, has terms of service that are similar to those of other streaming video services. That is, they are for personal, non-commercial use only. As you review the terms of service, you should take special note of terms such as "reproduce," "distribute," "derivative," and other terms that allude to any of the six exclusive rights. Generally, those uses are prohibited by the terms of service. Amazon has additional terms relating to the type and number of devices that users may use to access videos. Most online tools, including Amazon Prime, have a lower age limit of thirteen in order for users to be able to use the service. The implication of this is that users younger than thirteen are prohibited from using the service and thus are not able to make a fair use argument if they are able to access material from the service.

Brewer, M. & ALA Office for Instructional Technology Policy. (2008). *Fair use evaluator.* https://librarycopyright.net/resources/fairuse/index.php

An interactive tool that you can use to document your decision making that informs your use of copyrighted materials. It should not be considered legal advice. You can use it, though, to create a paper-trail of decisions you make as you use copyrighted material. Also useful for students to use as a scaffold as they practice their own fair use analysis efforts.

Canvas Terms of Use—https://www.instructure.com/policies/terms-of-use

In order for learning management systems to function properly, their terms of service must include provisions for the platform/company to be able to use copyrighted materials that users might upload. Canvas's illustrates this need. As you review the terms of use, you should take note of terms that allude to the six exclusive rights as well as terminology that describes acceptable use. Typically, acceptable use is defined in terms of service documents as use that does not violate the law and is not obscene.

CC search portal—https://search.creativecommons.org/

A repository of links, maintained by Creative Commons, that you can use to limit search for Creative Commons licensed items. You can search by type of license or by concrete and abstract concept terms. If you only use one source of Creative Commons licensed items, this is a good one, as it provides access to a variety of sites that house these sorts of materials.

Cease-and-Desist Letters—https://copyrightwitness.com/protect/cease-and-desist-letter#:~:text =It%20has%20come%20to%20our,the%20work%20and%20must%20stop

A short, easily understandable method to write cease-and-desist letters. Teachers can use this as a template for their students to write letters as a part of authentic projects.

Circular 21—Reproduction of Copyrighted Works by Educators and Librarians. https://www.copyright.gov/circs/circ21.pdf

The official documentation of the print guidelines that were the result of the Kastenmeier Report. This circular is able to be freely reproduced and distributed to teachers and students. It includes the sections of copyright law that were used to determine the guidelines, definitions of key terms, and an explanation of the guidelines for the use of print-based materials.

Copyright the Card Game—https://copyrightliteracy.org/resources/copyright-the-card-game/

A Creative Commons licensed downloadable set of playing cards that are a great way to scaffold students as they develop their fair use analysis skills. The game was originally created to correlate with UK copyright law. As of 2017, a US law version was made available (http://paulbond.info/blog/copyright-the-card-game-u-s-version/). Both versions are Creative Commons licensed, so are particularly useful to teachers of all levels who wish to use the game in their classrooms. As the game and cards are CC licensed, they can be customized by teachers who are using them in their classrooms.

Creative Commons Licenses—https://creativecommons.org/share-your-work/cclicenses/

Description of the six different Creative Commons licenses. This document provides information that creators of content can use when making a decision about which license they might want to apply to their work.

Creative Commons Licenses Explained—https://www.youtube.com/watch?v=2dw9MtyTunU

A three-minute video that explains the different Creative Commons licenses. The video itself is not CC licensed, so your use would need to be evaluated against fair use or appropriate guidelines. A printed version of the script is available, making it an effective item for those who might prefer reading text over hearing a narration.

Creative Commons: A History—https://scholarworks.boisestate.edu/sw_pubs/37/

A downloadable infographic that provides a snapshot of the history of Creative Commons. It is licensed CC BY 4.0, making it able to be used in whatever way you wish as long as you also include an appropriate attribution.

Disney+ Terms of Service—https://www.disneyplus.com/legal/subscriber-agreement

Disney+, a well-known streaming video service for movies that are especially popular with young children, has similar terms of use as other streaming video services. That is, they are for personal, non-commercial use only. As you review the terms of service, you should take special note of terms such as "reproduce," "distribute," "derivative," and other terms that allude to any of the six exclusive rights. Generally, those uses are prohibited by the terms of service. Most online tools, including Disney+, have a lower age limit of thirteen for users to be able to use the service. The implication of this is that users younger than thirteen are prohibited from using the service and thus are not able to make a fair use argument if they are able to access material from the service.

Dr. Seuss Goes After Photographer over Grinch-Themed Photo Shoot. (October 2, 2019). *Petapixel*—https://petapixel.com/2019/10/02/dr-seuss-goes-after-photographer-over-grinch-themed-photo-shoot/

This article describes one example of a cease-and-desist letter that users of copyrighted materials might receive. In this instance, the cease-and-desist request appears to be delivered via email rather than written letter.

Finding CC licensed materials from Eastern Michigan—https://guides.emich.edu/creativecommons/locating

A repository of several different sources of Creative Commons licensed materials. It is maintained by Eastern Michigan University libraries and so is likely to be most useful to university students and adults. A login is not required to access this document, although there might be links to resources internal to Eastern Michigan University that might require a username and password.

Flickr Terms of Use—https://www.flickr.com/help/terms

Rules that govern the use of the image hosting site Flickr.

Givony, S. (2017). "Stranger things have happened: Netflix writes funny cease and desist letter." *Sharon Givony Consulting: Turn Your Ideas into Assets.* https://sharongivoni.com.au/netflix-cease-desist-letter-copyright/

A humorous example of how a cease-and-desist letter might be written. The author is an Australian attorney specializing in intellectual property. Despite her not being based in the United States, her take and explanation for how copyright infringements can be handled provide a lighthearted explanation of the major elements of these sometimes scary-sounding letters.

Google Terms of Use—https://policies.google.com/terms

Rules that govern the use of Google and Google tools. Depending on which tool you're using, you may need to navigate through several documents to find the exact one that governs your use. Make sure to notice how users under the age of thirteen are or are not permitted to use Google services and tools.

Gould, M. (2024). "How to write choreography." *Mandi's Lindy Hop Blog*. https://dance.mandigould.com/choreography/

A clear and easy to consume essay describing how to write choreography. Choreography is protected by copyright, but only when it is in fixed and tangible format. The method by which choreography is fixed is unique, using symbology and music counts that are likely known only to dancers and choreographers.

"How to find Creative Commons licensed materials"—https://smartcopying.edu.au/how-to-find-creative-commons-licensed-materials/

A very brief tutorial on locating CC licensed materials.

Instagram Terms of Use—https://help.instagram.com/581066165581870

Rules that govern the use of the social media site Instagram.

Microsoft Terms of Use—https://www.microsoft.com/en-us/legal/terms-of-use

Rules that govern the use of Microsoft products. Depending on which specific application you're using, you may find that there are different terms that may apply. Make sure to notice how users under the age of eighteen are or are not permitted to use Microsoft services.

Moodle Terms of Service—https://apps.moodle.com/admin/tool/policy/view.php?versionid=3

In order for learning management systems to function properly, their terms of service must include provisions for the platform/company to be able to use copyrighted materials that users might upload. Moodle's illustrates this need. As you review the terms of use, you should take note of terms that allude to the six exclusive rights as well as terminology that describes acceptable use. Typically, acceptable use is defined in terms of service documents as use that does not violate the law and is not obscene.

Multimedia guidelines—http://files.eric.ed.gov/fulltext/ED402920.pdf

A primary source document of the multimedia guidelines that were created by the Subcommittee on reports and intellectual property of the Committee of the Judiciary in the US House of Representatives. Published in 1996, these multimedia guidelines continue to be referenced by courts, congress, and users of copyrighted materials.

Netflix Terms of Use—https://help.netflix.com/legal/termsofuse

Netflix, a well-known streaming video service, permits the use of its service for personal, non-commercial use only. As you review the terms of service, you should take special note of terms such as "reproduce," "distribute," "derivative," and other terms that allude to any of the six exclusive rights. Generally, those uses are prohibited by the terms of service. In addition to conditions relating to the use of content on the service, the terms address the age of users. Most online tools, including Netflix, have a lower age limit of thirteen in order for users to be able to use the service. The implication of this is that users younger than thirteen are prohibited from using the service and thus are not able to make a fair use argument if they are able to access material from the service.

Klein, Yvonne. "Searching and Finding Open Educational Resources (OER)"—https://oercommons.org/courseware/lesson/97649/overview

A short tutorial about finding CC licensed materials. It is maintained by the Open Educational Resources lab and so has a balanced perspective. Links to different sources of materials are included, but you are not able to conduct a "one step" search. You must navigate to the separate resources in order to search them for CC licensed materials.

Open AI Terms of Use—https://openai.com/policies/terms-of-use

Rules governing the use of Open AI tools such as ChatGPT. This is a relatively short document and does not explicitly address all aspects of copyright. Rather, it mentions intellectual property in a general fashion.

Pandora Terms of Use—https://www.pandora.com/legal

Rules governing the use of the music streaming service Pandora. The document is well organized and easily searchable using the find feature of web browsers. It is considered to be a primary source of information, as it is the actual document that users agree to when they establish their Pandora accounts.

Pearson Publishing Terms of Use—https://loginstatic.pearson.com/html/PearsonEULA.html and https://loginstatic.pearson.com/html/AcceptableUsePolicy.html

Primary source documentation for the terms and rules that users agree to when they use products published by Pearson. These documents control the use of Pearson products by both teachers and students, as they have accounts for different purposes.

Pinterest Terms of Service—https://policy.pinterest.com/en/terms-of-service

Rules that govern the use of the social media site Pinterest.

PowerSchool Terms of Use—https://www.powerschool.com/terms/

In order for learning management systems to function properly, their terms of service must include provisions for the platform/company to be able to use copyrighted materials that users might upload—PowerSchool's illustrates this need. As you review the terms of use, you should take note of terms that allude to the six exclusive rights as well as terminology that describes acceptable use. Typically, acceptable use is defined in terms of service documents as use that does not violate the law and is not obscene.

Smith, K. and Macklin, L. (2014). "A framework for analyzing any U.S. copyright problem." Creative Commons. https://kuscholarworks.ku.edu/bitstream/handle/1808/22723/Smith_Copyright_Analysis_Framework.pdf (License CC BY SA 4.0).

This concisely presented method for analyzing copyright problems provides readers with explicit questions that they can answer as they attempt to determine the status of any copyright situation that they encounter. It has been used by multiple scholars and authors as the basis for scaffolds and professional development throughout the United States.

Snapchat Terms of Use—https://snap.com/en-US/terms

Rules that govern the use of the social media site Snapchat.

Spotify Terms of Service—https://www.spotify.com/us/legal/end-user-agreement/

Rules governing the use of the music streaming service Spotify. The document is well organized and easily searchable using the find feature of web browsers. It is considered to be a primary source of information, as it is the actual document that users agree to when they establish their Spotify accounts.

The Story of Creative Commons—https://certificates.creativecommons.org/cccertedu/chapter/1-1-the-story-of-creative-commons/

The history of Creative Commons. Originally created for librarians and teachers enrolled in a certificate course, it is particularly useful for adult learners or those with sophisticated reading skills.

TikTok Terms of Use—https://www.tiktok.com/legal/page/us/terms-of-service/en

Rules that govern the use of the social media site TikTok. Be aware that some institutions limit access to TikTok, and you may not be able to access their terms even if you are not a user of TikTok. In the terms of service portion of TikTok, you can find a specific policy related to copyright, use of the service by children, and other details.

United States Copyright Law: A Guide for Music Educators. Retrieved May 4, 2024, https://nafme.org/resource/united-states-copyright-law-a-guide-for-music-educators/

Written by the National Association for Music Education, this website provides music educators with specific information regarding the use of music and related copyrighted works in instructional situations.

University of Minnesota Libraries. *Using existing works.* https://www.lib.umn.edu/copyright/fairuse

A short tutorial describing the four tests of fair use. Intended for university students and faculty, it may still be usable by older K–12 students. No username or password is required to access the site.

US copyright law, Title 17—https://www.copyright.gov/title17/92chap1.html

The text of the copyright law. As a primary source document, users can use it to see the actual language written into law. The law is hyperlinked, allowing users to quickly and easily navigate the different chapters and sections of the law.

Using Creative Commons Content—https://www.youtube.com/watch?v=1OULrgm4iW4&t=1s

A two-minute video using vocabulary and structure that is appropriate for intermediate grades and above. It is not CC licensed itself, so your use would need to be evaluated against fair use or appropriate guidelines.

Vondran, S. (2020a). *Attorney Steve® explains "willful" copyright infringement.* https://www.youtube.com/watch?v=P0Dli9uW2Jg

A six-minute video that explains what willful infringement is. The sound quality is reasonable, although not professional quality. There is a single image that the narrator uses to structure the information. It can be considered an audio-only item given the lack of moving images.

Vondran, S. (2020b). *Vicarious vs. contributory copyright infringement explained.* https://www.youtube.com/watch?v=OplosyyaAJ0

A four-minute video that defines the differences between contributory and vicarious infringement. The video is aimed at practicing attorneys, adult learners, and lay persons interested in legal topics. It is not to be considered legal advice. The images in the video are limited enough to consider this an audio-only resource. A transcript is available for viewing.

Wayne State University Library System. (2024). *Fair use checklist.* http://copyright.wayne.edu/checklist.php

An interactive checklist that documents the criteria you use to decide whether or not a particular use of copyrighted material can be considered fair use. It is not to be considered legal advice.

What are Creative Commons Licenses?—https://www.youtube.com/watch?v=srVPLrmlBJY

A two-minute video that introduces the different Creative Commons licenses. The language used is appropriate for students in intermediate grades and above. It is licensed CC BY NC SA, meaning that you may use it nearly however you want. You must NOT use it for commercial purposes, and you must share any derivative works under the same or a compatible license.

Why Was Creative Commons Created?—https://www.youtube.com/watch?v=tft3zNhzQHs

A four-minute narrated presentation giving a brief history of Creative Commons. It is licensed CC BY 4.0, making it able to be used in whatever way you wish as long as you also include an appropriate attribution.

Wiley Publishing Terms of Use—https://www.wiley.com/en-us/terms-of-use

Primary source documentation for the terms and rules that users agree to when they use products published by Wiley. These documents control the use of Pearson products by both teachers and students, as they have accounts for different purposes.

Wolston, M. (2018). *A brief history of Creative Commons.* https://vimeo.com/251525073 (Licensed CC BY 4.0).

An eight-minute video using lay-person terms to explain how the Creative Commons came into being. This video is a good example of using CC licensed materials to create a derivative work. It is also available on the Vimeo site. Included in the video is a linked document containing the citations for the media used within the video.

X (Formerly Twitter) Terms of Service—https://twitter.com/en/tos

Rules that govern the use of the social media site X.

Suggested Online Tools

Online Bingo Card Creator—bingobaker.com

An online tool that generates randomly structured bingo cards as well as call lists that can be used for a class bingo game. The free version limits printing or downloading to only eight different bingo cards. However, the tool has a one-time only paid membership that is advertised as being a lifetime membership of $24.95 (as of the publication of this text). Inclusion of pricing information here should not be considered to be formal endorsement or recommendation to register for the service. Rather, this information is provided for informational use only. Creating bingo cards is straightforward in Bingobaker. The interface to create a "base" card is easy and also permits the creation of question/answer style cell contents. Bingo cards can include text or images, permitting a wide variety of cards and games to be generated.

Plickers—plickers.com

An online tool that permits teachers to embed formative assessment into their lectures and other instructional activities. By creating scannable codes in the form of QR codes, teachers use the Plickers app to nearly instantaneously determine responses of the entire class or group. Results can be tabulated and tracked, as well as displayed in different chart forms so that students and teachers are able to see the accuracy of their responses.

Poll Everywhere—polleverywhere.com

An online tool that permits teachers to embed anonymous polls into their lectures and other instructional activities. Users may embed poll questions directly into presentations or may choose to have respondents provide answers after scanning a QR code. Users may elect to use either a free or a paid account, depending on the level of usage that is most appropriate to their needs.

Visual Metaphors

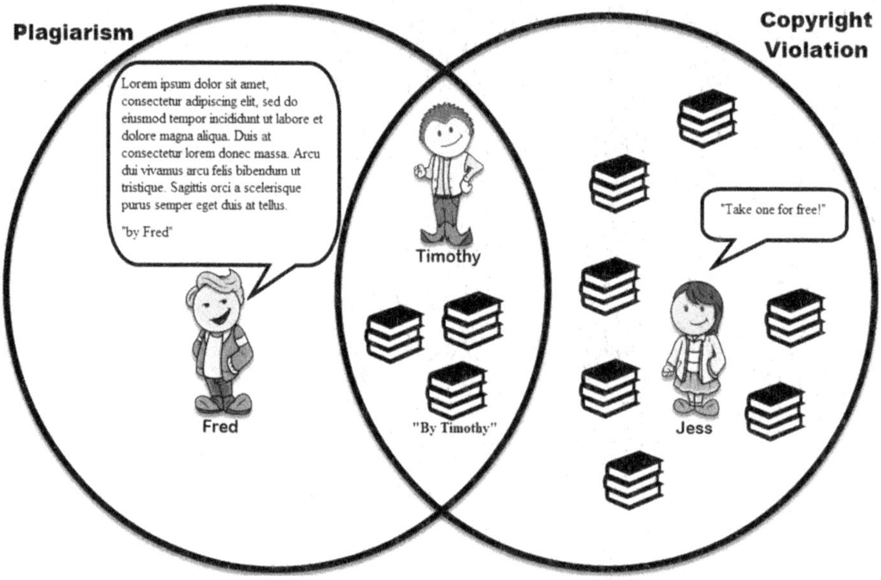

Plagiarism and Copyright Relationship. Source: Simpson & Wolf, 2021, p. 248, used with permission.

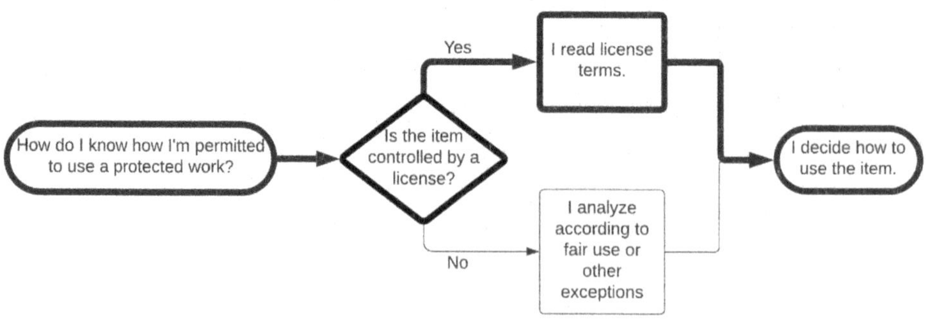

License Precedence over Fair Use.

5 Concordance

While most concordances are comprehensive lists or tables that indicate where words or concepts appear in a written work, this concordance serves as a reference for teachers who wish to be targeted in their selection of scenarios or objective questions when writing practice or assessment items such as tests or quizzes.

Questions by Lessons

Item Code	Bloom Classification	Lesson 1	Lesson 2	Lesson 3	Lesson 4	Lesson 5	Lesson 6	Lesson 7	Lesson 8	Lesson 9	Lesson 10	Lesson 11	Lesson 12	Lesson 13	Lesson 14
1.1	1A	✓	✓					✓							
1.2	1A	✓	✓												
1.3	1A	✓	✓												
1.4	2A	✓	✓												
1.5	1A	✓	✓												
1.6	1B	✓	✓												
1.7	2B	✓	✓					✓							
1.8	1B	✓	✓					✓							
1.9	1A	✓	✓												
1.10	1B	✓	✓												
1.11	1A	✓	✓												
1.12	1A	✓	✓												
1.13	1A	✓												✓	
1.14	1A	✓												✓	
1.15	2A	✓	✓												
1.16	2B	✓	✓												
1.17	2B	✓	✓												
1.18	2B	✓	✓												
1.19	2B	✓	✓												
1.20	2B	✓	✓												
1.21	2A	✓	✓												

Item Code	Bloom Classification	Lesson 1	Lesson 2	Lesson 3	Lesson 4	Lesson 5	Lesson 6	Lesson 7	Lesson 8	Lesson 9	Lesson 10	Lesson 11	Lesson 12	Lesson 13	Lesson 14
1.22	2B	✓	✓												
1.23	2B	✓	✓												
1.24	2B	✓						✓							
1.25	3B	✓						✓							
1.26	3B	✓									✓				
1.27	3B	✓									✓				
1.28	2B	✓	✓												
1.29	2A	✓	✓												
1.30	2A	✓	✓												
1.31	2B	✓												✓	
1.32	2A	✓												✓	
1.33	2A	✓												✓	
1.34	2A	✓												✓	
1.35	2A	✓												✓	
1.36	2B	✓												✓	
1.37	2B	✓												✓	
1.38	2A	✓												✓	
1.39	3A	✓	✓												
1.40	3A	✓						✓							
1.41	3A	✓						✓							
1.42	6A	✓	✓			✓									
1.43	6A	✓	✓			✓									
2.1	1A	✓		✓											
2.2	1A	✓		✓											
2.3	2A	✓		✓											
2.4	2A	✓		✓											
2.5	3B	✓		✓											
2.6	5B	✓		✓											
2.7	4B	✓		✓											
2.8	5C	✓		✓											
2.9	4C	✓		✓											
2.10	4C	✓		✓											

Item Code	Bloom Classification	Lesson 1	Lesson 2	Lesson 3	Lesson 4	Lesson 5	Lesson 6	Lesson 7	Lesson 8	Lesson 9	Lesson 10	Lesson 11	Lesson 12	Lesson 13	Lesson 14
2.11	4B	✓		✓											
2.12	4B	✓				✓									
2.13	4C	✓				✓									
2.14	4C	✓						✓							
2.15	4C	✓						✓							
2.16	3B	✓			✓			✓							
2.17	3B	✓			✓			✓							
2.18	3B	✓			✓			✓							
2.19	5B	✓		✓				✓							
2.20	5B	✓						✓							
2.21	5B	✓						✓							
2.22	5B	✓						✓							
2.23	6C	✓		✓											
2.24	6D	✓		✓											
2.25	6C	✓		✓											
2.26	6D	✓						✓							
3.1	1A	✓				✓		✓							
3.2	1A	✓				✓									
3.3	1A	✓				✓									
3.4	1A	✓				✓									
3.5	4A	✓				✓									
3.6	1A	✓				✓									
3.7	1A	✓				✓									
3.8	1A	✓			✓										
3.9	1A	✓			✓										
3.10	2A	✓			✓										
3.11	3A	✓				✓									
3.12	3A	✓				✓									
3.13	2A	✓				✓									
3.14	2A	✓				✓									
3.15	2A	✓				✓									
3.16	2A	✓			✓										

Item Code	Bloom Classification	Lesson 1	Lesson 2	Lesson 3	Lesson 4	Lesson 5	Lesson 6	Lesson 7	Lesson 8	Lesson 9	Lesson 10	Lesson 11	Lesson 12	Lesson 13	Lesson 14
3.17	2A	✓			✓										
3.18	2B	✓			✓										
3.19	2B	✓			✓										
3.20	2A	✓				✓									
3.21	2A	✓				✓									
3.22	2A	✓						✓							
3.23	2B	✓				✓									
3.24	2B	✓				✓									
3.25	2B	✓	✓			✓									
3.26	2B	✓	✓			✓									
3.27	3A	✓		✓											
3.28	3A	✓		✓											
3.29	3B	✓				✓									
3.30	4B	✓			✓										
3.31	4B	✓			✓										
3.32	5B	✓						✓							
3.33	6B	✓						✓	✓						
3.34	2B	✓			✓										
3.35	2A	✓						✓							
3.36	3A	✓						✓							
3.37	2A	✓			✓										
3.38	2A	✓			✓										
4.1	1A	✓					✓								
4.2	1A	✓					✓								
4.3	1A	✓					✓								
4.4	1A	✓					✓								
4.5	1A	✓					✓								
4.6	2A	✓					✓								
4.7	1A	✓					✓								
4.8	1A	✓					✓								

Item Code	Bloom Classification	Lesson 1	Lesson 2	Lesson 3	Lesson 4	Lesson 5	Lesson 6	Lesson 7	Lesson 8	Lesson 9	Lesson 10	Lesson 11	Lesson 12	Lesson 13	Lesson 14
4.9	5A	✓					✓								
4.10	2A	✓					✓								
4.11	2A	✓					✓								
4.12	2B	✓					✓								
4.13	2A	✓					✓								
4.14	2A	✓					✓								
4.15	2B	✓					✓								
4.16	2A	✓					✓								
4.17	3B	✓						✓							
4.18	4B	✓						✓							
4.19	4B	✓						✓							
4.20	4B	✓						✓							
4.21	4B	✓						✓							
4.22	5B	✓						✓							
4.23	6C	✓								✓					
4.24	6D	✓					✓								
5.1	1A	✓						✓		✓					
5.2	2A	✓						✓							
5.3	1A	✓						✓							
5.4	1A	✓						✓							
5.5	2A	✓						✓							
5.6	3A	✓						✓							
5.7	3B	✓						✓		✓	✓		✓		
5.8	3D	✓						✓	✓						
5.9	5B	✓						✓							
5.10	5B	✓						✓							
5.11	5B	✓						✓					✓		
5.12	3B	✓						✓							
5.13	3B	✓						✓							
5.14	2B	✓						✓							

Item Code	Bloom Classification	Lesson 1	Lesson 2	Lesson 3	Lesson 4	Lesson 5	Lesson 6	Lesson 7	Lesson 8	Lesson 9	Lesson 10	Lesson 11	Lesson 12	Lesson 13	Lesson 14
5.15	5B	✓						✓							
5.16	2B	✓						✓							
5.17	6C	✓								✓					
5.18	6C	✓								✓					
5.19	6D	✓								✓					
6.1	1A	✓							✓		✓	✓	✓		
6.2	1A	✓							✓		✓	✓	✓		
6.3	1A	✓									✓	✓	✓		
6.4	1A	✓									✓	✓	✓		
6.5	1A	✓									✓	✓	✓		
6.6	1A	✓									✓	✓	✓		
6.7	2A	✓									✓	✓	✓		
6.8	2A	✓									✓	✓	✓		
6.9	2A	✓									✓	✓	✓		
6.10	2A	✓									✓	✓	✓		
6.11	2A	✓							✓						
6.12	2A	✓							✓						
6.13	2D	✓							✓						
6.14	2A	✓													
6.15	2A	✓													
6.16	3A	✓							✓	✓					
6.17	2A	✓								✓					
6.18	4A	✓									✓				
6.19	5B	✓									✓				
6.20	5B	✓									✓				
6.21	4C	✓							✓	✓					
6.22	4C	✓							✓	✓					
6.23	6B	✓					✓								
6.24	6C	✓					✓	✓							
6.25	6D	✓					✓	✓							

Item Code	Bloom Classification	Lesson 1	Lesson 2	Lesson 3	Lesson 4	Lesson 5	Lesson 6	Lesson 7	Lesson 8	Lesson 9	Lesson 10	Lesson 11	Lesson 12	Lesson 13	Lesson 14
7.1	1A	✓									✓	✓	✓		
7.2	1A	✓									✓	✓	✓		
7.3	1A	✓									✓	✓	✓		
7.4	1A	✓									✓	✓	✓		
7.5	1A	✓									✓	✓	✓		
7.6	1A	✓									✓	✓	✓		
7.7	1A	✓									✓	✓	✓		
7.8	2A	✓									✓	✓	✓		
7.9	2A	✓									✓	✓	✓		
7.10	2A	✓									✓	✓	✓		
7.11	2A	✓									✓	✓	✓		
7.12	3B	✓									✓	✓	✓		
7.13	2B	✓									✓	✓	✓		
7.14	3A	✓									✓	✓	✓		
7.15	3A	✓									✓	✓	✓		
7.16	2B	✓										✓	✓		
7.17	2B	✓										✓	✓		
7.18	2B	✓										✓	✓		
7.19	4B	✓										✓	✓		
7.20	5B	✓										✓	✓		
7.21	6D	✓										✓	✓		
7.22	2A	✓									✓	✓	✓		
8.1	1A	✓												✓	✓
8.2	2A	✓												✓	✓
8.3	1A	✓												✓	✓
8.4	1A	✓												✓	✓
8.5	1A	✓												✓	✓
8.6	2A	✓												✓	✓
8.7	2A	✓												✓	✓
8.8	3A	✓												✓	

Item Code	Bloom Classification	Lesson 1	Lesson 2	Lesson 3	Lesson 4	Lesson 5	Lesson 6	Lesson 7	Lesson 8	Lesson 9	Lesson 10	Lesson 11	Lesson 12	Lesson 13	Lesson 14
8.9	2A	✓												✓	
8.10	1A	✓												✓	
8.11	1A	✓												✓	
8.12	2A	✓												✓	
8.13	2B	✓												✓	
8.14	2B	✓												✓	
8.15	1A	✓												✓	
8.16	2B	✓												✓	
8.17	2B	✓												✓	✓
8.18	2B	✓												✓	✓
8.19	2B	✓												✓	✓
8.20	2B	✓												✓	✓
8.21	3B	✓												✓	✓
8.22	2B	✓												✓	✓
8.23	6D	✓												✓	✓
8.24	2B	✓												✓	
8.25	2B	✓												✓	
8.26	3B	✓												✓	
8.27	2B	✓												✓	
8.28	3B	✓												✓	
8.29	4B	✓												✓	✓
8.30	4B	✓												✓	✓
8.31	5B	✓												✓	
8.32	5B	✓												✓	
8.33	6C	✓												✓	✓
8.34	6B	✓												✓	✓

Scenarios by Concept

The following concordance chart helps readers select scenarios to use as practice or assessment items within different lessons. Each scenario is numbered within the Scenario Bank. Each court case has a separate number, beginning with the capital letter "G." Each lesson has a number assigned to it, appearing at the beginning of the lesson title in Chapter 2. The exclusive rights, infringement type, and character columns use codes to indicate which of the rights or infringement are illustrated in the given scenario. The key for those codes appears at the top of the chart. Lessons 1, 3, and 7 are all appropriate for all scenarios. Therefore, only additional lesson numbers are listed in that column. If no other lessons are appropriate for a scenario, I've repeated 1, 3, and 7 indicators.

Key:
Exclusive rights: R = Reproduction; D = Distribution; A = Adaptation; PD = Public Display; PP = Public Performance; DAT = Public Performance through Digital Audio Transmission.
Infringement type: S = Standard; I = Innocent; W = Willful; C = Contributory; V = Vicarious; D = Direct
Characters: T = Teachers; S = Students; A = Administrators; L = Librarians; P = Parents

Scenario #	Exclusive Rights	Concepts	Infringement Type	Court Case #	Characters	Lesson # 1, 3, 7 plus:
1	D, PP	Video; fair use	W; D	G32	T	11, 12, 13, 14
2	DAT; PP	Supplemental resources; licenses; fair use	S	G2	T	4, 10, 11, 12, 13, 14
3	D	Supplemental resources	0	–	S; T	2, 4
4	PD; A; R	Transformative use; direct instruction; anthologies	0	–	T	3
5	A; PD	Supplemental instruction	I; S	G12	T; S	6, 11, 12, 13, 14
6	A; R	Music; sound recordings	S	G29	T; L	11, 12, 13, 14
7	PD; R; PP; A	Sound recording	0	G1; G6	S	8, 11, 12
8	R	Sound recording	S	–	T	6, 13, 14
9	R; PD	Photographs; enforcement	S	–	T	13, 14
10	R; D	Public domain; fair use; gov't doc.	I	–	T; S	2, 13, 14

Key:
Exclusive rights: R = Reproduction; D = Distribution; A = Adaptation; PD = Public Display; PP = Public Performance; DAT = Public Performance through Digital Audio Transmission.
Infringement type: S = Standard; I = Innocent; W = Willful; C = Contributory; V = Vicarious; D = Direct
Characters: T = Teachers; S = Students; A = Administrators; L = Librarians; P = Parents

Scenario #	Exclusive Rights	Concepts	Infringement Type	Court Case #	Characters	Lesson # 1, 3, 7 plus:
11	PP; DAT	Licensing; sound recording	S	G2	T; S	11, 12, 13, 14
12	R: D; PP	Disabilities; fair use; blind	0	G4	T; S	11, 12
13	R; D	Replacement copies; standardized test exigent use; current use damaged materials	0	–	T	9
14	A	Transformative use; direct instruction	0	–	T; S	2
15	R; A; PP	Blind	0	G21	T; S	10, 11, 12
16	D; R	Software; licensing	S; W	G31	P; T	6, 11, 12, 13, 14
17	A; PP	Direct instruction	S	–	T	8, 9, 13, 14
18	R; PD	Distance ed. Fair use; professional development	S	–	T; S	6, 13, 14
19	R; D	Orphan work; out of print; fair use; copyright expiration	I	–	T; P	2, 13, 14
20	PP	Video fair use; reward; exceptions	S	–	T	6, 13, 14
21	R; D	Replacement copies; fair use; damaged originals	I; S	–	T; S	13, 14
22	PD	Fair use; direct instruction; copyright ownership	0	–	T: S	1, 3, 7
23	PP; R; PD	Exceptions; enforcement	S	–	T; S	13, 14
24	R	Personal use; fair use	0	–	T; S	1, 3, 7
25	R: D: A	Fair use; saving money	S	–	T; S	13, 14

Key:
Exclusive rights: R = Reproduction; D = Distribution; A = Adaptation; PD = Public Display; PP = Public Performance; DAT = Public Performance through Digital Audio Transmission.
Infringement type: S = Standard; I = Innocent; W = Willful; C = Contributory; V = Vicarious; D = Direct
Characters: T = Teachers; S = Students; A = Administrators; L = Librarians; P = Parents

Scenario #	Exclusive Rights	Concepts	Infringement Type	Court Case #	Characters	Lesson # 1, 3, 7 plus:
26	PP; R: A	Fair use; instructional use	S	–	T: S	4, 8, 9, 13, 14
27	R: A: PD	Anthology; fair use; instructional use	S; C	–	T; P	13, 14
28	R; D	Exigent circumstances; fair use; damaged original	0	–	T: A	1, 3, 7
29	PP	Reward; video fair use; license	V; S	–	T: A	6, 13, 14
30	R; D	Gov't document; public domain; fair use; multiple copies	I	–	L	2, 13, 14
31	R: D	Directed copying; fair use	S; C	–	T; A	13, 14
32	PP	Linking; fair use	0	G2; G23	T; S	11, 12
33	R: D	Instructional use; fair use; multiple copying	0	–	T; S; A	1, 3, 7
34	R	Professional development; directed copying; fair use	S	–	A; P	13, 14
35	R; PD: A; PP	Decoration; fair use; derivative use	0	G6	L	9, 11, 12
36	None	Licensing; saving money	W	G32	S; A	4, 11, 12, 13, 14
37	PP; PD; R; D	Distance ed.; licensing	0	G2	S; A	4, 6, 11, 12
38	PP	Music; entertainment	S	–	T; S	13, 14
39	PD	Decoration; using original items	0	–	L	1, 3, 7
40	R	Fair use; punishment; hand copying	S	–	T; S	13, 14
41	PP	Parody; fair use	S	G5; G7	S	13, 14

Key:
Exclusive rights: R = Reproduction; D = Distribution; A = Adaptation; PD = Public Display; PP = Public Performance; DAT = Public Performance through Digital Audio Transmission.
Infringement type: S = Standard; I = Innocent; W = Willful; C = Contributory; V = Vicarious; D = Direct
Characters: T = Teachers; S = Students; A = Administrators; L = Librarians; P = Parents

Scenario #	Exclusive Rights	Concepts	Infringement Type	Court Case #	Characters	Lesson # 1, 3, 7 plus:
42	PD	VARA; Integrity; minors w/ copyright	W	G8; G10	T; S	13, 14
43	R; A	Derivative use; fair use	S	G9; G11	P; A	2, 11, 13, 14
44	R; A	Derivative use; integrity	W	G9; G11	T	2, 11, 13, 14
45	PD; A	Fair use	W	G12	T; A	11, 13, 14
46	R	Fair use; Creative Commons; licenses	S	G13; G24	T	5, 11
47	R; D; PD	Ownership	S	G15	T; S	11, 13, 15
48	PD; A	Derivative use; fair use	0	G19	T; S	6, 11
49	R; D	Work made for hire	0	G20; G27; G33	T; A	11
50	PP; R; D	Work made for hire	0	G20; G27; G33	T; A	11

6 Glossary and Acronyms

In this chapter, you will find common copyright and instructional terms used within the lessons contained in this book. The glossary will be particularly useful to instructors who might not have had formal preparation in the teaching fields. Users should feel free to add to this glossary as they encounter terms and definitions that they feel should be memorialized for their own personal use. It is important to note that the definitions provided in this glossary are suitable for use by lay persons, that is, by non-lawyers. If teachers or students have interest or need for "official" definitions for copyright-related terms as they are used within the law, they can find more detailed definitions in Chapter 1 of the copyright law at https://www.copyright.gov/title17/92chap1.html, as well as in dedicated law dictionaries such as *Black's Law Dictionary*, available in both print and online at https://thelawdictionary.org/

Acronyms

ADA The Americans with Disabilities Act

CC Creative Commons

CONFU Conference on Fair Use

CTEA Copyright Term Extension Act—Also known as the Sonny Bono Copyright Term Extension Act

DMCA Digital Millenium Copyright Act

MMA Music Modernization Act

MTIA Marrakesh Treaty Implementation Act

NOI Notice of Intention

PETA People for the Ethical Treatment of Animals

RIOA Brand of audio players produced by Diamond Multimedia

SCOTUS Supreme Court of the United States

TEACH Act Technology, Education, and Copyright Harmonization Act

USOC United States Olympic Committee

VARA Visual Artists Rights Act

Glossary

Adapt/adaptation Any change to a work that is protected by copyright. Common types of adaptations include format (analog to digital, black-and-white to colorized, etc.).

Appeal An appeal is when one party of a court case asks the next higher level of jurisdiction to revisit the case and ruling. The highest court of appeal in the United States is the Supreme Court of the United States (SCOTUS).

Berne Convention An international treaty that the United States joined in 1987. Three governing principles serve as the minimum protections that signatories must ensure in order to be in compliance. First, protected works in one signatory will be protected in other signatories as if protected by themselves. For instance, England will protect US works in the same way that other works in England are protected. Second, protection must be automatic and not require regulatory adherence. Lastly, protection must be independent of the country of origin. That is, protection by members will continue for the length of time a work is protected in the original country (as long as it's longer than the treaty minimums), but not longer.

Cease-and-desist letter An official letter, usually from an attorney, that directs someone to stop a specific infringement. These sorts of letters also spell out the next legal steps that will be taken if the infringement persists.

Copyright A type of intellectual property applied to creative works that have authorship or are created by artists.

Creative Commons A source of licensed materials that are copyright-protected and possess certain permissions that are "pre-granted" by the authors/artists of those materials. Licenses in the Creative Commons must be followed, or the use is not considered to be fair use.

Damage(s) Monetary fines that infringers must pay as punishment for infringing someone's copyright protection. Damages are determined by judges and can vary from case to case. Sometimes, damages are considered "potential"—hypothetical amounts that would result if everyone, everywhere, were to exhibit the infringing behavior. Other times, damages are considered "actual"—the specific amount of money that the copyright owner lost, or the infringer inappropriately gained, because of the infringement. Damages can also be considered "statutory"—specific amounts for certain types of infringement that are written into the law itself.

Defendant Person or party being sued.

Derivative Work A type of creative work that grows from, is a modification of, or is a combination of other copyright-protected works. Examples include "mashups," translations, or adaptations, as in films or plays.

Display Placing a copyrighted work in a space where members of the public can see it. Hanging pictures on a wall, loading images onto webpages, painting pictures or murals directly onto walls, or placing artwork/sculptures in museums or open-air spaces are all examples of display. Only items that do not move or are not dependent on time to be perceived can be displayed.

Distribute/distribution To cause or permit other people to possess an item. Students may use "pass out" or "pass around" as synonymous terms.

Exception A codified departure from the ability of a copyright holder to enforce their copyright protections pertaining to the six exclusive rights on users. The most well-known exception is fair use. Other exceptions are written into the law for libraries, classrooms, and persons with disabilities.

Fair Use The most well-known exception to the six exclusive rights of copyright ownership. For a user to claim that a particular use is considered to be "fair," their use must pass four factors. First, the purpose and character of the use: Is the use for educational/not for profit use or is the use commercial? Included in the first factor is the concept of transformative use. Second, the nature of the copyrighted work; works that are strictly factual in nature, such as lists of dates, states/capitals, and so on, are not eligible for copyright protection, while creative works such as novels and consumable works such as student workbooks are eligible for copyright protection. Third, the proportionality of the amount used in relation to the work as a whole; in general, the more of something that is used, the stronger the justification should be for its use. Last, the effect of the use on the market for or the value of the original; in general, if the use would prevent money from flowing to the copyright owner, the use is likely not to be considered fair.

Far Hit A non-obvious example of a particular concept. For instance, "whale" is a far hit for the concept of mammal. Likewise, database-held data is a far hit for literary work that is eligible for copyright protection.

Gallery Walk A strategy to increase student engagement during practice activities in class. Students work in small groups on a task and then display the results of their work. Groups then rotate to the displays of their peers, revise or comment on the displays, and then return to their starting places.

Guideline(s) Sets of agreed-upon limits that provide users with guidance about how much of a specific sort of copyrighted work may be used without going beyond the bounds of fair use. Guidelines do not have the force of law, but when they are followed, courts generally see the uses in question more favorably.

Injunction An order from a judge that prevents someone from doing a specific thing. In copyright-related situations, a judge might issue an injunction to someone that prevents them from recording videos or copying materials. The purpose of an injunction is to cause the infringing behavior to stop.

Intellectual property Creative products such as inventions, artistic or literary items, or commercially used products such as signs, symbols, or logos. An overarching term to describe those items that are protected by copyright law, trademark law, or patent law.

Jurisdiction The controlling authority of a particular case, usually geographical (districts, circuits, etc.).

License A special set of rules or permissions that control the use of copyrighted materials. Licenses supersede the permissions that can arise from the application of guidelines or exceptions to the use of copyrighted materials. Using copyrighted works in contravention of a license means that the user is subject to breach of contract consequences as well as being unable to consider the use as fair.

Moral Rights A special type of copyright protection granted to visual artists, a type of creator of specific types of copyrighted works: paintings (including murals and some graffiti), drawings, prints, sculptures, or photographs that have been created for display and not publication, provided they are of recognized stature. Moral rights include the right of attribution; the right to include the artist's name, the right to remove the artist's name if the artist wishes not to claim ownership, and the right to prevent the artist's name from being included if the artwork is modified in a way that would harm the artist's reputation or honor. Moral rights also include the right to integrity; the right to prevent the intentional or negligent destruction of work.

Near Hit An obvious example of a concept. Near hits are examples that most people would recognize as being representative of a particular concept. For instance, "dog" is a near hit for the concept of mammal. Likewise, a book is a near hit for the concept of a literary work that is eligible for copyright protection.

Non-commercial use Use of an item in a manner that does not attempt to earn money. Attempting to earn money but failing to do so (being bad at business or an endeavor) does NOT make a use non-commercial.

Non-exclusive license A set of permissions to access a website or use a creative product that is shared with another person.

Notice of Intention (NOI) A document filed with the Copyright Office to notify the intent to play, record, or distribute a digital song. It allows you to learn the cost of the fee needed in order to do what you intend to do with the song.

Orphan Work A work that is protected by copyright and has not entered the public domain, but for which no copyright owner can be identified or located.

Patent A type of intellectual property that is granted to processes or business practices.

People for the Ethical Treatment of Animals (PETA) An organization concerned with animal rights.

Perform/Performance Acting out (for items like plays or pantomimes), showing (for items such as movies, songs, or presentations) in a public place or space. Only items that depend on the passage of time to be perceived (movies, concerts, plays, etc.) can be performed.

Permissions Found in licenses that control copyrighted works; written descriptions of the behaviors, and conditions under which, users are allowed to perform copyright-protected actions. These permissions may be more or less restrictive than what might be determined through a fair use analysis. When found in professional or leisure licenses, they describe the activities that the license holder is allowed to undertake with regard to that specific type of activity.

Personal use Private use or viewing of an item. For instance, viewing a motion picture at home is considered to be personal use. Photocopying an article from a journal to use as a reference resource in a study is personal use.

Plaintiff Person or party bringing a suit against another person or party.

Proficiencies Level of skill that some leisure or professional licenses require in order to be eligible for those licenses. Common examples include academic preparation for professional licenses, safety courses for leisure activities, and continuing education for some professional licenses. This element of licensing is not commonly found in licenses that control the use of copyrighted materials.

Prohibitions Found in licenses that control copyrighted works; written descriptions of the behaviors, and conditions under which users are NOT allowed to perform copyright-protected actions. These permissions may be more or less restrictive than what might be determined through a fair use analysis. When found in professional or leisure licenses, they describe the activities that the license holder is NOT allowed to do regarding that specific type of activity.

Public A type of space that is open to the general public and where a gathering of people outside of a normal circle of friends or family can occur. Classrooms are public spaces.

Public Domain The public domain is not a place. The public domain describes the set of creative materials that were eligible for copyright protection, but that protection is no longer in place. Materials enter the public domain after specified periods of time depending upon the year in which they were created, the date of the creator's death, whether the work was made "for hire," as well as whether the author directed the work to enter the public domain. Works that are in the public domain no longer have protections over the six exclusive rights of the copyright owner.

Reproduce/reproduction To duplicate or cause to be duplicated. Students may use "copy" as a synonymous term.

Think-Aloud Protocol Narrating out loud the thoughts and decisions that one engages in while completing a complex task. The verbal narration permits other people to know how you think, on what you focus, the decisions you make, and where you click during online navigation.

Trademark A type of intellectual property that protects symbols and slogans of brands, with the purpose of preventing consumer confusion.

Transformative A type of derivative work of a copyright-protected work. Transformative uses imbue new thought, creativity, meaning, or purpose to the original work.

Work Made for Hire A type of copyright-protected work that is created as part of one's job, or as part of a contract. The employer owns the copyright for works made for hire, not the author or artist.

7 Appendices

Appendix A—Analysis Scaffold
Appendix B—Exceptions Analysis Scaffold
Appendix C—Does a License Permit My Use?
Appendix D—License Use Scaffold
Appendix E—Is My Use Permitted by Specific Fair Use Guidelines?
Appendix F—Fair Use Checklist
Appendix G—Key Court Cases—Copyright
Appendix H—Scavenger Hunt Example Clue List
Appendix I—Sample Bingo Card and Concentration Game Concept Pairs
Appendix J—Multimedia Guidelines Cheat Sheet
Appendix K—Guidelines and Laws Quick Reference
Appendix L—Questions for Plicker Cards or Poll Everywhere Activities

Note: The appendices included here are low-resolution versions of the complete documents. Downloadable, full-sized, and printable versions are available on the companion website: https://bloomsbury.pub/teaching-copyright.

Appendix A
Analysis Scaffold

Analysis Scaffold

Note: a downloadable version of this scaffold is available at the text website.

Scenario	Rights	Works	Exceptions	Licenses	Risk Level	Fair Use
Indicate which scenario you're analyzing (number, brief key words, etc.). Use one row for each scenario.	List the exclusive rights of a copyright owner that are affected in this scenario.	List the type of copyrighted work that is described in this scenario.	List any exceptions to the exclusive rights of a copyright owner that apply to this scenario	List any licenses that would control the actions being described in this scenario.	Rate the actions described in this scenario in terms of how risky they are: Low/Medium/High Scale of 1-5 Scale of 1-10	Determine whether the action or activity described in this scenario is likely to be considered fair use.
	Write any assumptions you made in coming to your risk determination.					
	Write any assumptions you made in coming to your fair use determination.					
	Write any questions you need answered in order to be able to come to a more accurate/confident determination of risk or fair use assessment.					

This scaffold is based on the Smith and Macklin (2014) document, A framework for analyzing any U.S. copyright problem.

Scenario	Rights	Works	Exceptions	Licenses	Risk Level	Fair Use
	Write any assumptions you made in coming to your risk determination.					
	Write any assumptions you made in coming to your fair use determination.					
	Write any questions you need answered in order to be able to come to a more accurate/confident determination of risk or fair use assessment.					
Scenario	**Rights**	**Works**	**Exceptions**	**Licenses**	**Risk Level**	**Fair Use**
	Write any assumptions you made in coming to your risk determination.					
	Write any assumptions you made in coming to your fair use determination.					
	Write any questions you need answered in order to be able to come to a more accurate/confident determination of risk or fair use assessment.					

p. 2

This scaffold is based on the Smith and Macklin (2014) document, A framework for analyzing any U.S. copyright problem.

Appendix B
Exceptions Analysis Scaffold

Note: a downloadable version of this scaffold is available at the text website.

<table>
<tr><th>Scenario</th><th>Type of Activity</th><th>Works</th><th>Type of People</th><th>Environment of Use</th><th>Exceptions</th></tr>
<tr><td>Indicate which scenario you're analyzing (number, brief key words, etc.). Use one row for each scenario.</td><td>List the exclusive rights of a copyright owner that are affected in this scenario.</td><td>List the type of copyrighted work that is described in this scenario.</td><td>List the type of people in the scenario (e.g. teachers, students)</td><td>List where or how the use is happening in the scenario (e.g. online, teaching, public, etc.)</td><td>List the exceptions that apply to the scenario.</td></tr>
<tr><td rowspan="4"></td><td></td><td></td><td></td><td></td><td></td></tr>
<tr><td colspan="4">Write any information that would need to be added to the scenario in order to make an informed risk assessment decision.</td><td></td></tr>
<tr><td colspan="4">Based on the information in the scenario, and the provisions of the exception(s) that you identified, is the activity in the scenario permitted?</td><td></td></tr>
<tr><td colspan="4">Write any questions you need answered in order to be able to come to a more accurate/confident determination of permissibility.</td><td></td></tr>
</table>

This scaffold is based on the Smith and Macklin (2014) document, A framework for analyzing any U.S. copyright problem.

Scenario	Type of Activity	Works	Type of People	Environment of Use	Exceptions
	Write any information that would need to be added to the scenario in order to make an informed risk assessment decision.				
	Based on the information in the scenario, and the provisions of the exception(s) that you identified, is the activity in the scenario permitted?				
	Write any questions you need answered in order to be able to come to a more accurate/confident determination of permissibility.				

This scaffold is based on the Smith and Macklin (2014) document, A framework for analyzing any U.S. copyright problem.

Appendix C
Does a License Permit My Use?

Does a License Permit My Use?

Note: a downloadable version of this checklist is available at the text website.

Is my item in the public domain?

☐ Yes (I can do whatever I want) ☐ No (Go to next question)

Did I get my item from a database at my school or institution?

☐ Yes (My use is probably permitted, but if I have questions, I should ask my teacher or librarian.) ☐ No (Go to next question)

Did I get my item from a web-based resource that has a Terms of Service or Use document?

☐ Yes (See additional question) ☐ No (Go to next question)

Is my use permitted by the Terms of Service (age, type and place of use, etc.)?

☐ Yes (Stop analysis, use the item) ☐ No (Go to next question)

Does my item have a Creative Commons license?

☐ Yes (See additional questions) ☐ No (Go to next question)

Have I given proper attribution for the item in my project?

☐ Yes (See next question) ☐ No (Create attribution, then go to next question)

Is my use permitted by the Terms of the Creative Commons license?

☐ Yes (Stop analysis, use the item) ☐ No (Find a different item, or revise use to be in compliance with terms)

Appendix D
License Use Scaffold

License Use Scaffold

My Item (title/source/URL): ______________________________

License controlling my item:

☐ None (skip to the bottom of the page)

☐ Creative Commons – Type of CC license: ______________________

☐ Other – Name & URL: ______________________________

My use is or will be		**License permits my use**	
☐ Reproduction		☐ Yes	☐ No
☐ Distribution		☐ Yes	☐ No
☐ Adaptation		☐ Yes	☐ No
☐ Derivative		☐ Yes	☐ No
☐ Display		☐ Yes	☐ No
☐ Performance		☐ Yes	☐ No
☐ Digital audio transmission		☐ Yes	☐ No
Choose only one type-of-use option each of the next 2 rows			
☐ Public	☐ Private	☐ Yes	☐ No
☐ Commercial	☐ Non-Commercial	☐ Yes	☐ No

Given my age, I am permitted to access/use my item at the location I found it.	☐ Yes	☐ No
I have legally accessed my item (logging in, paying appropriate fees, etc.).	☐ Yes	☐ No

Based on my answers here, my use is

☐ Permitted / ☐ Not permitted **by a license.** *(If I checked "No" to any item, my use is not permitted)*

If I checked "none" at the top of the page, my use is not controlled by a license, and I should continue with my use analysis according to fair use and other applicable exceptions to the exclusive rights of a copyright holder.

Appendix E
Is My Use Permitted by Specific Fair Use Guidelines?

Is My Use Permitted by Specific Fair Use Guidelines?

Note: a downloadable version of this checklist is available at the text website.

Directions: For each section, circle the appropriate descriptor of the use of copyrighted material as indicated in the scenario in question. Write in the specific amount being used in the blanks labeled "number". Use the information you've provided to make a final determination about the permissibility of the use described in the scenario.

Reason/Nature of Use: Teaching Project/Assignment Commercial Private

Type of User: Teacher Student General Public

Type of Work	Examples
Text	*Prose, print, poetry, book, periodical, printed music*
Image	*Illustration, photograph, graph, cartoon, picture*
Visual art	*Painting, drawing, prints, photographs, sculpture (unique and fewer than 200 made)*
Music	*Scores, lyrics, recordings, music video*
Audio-visual	*Motion pictures*
Multi-media	*Web presentations, electronic presentations, etc.*

What & How Much Was Used?

_______ of pages / words / chapters / seconds / minutes / items (poems, images, excerpts, etc.)
Number

_______ of artist(s) / photographer(s)
Number

Where Did It Come From?

Y / N Collection or Anthology?

_______ of pages / words / chapters / seconds / minutes / items (poems, images, etc.)
Number

Y / N **The use is permissible.**

Appendix F
Fair Use Checklist

Fair Use Checklist

Name:	
Institution/Department:	
Description of project:	
Description of copyrighted work used and manner of use:	

Based on this evaluation of my use of copyrighted materials for the described project, I believe I have acted in good faith to determine this is a fair use of the copyrighted materials.

Signature:______________________________ Date:____________________

To determine whether your use of material is likely to be protected under the Fair Use doctrine (Section 107 in the copyright code), check all applicable factors below. You should print this form, complete it, and keep it on file for future reference.
The information presented is not a substitute for legal advice obtained from a licensed attorney. Please see Auburn University's Copyright policy and web site for further information about our copyright policies.

Factor 1: Purpose and Character of the Use

Weighs in Favor of Fair Use	Weighs Against Fair Use
☐ Nonprofit Educational	☐ Commercial Activity
☐ Teaching (including multiple copies for classroom use)	☐ Profiting from use
☐ Research or Scholarship	☐ Entertainment
☐ Criticism, Comment, News Reporting, or Parody	☐ Non-transformative
☐ Transformative (use changes work for new utility or purpose)	☐ For publication
☐ Personal Study	☐ For public distribution
☐ Use is necessary to achieve your intended educational purpose	☐ Use exceeds intended educational purpose

Factor 2: Nature of Copyrighted Work

Weighs in Favor of Fair Use	Weighs Against Fair Use
☐ Published Work	☐ Unpublished work
☐ Factual or nonfiction work	☐ Highly creative work (art, music, novels, films, plays, poetry, fiction)
☐ Important to educational objectives	☐ Consumable work (workbook, test)

Factor 3: Amount and Substantiality of Portion Used

Weighs in Favor of Fair Use	Weighs Against Fair Use
☐ Small portion of work used	☐ Large portion or entire work used
☐ Portion used is not central or significant to entire work as a whole	☐ Portion used is central or "heart of work"
☐ Amount taken is narrowly tailored to educational purpose such as criticism, comment, research, or subject being taught	☐ Amount taken is more than necessary for criticism, comment, research, or subject being taught

Factor 4: Effect on Market for Original

Weighs in Favor of Fair Use	Weighs Against Fair Use
☐ No significant effect on market or potential market for copyrighted work	☐ Significantly impairs market or potential market for copyrighted work or derivative
☐ Use stimulates market for original work	☐ Licensing or permission reasonably available
☐ No similar product marketed by copyright holder	☐ Numerous copies made or distributed
☐ No longer in print	☐ Repeated or long term use that demonstrably affects the market for the work
☐ Licensing or permission unavailable	☐ Required classroom reading
☐ Supplemental classroom reading	☐ User does not own lawfully acquired or purchased copy of original work
☐ One or few copies made or distributed	☐ Unrestricted access on the web or other public forum
☐ User owns lawfully acquired or purchased copy of original work	
☐ Restricted access (to students or other appropriate group)	

Appendix G
Key Court Cases—Copyright

This list of court cases is not exhaustive. It was drawn from the list of cases referenced in Simpson and Wolf (2021). Landmark cases are indicated by bolded titles. The other cases have been chosen due to their influence on accepted practice and common guidelines for using copyrighted works as well as the nature of regularly applied copyright concepts. Teachers and other instructors who are interested in a detailed examination of these cases should be sure to seek out the primary case documents or other interpretations written by legal scholars. The information provided here is intended to be sufficient for laypeople to understand the conflict between the parties as well as the significant aspects of the final rulings by the courts. The information provided here is NOT intended to be anything other than an overview and broad understanding. It should NOT be considered to be specific legal analysis nor interpretation of the legal ramifications.

I've chosen four main sources for online information about the cases listed here. The first is the US Copyright Office Fair Use Index. The Fair Use Index is maintained by the US Copyright Office with a stated goal of "to make the principles and application of fair use more accessible and understandable to the public by presenting a searchable database of court opinions, including by category and type of use" (US Copyright Office, para. 1). For less experienced learners, the sources from the US Copyright Office are particularly useful, as they are written in summary form and use language that laypeople can easily understand. The second is Justia. Justia strives to provide "free and open access to the law" (Justia, para. 1) for all people. While there is an access level that is available for a subscription fee, the links provided here do not require a login nor a subscription. The links provided here provide the text of the cases in each entry. As source for primary source documents, the information in Justia is particularly useful for more experienced learners who are more adept at navigating longer, more complex documents than less experienced learners might be. The third resource is Casetext. Casetext is an artificial intelligence (AI) augmented resource targeted to attorneys and law offices. The readings here are direct links to the full text of the opinions that are linked. You should be aware that full functionality of Casetext is only available via a subscription. The last main source that I've linked to is Oyez. Oyez is "a multimedia archive devoted to making the Supreme Court of the United States accessible to everyone. It is the most complete and authoritative source for all of the Court's audio" (Oyez, 2024, para. 1). Be aware that only cases that were heard by the US Supreme Court are available via the Oyez resource.

Access is free and does not require a subscription. Each of the direct links provided here was functional and accurate as of the printing of this book. However, access to the documents linked here cannot be guaranteed beyond the time of publication. Finally, there are several cases where online access to accurate information is provided outside of the three main resources described here. Do not assume that the lack of links to the main resources has any significance. Links are provided to primary source documents when possible and trustworthy summary sources when primary documents are not available.

G1 **Official Title:**	**A & M Records, Inc. v. Napster, Inc.**
Online Reading Sources	From Copyright Office (summary document) https://www.copyright.gov/fair-use/summaries/a&mrecords-napster-9thcir2001.pdf From Justia (final ruling): https://law.justia.com/cases/federal/appellate-courts/F3/239/1004/636120/ From Findlaw (final ruling): https://caselaw.findlaw.com/court/us-9th-circuit/1047162.html
Lay Person's Title:	N/A
Landmark?	No
Year:	2002
Plaintiff (person doing the "suing"):	A & M Records
Defendant (Person getting sued):	Napster, Inc.
Problem/Conflict:	Napster, a music sharing platform, permitted the downloading of music files.
Major finding(s):	Permitting the sharing of copyrighted music on a file-sharing platform violates artists' copyrights. Uploaders violate the right of distribution. Downloaders violate the right of reproduction.
Key Concepts:	Right of distribution; right of reproduction; fair use
Jurisdiction:	9th circuit (includes CA)

G2 **Official Title:**	**Allman v. Capricorn Records**
Online Reading Sources	From Casetext: https://casetext.com/case/allman-v-capricorn-records
Lay Person's Title:	N/A
Landmark?	No

Year:	2002
Plaintiff (person doing the "suing"):	Allman (a musician)
Defendant (Person getting sued):	Capricorn Records
Problem/Conflict:	Did Capricorn Records exceed the scope of the licenses they were granted by Allman in the reproduction and distribution of records?
Major finding(s):	Licensed behavior is controlled by contract law, so defendants can't be sued for copyright infringement if engaging in license-controlled behavior, just breach of contract. However, if the behavior is outside the scope of the license granted, the defendant can be sued for copyright infringement.
Key Concepts:	Licenses trump copyright
Jurisdiction:	9th circuit (includes CA)

G3	
Official Title:	**Authors Guild v. Google, Inc.**
Online Reading Sources	From Copyright Office (summary): https://www.copyright.gov/fair-use/summaries/authorsguild-google-2dcir2015.pdf From Justia: https://law.justia.com/cases/federal/appellate-courts/ca2/13-4829/13-4829-2015-10-16.html From Casetext: https://casetext.com/case/guild-v-google-inc-1
Lay Person's Title:	N/A
Landmark?	Yes
Year:	2015
Plaintiff (person doing the "suing"):	Author's Guild
Defendant (Person getting sued):	Google
Problem/Conflict:	Google scanned portions of copyrighted books to include in search results, also permitting limited full-text search. Google asserted that its use should be considered fair use.
Major finding(s):	Transformative use requires complex thought and creativity. The public benefit of Google's actions outweighed the author's benefit of copyright protection.
Key Concepts:	Transformative Use; fair use: "Advancing the public welfare"
Jurisdiction:	2nd circuit (includes NY)

G4

Official Title:	**Authors Guild, Inc. v. HathiTrust**
Online Reading Sources	From Copyright Office (Summary): https://www.copyright.gov/fair-use/summaries/authorsguild-hathitrust-2dcir2014.pdf From Justia: https://law.justia.com/cases/federal/appellate-courts/ca2/12-4547/12-4547-2014-06-10.html From Casetext: https://casetext.com/case/authors-guild-inc-v-hathitrust-1/analysis?citingPage=1&sort=relevance&sortCiting=date-ascending
Lay Person's Title:	N/A
Landmark?	No
Year:	2014
Plaintiff (person doing the "suing"):	Author's Guild
Defendant (Person getting sued):	HathiTrust
Problem/Conflict:	HathiTrust worked in partnership with Google to make public domain as well as copyright-protected works available to users with print-disabilities as part of a larger project to archive works for public access.
Major finding(s):	Adapting (scanning and making available in screen-reader format) works in order to make them accessible to persons with visual disabilities is considered to be fair use.
Key Concepts:	Adaptation; Accessibility
Jurisdiction:	2nd circuit (includes NY)

G5

Official Title:	**Berlin v. E.C. Pubs., Inc.**
Online Reading Sources	From Copyright Office (summary): https://www.copyright.gov/fair-use/summaries/berlin-ecpublins-2dcir1964.pdf From Casetext: https://casetext.com/case/berlin-v-ec-publications-inc From Justia: https://law.justia.com/cases/federal/district-courts/FSupp/219/911/1438356/
Lay Person's Title:	N/A
Landmark?	No
Year:	1964
Plaintiff (person doing the "suing"):	Berlin
Defendant (Person getting sued):	E. C. Publications (distributors of *Mad Magazine*)

Problem/Conflict:	*Mad Magazine* published satirical parodies of the lyrics to upwards of 25 different songs.
Major finding(s):	Parody is considered to be fair use.
Key Concepts:	Parody; fair use
Jurisdiction:	2nd circuit (includes NY)

G6	
Official Title:	**Blanch v. Koons**
Online Reading Sources	From Copyright Office (Summary): https://www.copyright.gov/fair-use/summaries/blanch-koons-2dcir2006.pdf From FindLaw: https://caselaw.findlaw.com/court/us-2nd-circuit/1374144.html From Harvard (abridged, but detailed, summary): https://cyber.harvard.edu/people/tfisher/IP/2006%20Blanch%20Abridged.pdf
Lay Person's Title:	N/A
Landmark?	No
Year:	2006
Plaintiff (person doing the "suing"):	Blanch (a photographer)
Defendant (Person getting sued):	Koons (an artist)
Problem/Conflict:	Koons used a portion of a photograph created by Blanch as part of a contracted work.
Major finding(s):	Other factors beyond the four tests of fair use can be used to determine whether a particular use is fair (bad faith, etc.). An early example where a broader interpretation of transformative use was used in a judicial finding. The rights of author/creator must be balanced with the rights of user.
Key Concepts:	Transformative use; fair use
Jurisdiction:	2nd circuit (includes NY)

G7	
Official Title:	**Campbell v. Acuff-Rose Music, Inc.**
Online Reading Sources	From Copyright Office (Summary): https://www.copyright.gov/fair-use/summaries/campbell-acuff-1994.pdf From Justia: https://supreme.justia.com/cases/federal/us/510/569/ From Casetext: https://casetext.com/case/acuff-rose-music
Lay Person's Title:	Pretty Woman Case
Landmark?	Yes
Year:	1994

Plaintiff (person doing the "suing"):	Acuff-Rose Music
Defendant (Person getting sued):	Campbell (2 Live Crew & Music Company)
Problem/Conflict:	2 Live Crew used Roy Orbison's "Oh Pretty Woman" to create a parody. (https://youtu.be/rMqnPVU207M?si=S_G5xaErZtWk5ShX)
Major finding(s):	Parody as a format can be considered to be fair use, even though parody sometimes is for a commercial purpose.
Key Concepts:	Parody; fair use
Jurisdiction:	6th Circuit (includes TN)

G8	
Official Title:	**Carter v. Helmsley-Spear, Inc.**
Online Reading Sources	From Justia: https://law.justia.com/cases/federal/district-courts/FSupp/861/303/2261919/ From Casetext: https://casetext.com/case/carter-v-helmsley-spear-inc
Lay Person's Title:	N/A
Landmark?	No
Year:	1994
Plaintiff (person doing the "suing"):	Carter (plus Swing and Veronis—Artists)
Defendant (Person getting sued):	Helmsley-Spear (property managers)
Problem/Conflict:	Carter and his associates had been contracted to create murals for a building. They retained the copyrights for their murals. That building came under the management of the Helmsley-Spear company. Helmsley-Spear retracted the permission to install art on the building and stated that the existing art was going to be removed.
Major finding(s):	Artists have moral rights of integrity and attribution (VARA, passed in 1990). However, as the artwork was found to be a "work made for hire," the art did not receive VARA protection.
Key Concepts:	VARA; Work Made for Hire
Jurisdiction:	2nd circuit (includes NY)

G9	
Official Title:	**Clean Flicks of Colo. v. Soderbergh**
Online Reading Sources	From Copyright Office (Summary): https://www.copyright.gov/fair-use/summaries/cleanflicks-soderbergh-dcolo2006.pdf From Casetext: https://casetext.com/case/clean-flicks-of-colorado

Lay Person's Title:	N/A
Landmark?	No
Year:	2006
Plaintiff (person doing the "suing"):	Soderbergh
Defendant (Person getting sued):	Clean Flicks
Problem/Conflict:	Clean Flicks removed content (profanity, drugs, sexual references, etc.) from films and then sold the redacted films.
Major finding(s):	The redaction of films does not constitute fair use, as the activity is not transformative. Also, the intent of the film's creators was altered with the redaction process, thus altering the films.
Key Concepts:	Adaptation; fair use; transformative use
Jurisdiction:	DC District Court

G10 **Official Title:**	**Cohen v. G & M Realty L. P.**
Online Reading Sources	From Casetext: https://casetext.com/case/cohen-v-gm-realty-lp From Justia: https://law.justia.com/cases/federal/district-courts/new-york/nyedce/1:2013cv05612/347782/172/
Lay Person's Title:	N/A
Landmark?	No
Year:	2017
Plaintiff (person doing the "suing"):	Cohen
Defendant (Person getting sued):	G & M Realty
Problem/Conflict:	G & M Realty painted over graffiti work that Cohen had painted on the side of a building in NY.
Major finding(s):	Graffiti is eligible for VARA protections provided it can be shown to be of "recognized stature." Clarified that the medium used to create visual art should be liberally interpreted, as artists can use a wide variety of media to create such art.
Key Concepts:	VARA; recognized stature
Jurisdiction:	Eastern District of NY

G11

Official Title:	**Disney Enter's, Inc. et al. v. VidAngel, Inc.**
Online Reading Sources	From Copyright Office (Summary): https://www.copyright.gov/fair-use/summaries/disney-vidangel-9thcir2017.pdf From Justia: https://law.justia.com/cases/federal/appellate-courts/ca9/16-56843/16-56843-2017-08-24.html From Casetext: https://casetext.com/case/disney-enters-inc-v-vidangel-inc-5
Lay Person's Title:	N/A
Landmark?	No
Year:	2017
Plaintiff (person doing the "suing"):	Disney
Defendant (Person getting sued):	VidAngel
Problem/Conflict:	VidAngel removed objectionable content from motion pictures and did so by circumventing control measures meant to control access to copyrighted material under the DMCA. They then streamed the results of their actions to consumers.
Major finding(s):	Redacting content from motion pictures is not fair use. Streaming redacted movies is not fair use.
Key Concepts:	Adaptation; DMCA protections
Jurisdiction:	9th circuit (includes CA), on appeal. Note: the disposition of this case was very long, and ultimately, VidAngel decided to drop their appeal. Instead, they settled for a smaller amount of fines than what they were originally found liable for.

G12

Official Title:	**DynaStudy, Inc. v. Houston Indep. Sch. Dist.**
Online Reading Sources	From Casetext: https://casetext.com/case/dynastudy-inc-v-hous-indep-sch-dist From Justia: https://dockets.justia.com/docket/texas/txsdce/4:2016cv01442/1361442
Lay Person's Title:	DynaStudy Case
Landmark?	No
Year:	2017
Plaintiff (person doing the "suing"):	DynaStudy
Defendant (Person getting sued):	Houston Independent School District (and specific employees)

Problem/Conflict:	A teacher scanned copyrighted test preparation materials, removed the copyright information, and then posted those scanned materials on a publicly accessible website. Administrators were made aware of the acts and did not take action to prevent them from occurring.
Major finding(s):	Administrators can be held responsible for the actions of teachers in their buildings. Removal of copyright notification demonstrates willful infringement.
Key Concepts:	Willful infringement; fair use; vicarious infringement
Jurisdiction:	Southern District of TX

G13

Official Title:	**Eldred v. Ashcroft**
Online Reading Sources	From Copyright Office (Summary): https://www.copyright.gov/docs/eldredd1.pdf From Oyez: https://www.oyez.org/cases/2002/01-618 From Justia: https://supreme.justia.com/cases/federal/us/537/186/#top
Lay Person's Title:	N/A
Landmark?	Yes
Year:	2003
Plaintiff (person doing the "suing"):	Eldred (a publisher)
Defendant (Person getting sued):	Ashcroft
Problem/Conflict:	Challenged the CTEA; asserted that the term of copyright protection was so long as to practically be "forever."
Major finding(s):	Finite term of copyright protection satisfies "limited time" of protection.
Key Concepts:	CTEA; Creative Commons (as a result of this case, Eldred went on to found the Creative Commons)
Jurisdiction:	SCOTUS

G14

Official Title:	**Faulkner Press, L.L.C. v. Class Notes L. L. C.**
Online Reading Sources	From Casetext: https://casetext.com/case/faulkner-press-llc-v-class-notes-4 From Justia: https://law.justia.com/cases/federal/district-courts/florida/flndce/1:2008cv00049/49611/55/
Lay Person's Title:	N/A

Landmark?	No
Year:	2010
Plaintiff (person doing the "suing"):	Faulkner Press (and Michael Moulton, a professor)
Defendant (Person getting sued):	Class Notes
Problem/Conflict:	Students were selling their class notes to "Class Notes" to be packaged and resold by other students.
Major finding(s):	Students have an implied license to take class notes in classes in which they are enrolled. Packaged class notes are considered to be derivative works. Selling those derivative works as a right is still murky.
Key Concepts:	Derivative Works; implied license
Jurisdiction:	Northern District of FL

G15	
Official Title:	**Feist Publ'ns, Inc. v. Rural Tel. Serv. Co.**
Online Reading Sources	From Justia: https://supreme.justia.com/cases/federal/us/499/340/ From Oyez: https://www.oyez.org/cases/1990/89-1909 From Casetext: https://casetext.com/case/feist-publications-inc-v-rural-telephone-service-company-inc?sort=relevance&q=Feist%20v.%20Rural%20Tel&p=1&tab=keyword&jxs=&type=case
Lay Person's Title:	N/A
Landmark?	Yes
Year:	1991
Plaintiff (person doing the "suing"):	Rural Telephone Services Company
Defendant (Person getting sued):	Feist (another telephone directory publisher)
Problem/Conflict:	Feist was creating a regional telephone directory comprising information from a variety of locales in KS. All locales except Rural licensed their material for inclusion in the aggregated directory. Feist reproduced Rural's white pages without a license.
Major finding(s):	Minimal levels of creativity are needed in order to qualify for copyright protection. A simple alphabetical listing of names, addresses, and phone numbers does not meet this threshold.
Key Concepts:	Copyrightable works
Jurisdiction:	SCOTUS

G16

Official Title:	**Harper & Row, Pubs. V. Nation Enters.**
Online Reading Sources	From Oyez: https://www.oyez.org/cases/1984/83-1632 From Justia: https://supreme.justia.com/cases/federal/us/471/539/ From Copyright Office (Summary): https://www.copyright.gov/fair-use/summaries/harperrow-nationmagazine-1985.pdf From Casetext: https://casetext.com/case/harper-row-publishers-inc-v-nation-ent
Lay Person's Title:	N/A
Landmark?	Yes
Year:	1985
Plaintiff (person doing the "suing"):	Harper & Row
Defendant (Person getting sued):	*Nation* (a magazine)
Problem/Conflict:	*Nation* published an excerpt from a book that President Ford had written and licensed to Harper & Row for publication. Harper & Row contracted with *Time* magazine to publish excerpts of the work. When *Nation* published excerpts in its magazine, *Time* backed out of the contract with H & R.
Major finding(s):	The nature of the excerpted material as well as the amount used did not align with fair use principles. The right of first publication is important and wouldn't garner protection for unpublished works if it could be overridden using "fair use" as a defense. SCOTUS used the four tests of fair use, all of which were found not to support fair use.
Key Concepts:	Four fair use tests; substantiality of amount used (third test)
Jurisdiction:	SCOTUS

G17

Official Title:	**Hern v. Meyer**
Online Reading Sources	From Justia: https://law.justia.com/cases/federal/district-courts/FSupp/664/832/1504043/ From vLex: https://case-law.vlex.com/vid/hearn-v-meyer-no-889166355
Lay Person's Title:	N/A
Landmark?	No
Year:	1987
Plaintiff (person doing the "suing"):	Hearn
Defendant (Person getting sued):	Meyer (an author)

Problem/Conflict:	Meyer reproduced illustrations in a book she wrote that appeared in a book that Hearn wrote. Those illustrations were not original to Hearn but rather, reproduced using exacting technique.
Major finding(s):	Despite the exacting technique and close replication, the reproduction by Hearn of the illustrations in question meant that he did not have standing to sue for copyright. Insufficient creativity was present in his reproductions. The court found that slavish reproductions did not merit copyright protections of results.
Key Concepts:	Copyrightable works.
Jurisdiction:	Southern District of NY

G18	
Official Title:	**Hines v. Overstock.com**
Online Reading Sources	From Casetext: https://casetext.com/case/hines-v-overstockcom From Justia: https://law.justia.com/cases/federal/district-courts/new-york/nyedce/1:2009cv00991/289858/121/
Lay Person's Title:	N/A
Landmark?	No
Year:	2009
Plaintiff (person doing the "suing"):	Hines
Defendant (Person getting sued):	Overstock
Problem/Conflict:	Overstock applied a restocking fee to returned merchandise, which Hines asserted constituted a breach of contract. Hines asserted that she was unaware that the restocking fee would be applied.
Major finding(s):	Terms and conditions of websites are applicable to users once they use the site. Use of a website implies agreement to the terms and conditions.
Key Concepts:	Terms & Conditions
Jurisdiction:	Eastern District of NY

G19	
Official Title:	**Kirtsaeng v. John Wiley & Sons, Inc.**
Online Reading Sources	From Oyez: https://www.oyez.org/cases/2012/11-697 From Justia: https://supreme.justia.com/cases/federal/us/579/15-375/ From Casetext: https://casetext.com/case/john-wiley-sons-inc-v-kirtsaeng

Lay Person's Title:	N/A
Landmark?	Yes
Year:	2013
Plaintiff (person doing the "suing"):	John Wiley & Sons
Defendant (Person getting sued):	Kirtsaeng
Problem/Conflict:	Kirtsaeng purchased copies of books published by John Wiley & Sons from international booksellers. He then resold those books in the United States.
Major finding(s):	First Sale doctrine applies even to those items purchased abroad; it doesn't stop at the US border.
Key Concepts:	First Sale
Jurisdiction:	SCOTUS

G20 **Official Title:**	**Molinelli-Freytas v. Univ. of Puerto Rico**
Online Reading Sources	From Casetext: https://casetext.com/case/molinelli-freytes-v-univ-of-pr From Justia: https://law.justia.com/cases/federal/district-courts/puerto-rico/prdce/3:2009cv01655/74681/445/
Lay Person's Title:	N/A
Landmark?	No
Year:	2010
Plaintiff (person doing the "suing"):	Molinelli-Freytes (and Lillian Bird-Canals)
Defendant (Person getting sued):	University of Puerto Rico (and Puerto Rico Council on Higher Education)
Problem/Conflict:	Molinelli-Freytes and Bird-Canals created an original manuscript that the University then used for the creation of a new graduate program. The proposal was written during non-working hours.
Major finding(s):	Work created during non-working hours can be considered a work made for hire, especially if it is substantially similar to the type of work for which the author is employed.
Key Concepts:	Work made for hire
Jurisdiction:	District Court of Puerto Rico

G21 **Official Title:**	**Nat'l Ass'n of the Deaf v. Netflix Inc.**
Online Reading Sources	From Casetext: https://casetext.com/case/natl-assn-of-the-deaf-v-netflix-inc

Lay Person's Title:	N/A
Landmark?	No, w/ relation to copyright, but Deaf advocacy groups may consider it landmark for accessibility reasons
Year:	2012
Plaintiff (person doing the "suing"):	National Association of the Deaf
Defendant (Person getting sued):	Netflix
Problem/Conflict:	Netflix did not provide closed captioning on its streaming programming, making it inaccessible to people with hearing deficits. Netflix asserted that since it was not a physical location, being only available via the Web, the ADA didn't apply to its services.
Major finding(s):	Netflix constituted a "place of business," as it sells services to the public. As such, website-only businesses are subject to the requirements of the ADA.
Key Concepts:	Adaptation; Accessibility
Jurisdiction:	District Court of MA

G22

Official Title:	**Naruto v. Slater**
Online Reading Sources	From Justia: https://law.justia.com/cases/federal/appellate-courts/ca9/16-15469/16-15469-2018-04-23.html From 9th Circuit: https://cdn.ca9.uscourts.gov/datastore/opinions/2018/04/23/16-15469.pdf From Casetext: https://casetext.com/case/naruto-v-slater-2?sort=relevance&q=naruto%20v.%20slater&p=1&tab=keyword&jxs=&type=case
Lay Person's Title:	Monkey Selfies Case
Landmark?	No
Year:	2018
Plaintiff (person doing the "suing"):	Naruto (a crested macaque—a type of monkey), represented by PETA
Defendant (Person getting sued):	Slater (a wildlife photographer)
Problem/Conflict:	PETA sued Slater for copyright infringement for photos that were taken when Naruto the monkey snapped the shutter on a camera that had been left unattended in the wild.
Major finding(s):	Naruto the monkey did not have standing (wasn't eligible) to assert copyright ownership because the copyright law doesn't give animals the right to do so. Copyright ownership may only be held by humans.

Key Concepts:	Copyrightable Works; Copyright Ownership
Jurisdiction:	9th circuit (includes CA)

G23

Official Title:	**Pearson Educ., Inc. v. Ishayev**
Online Reading Sources	From Justia: https://law.justia.com/cases/federal/district-courts/new-york/nysdce/1:2011cv05052/382350/73/ From Casetext: https://casetext.com/case/pearson-educ-3
Lay Person's Title:	N/A
Landmark?	No
Year:	2013
Plaintiff (person doing the "suing"):	Pearson
Defendant (Person getting sued):	Ishayev
Problem/Conflict:	Ishayev sold copyrighted works to a third party both by attaching files as zip files to emails and by sending hyperlinked addresses in an email.
Major finding(s):	Several aspects of the case were considered, including whether the files in question qualified as derivative works. Importantly, the court likened the sending of hyperlinks to giving of a set of driving directions. Thus, text-based hyperlinks cannot be infringing materials.
Key Concepts:	Copyrightable Works
Jurisdiction:	Southern District of NY

G24

Official Title:	**Philpot v. WOS, Inc.**
Online Reading Sources	From Copyright Office (Summary): https://www.copyright.gov/fair-use/summaries/philpot-wosinc-wdtexas2019.pdf From Casetext: https://casetext.com/case/philpot-v-wos-inc-1 From Justia: https://dockets.justia.com/docket/texas/txwdce/1:2018cv00339/938619
Lay Person's Title:	N/A
Landmark?	No
Year:	2019
Plaintiff (person doing the "suing"):	Philpot (a freelance photographer)
Defendant (Person getting sued):	WOS (Wide Open Country—a media company)
Problem/Conflict:	WOS published photographs taken by Philpot without proper attribution and after scrubbing the metadata from the photos prior to publication.

Major finding(s):	The photographs in question were Creative Commons licensed. All CC licenses require, at minimum, appropriate attribution. The court ruled that use of copyrighted materials falling under a license is controlled by that license. If a work is used outside of the terms of a license, the use cannot be considered fair use.
Key Concepts:	Licenses; Creative Commons; Attribution; Fair Use
Jurisdiction:	Western District of TX

G25	
Official Title:	**Recording Indus. Ass'n of Am. V. Diamond Multimedia Sys. Inc.**
Online Reading Sources	From Castext: https://casetext.com/case/recording-indust-of-america-v-diamond-multimedia
Lay Person's Title:	N/A
Landmark?	No
Year:	1999
Plaintiff (person doing the "suing"):	Recording Industry of America
Defendant (Person getting sued):	Diamond Multimedia Systems (producers of the RIO digital audio player)
Problem/Conflict:	The RIO device permitted consumers to record digital copies of music that were stored on their computer hard drives. RIAA asserted that the device in question did not qualify as a recording device as Diamond hadn't paid appropriate fees for it to be considered as such.
Major finding(s):	"Space shifting" of personally owned music files is considered fair use, but the files must be physically owned by the consumer and not recorded from a streaming service.
Key Concepts:	Audio Home Recording Act; Time Shifting/Space Shifting
Jurisdiction:	9th circuit (Includes CA)

G26	
Official Title:	**San Francisco Arts & Athletics, Inc. v. U.S. Olympic Comm.**
Online Reading Sources	From Justia: https://supreme.justia.com/cases/federal/us/483/522/ From Casetext: https://casetext.com/case/san-francisco-arts-athletics-inc-v-united-states-olympic-committee
Lay Person's Title:	N/A
Landmark?	No

Year:	1987
Plaintiff (person doing the "suing"):	US Olympic Committee
Defendant (Person getting sued):	San Francisco Arts & Athletics
Problem/Conflict:	San Francisco Arts & Athletics wished to use "Olympics" as a part of a gay-related set of games they were organizing. The US Olympic Committee sued under trademark law protection.
Major finding(s):	Congress intentionally granted the USOC exclusive use of the word "Olympic" without regard to whether use of the word tends to cause confusion. Additionally, the word "Olympic" is not generic, so not just anyone can use the term. Any First Amendment argument that anyone can use the term in political speech does not prohibit Congress from permitting the USOC to have exclusive use of the term in particular settings.
Key Concepts:	Translations; Adaptation; Derivative Work
Jurisdiction:	SCOTUS

G27

Official Title:	**Shaul v. Cherry Valley-Springfield Cent. Sch. Dist.**
Online Reading Sources	From Justia: https://law.justia.com/cases/federal/district-courts/FSupp2/218/266/2359991/ From Casetext: https://casetext.com/case/shaul-v-cherry-valley-springfield-cent-sch
Lay Person's Title:	N/A
Landmark?	No
Year:	2004
Plaintiff (person doing the "suing"):	Shaul (a teacher)
Defendant (Person getting sued):	Cherry Valley-Springfield Central School District
Problem/Conflict:	Shaul was dismissed from his position for a matter unrelated to copyright. In the course of retrieving his materials from his classroom, several items were not removed and were then seized or disposed of by the principals of his school. Shaul asserted that the copyright-protected items that were seized (tests, quizzes, lessons, etc.) were his to have and that they were illegally seized.
Major finding(s):	The court found that the items were created as a work made for hire and were not illegally seized; that those items were created as a part of Shaul's employment and he did not possess documentation granting him ownership of those documents.

Key Concepts:	Work Made for Hire
Jurisdiction:	Northern District of NY

G28 **Official Title:**	**Shepard Fairey v. Assoc. Press**
Online Reading Sources	From Justia: https://docs.justia.com/cases/federal/district-courts/new-york/nysdce/1:2009cv01123/340121/1 From Casetext: https://casetext.com/case/fairey-v-associated-press
Lay Person's Title:	N/A
Landmark?	No
Year:	2009
Plaintiff (person doing the "suing"):	Shepard Fairey (an artist)
Defendant (Person getting sued):	Associated Press
Problem/Conflict:	The Associated Press accused Fairey of violating the copyright they held for a photograph of President (then candidate) Obama by using it as part of another work of visual art.
Major finding(s):	Fairey said he thought the Associated Press was wrong about which photo he used to create his posters, but when he realized they were right, he settled the suit on unfavorable terms. Both parties agreed that neither side surrendered their interpretation of the law.
Key Concepts:	Adaptation; Fair Use
Jurisdiction:	Southern District of NY

G29 **Official Title:**	**Sony Corp. of Am. V. Universal City Studios, Inc.**
Online Reading Sources	From Copyright Office (Summary): https://www.copyright.gov/fair-use/summaries/sonycorp-universal-1984.pdf From Oyez: https://www.oyez.org/cases/1982/81-1687 From Justia: https://supreme.justia.com/cases/federal/us/464/417/ From Casetext: https://casetext.com/case/universal-city-studios-v-sony-corp-of-amer
Lay Person's Title:	Betamax Case
Landmark?	No
Year:	1984

Plaintiff (person doing the "suing"):	Universal City Studios
Defendant (Person getting sued):	Sony (makers of Betamax video tape recording/playing machines)
Problem/Conflict:	Universal City sued Sony for contributory infringement because Sony made devices that were capable of copying and therefore infringing on copyright.
Major finding(s):	Recording publicly available information for time-shifting purposes is fair use, supported by the "access" aspect of the First Amendment.
Key Concepts:	Fair Use; Home Recording
Jurisdiction:	SCOTUS

G30	
Official Title:	**Tresona Multimedia, LLC v. Burbank High Sch. Vocal Music Ass'n**
Online Reading Sources	From Copyright Office: https://www.copyright.gov/fair-use/summaries/tresona-multimedia-burbank-highschool-vocal-music-assn-9thcir2020.pdf From Casetext: https://casetext.com/case/tresona-multimedia-llc-v-burbank-high-sch-vocal-music-assn
Lay Person's Title:	N/A
Landmark?	No
Year:	2020
Plaintiff (person doing the "suing"):	Tresona Multimedia, LLC
Defendant (Person getting sued):	Burbank High School Vocal Music Association
Problem/Conflict:	The vocal director at Burbank High School used various pieces or portions of pieces of protected works in the creation of the show choir performance. Tresona asserted that the use of those portions required licensing.
Major finding(s):	The use of the works by the choir was determined to be fair use due to the educational nature of the use as well as the transformative nature in which they were used.
Key Concepts:	Transformative; Fair Use
Jurisdiction:	9th circuit (Includes CA)

G31	
Official Title:	**Vernor v. Autodesk, Inc.**
Online Reading Sources	From Casetext: https://casetext.com/case/vernor-v-autodesk-inc-2 From Justia: https://law.justia.com/cases/federal/district-courts/washington/wawdce/2:2007cv01189/145432/71/

Lay Person's Title:	N/A
Landmark?	No
Year:	2010
Plaintiff (person doing the "suing"):	Vernor
Defendant (Person getting sued):	Autodesk
Problem/Conflict:	Vernor wanted to be able to resell copies of software that he had purchased. Autodesk asserted that software wasn't sold, it was licensed, and carried restrictions on how it could be used or redistributed.
Major finding(s):	Court acknowledged some potentially thorny issues, as the First Sale doctrine isn't protected by licensed activities. It found that software purchasers are licensees and subject to the terms of those licenses.
Key Concepts:	License; distribution; First Sale
Jurisdiction:	Western District of WA

G32

Official Title:	**Viacom Int'l Inc. v. YouTube, Inc.**
Online Reading Sources	From Casetext: https://casetext.com/case/viacom-intl-inc-v-youtube-inc-2 From Justia: https://law.justia.com/cases/federal/district-courts/new-york/nysdce/1:2007cv02103/302164/364/
Lay Person's Title:	N/A
Landmark?	Yes
Year:	2012 (9th Cir.), 2013 (S.D.N.Y.)
Plaintiff (person doing the "suing"):	Viacom
Defendant (Person getting sued):	YouTube
Problem/Conflict:	Viacom sued YouTube, saying that YouTube violated reproduction, distribution, and public display of copyrighted works. Viacom asserted that YouTube should be held responsible for what users uploaded to the platform in a similar way that Grokster was held responsible for uploaded music files.
Major finding(s):	Willful blindness threshold established as requiring specific knowledge regarding content uploaded, the persons doing the uploading, and the presence or absence of instructional material for the circumvention of copyright protections in the upload process. Evidence of a lack of specific knowledge included no formal review or cataloging of uploaded material. Burden of enforcing copyright rests primarily with the copyright owner.

Key Concepts:	Willful blindness
Jurisdiction:	2nd circuit (includes NY)

G33 **Official Title:**	**Woodson v. Atl. City Bd. Of Educ.**
Online Reading Sources	From Casetext: https://casetext.com/case/woodson-v-bd-of-educ#:~:text=Plaintiff%20initially%20filed%20a%20complaint,Infringement%20(Count%20III)%2C%20and From Justia: https://law.justia.com/cases/federal/district-courts/new-jersey/njdce/1:2019cv14572/411127/29/
Lay Person's Title:	N/A
Landmark?	No
Year:	2020
Plaintiff (person doing the "suing"):	Woodson (a teacher)
Defendant (Person getting sued):	Atlanta Board of Education
Problem/Conflict:	Woodson completed work that was determined NOT to be a work made for hire. The principal of Woodson's school used her work in an article that was submitted to a professional journal. Woodson sued the principal and school board for copyright infringement.
Major finding(s):	The work was not a work made for hire; therefore, Woodson retained the copyright. However, she waited too long to sue for damages, so did not prevail.
Key Concepts:	Copyright v. Plagiarism; timeline to recover damages
Jurisdiction:	District of NJ

Appendix H
Scavenger Hunt Example Clue List

The clues for a scavenger hunt yielding various items possessing Creative Commons licenses presented here can be adapted in limitless ways. Generally, the clues below are organized from simple to complex. Teachers should select items that are appropriate for their learners.

Teachers may choose to have students use specific sources of Creative Commons licensed materials, or have students conduct online searches themselves. The decision to provide the sources or have students search for the sources should be based on the skill and developmental level of the students. Younger, less experienced students will benefit from having the sources of items provided for them, while more skillful learners should be able to conduct searches for licensed items on their own.

Sources of Creative Commons Licensed Materials

The following list of sources containing Creative Commons licensed materials is not exhaustive. It does contain reputable sites that have been in existence long enough to be considered as persistent as possible, given that all items on the internet are inherently transient. Some of these sources permit relatively simple searching, while others require users to use special filters or procedures to find Creative Commons licensed materials within a more comprehensive set of items. Teachers may need to provide explicit instruction to students on the use of these resources.

- Community Audio—https://archive.org/details/opensource_audio
- Creative Commons Search—https://search.creativecommons.org/
- Europeana—https://www.europeana.eu/en
- Flickr—https://www.flickr.com/creativecommons/
- Merlot—https://www.merlot.org/merlot/index.htm
- Mixter—http://ccmixter.org/
- Pixabay—https://pixabay.com/
- Vimeo—https://vimeo.com/creativecommons
- Wikimedia Commons—https://commons.wikimedia.org/wiki/Main_Page
- YouTube—https://www.youtube.com/

Clues for Creative Commons Scavenger Hunt

Simple

Simple items ask students to locate single concept items by either license or media type.

1. Find any CC licensed image.
2. Find any CC licensed text-based item (webpage, document, etc.).
3. Find any CC licensed video.
4. Find any CC licensed audio item (music clip, sound effect, podcast, etc.).
5. Find any CC0 licensed item.
6. Find any CC BY licensed item.
7. Find any CC BY SA licensed item.
8. Find any CC BY NC licensed item.
9. Find any CC BY ND licensed item.
10. Find any CC BY NC SA licensed item.
11. Find any CC BY NC ND licensed item.

Moderate

Moderate items ask students to locate multiple concept items, combining two different concepts. The addition of specific concrete topics adds a level of complexity to the clue items. Concrete topics are those that yield a common understanding of what the result should be. Typically, these are nouns that have easily identified representations. Subjects or concepts that could be illustrated in a variety of ways should be avoided for this level of clue ("race"—could be an event or a descriptor of people; "home"—could be a house, a trailer, an apartment, or even the landing page of a website, etc.).

1. Find any image with a CC0 license.
2. Find any image with a CC BY license.
3. Find any image with a CC BY SA license.
4. Find any image with a CC BY NC license.
5. Find any image with a CC BY ND license.
6. Find any image with a CC BY NC SA license.
7. Find any image with a CC BY NC ND license.
8. Repeat clues 1–7, replacing "image" with the media type of your choice (text item, audio, video, etc.).

9. Find any CC licensed image that illustrates [*insert concrete subject here*] ("apple," "house," "book," etc.).
10. Repeat clue 9, replacing "CC" with the license type of your choice.

Complex

Complex items ask students to locate multiple concept items, combining more than two different concepts. The addition of abstract topics adds an additional level of complexity to the clue items. Abstract topics or subjects are those that yield multiple representations of what the result would be. All parts of speech are appropriate, as long as they have multiple representations or are inherently abstract (e.g., "race," "home," as shown above, or "love," "work," or "honesty").

1. Find any CC0 licensed image that illustrates [*insert abstract subject/concept here*].
2. Find any CC BY licensed image that illustrates [*insert abstract subject/concept here*].
3. Find any CC BY SA licensed image that illustrates [*insert abstract subject/concept here*].
4. Find any CC BY NC licensed image that illustrates [*insert abstract subject/concept here*].
5. Find any CC BY ND licensed image that illustrates [*insert abstract subject/concept here*].
6. Find any CC BY NC SA licensed image that illustrates [*insert abstract subject/concept here*].
7. Find any CC BY NC ND licensed image that illustrates [*insert abstract subject/concept here*].
8. Repeat clues 1–7, replacing "image" with the media type of your choice.
9. Find any CC licensed image that illustrates [*insert abstract subject/concept here*] ("apple," "house," "book," etc.).
10. Repeat clue 9, replacing "CC" with the license type of your choice.

Clues for Copyright Concept Scavenger Hunt

The clues in this section are designed to provide students the opportunity to locate primary or secondary sources of information relating to copyright concepts or copyright-related court cases.

Teachers may choose to have students use trusted sources that curate information about court cases dealing with copyright issues or to have students conduct online searches themselves. The decision to provide the sources or have students search for the sources should be based on the skill and developmental level of the students. Younger, less experienced students will benefit from having the sources of items provided for them, while more skillful learners should be able to conduct searches for licensed items on their own.

Teachers may wish to limit the scavenger hunt to court cases, or they may wish to expand the hunt to include broad copyright concepts. In situations where copyright concepts are included in the hunt, teachers will need to decide whether to limit students' results to primary source documents or to permit them also to use secondary sources. Lessons that teach students how to conduct online searches for broad concepts are outside the scope of this text, so teachers should be prepared to provide those lessons as needed for their students if they so desire.

Trustworthy Sources of Court Case Information

- Casetext—https://casetext.com/
- Justia—https://www.justia.com/
- Oyez—https://www.oyez.org/
- US Copyright Office Fair Use Index—https://www.copyright.gov/fair-use/

Simple

Simple items ask students to locate single-concept items, whether that is a court case, a primary source of information, or a secondary source of information.

1. Find a court case that dealt PRIMARILY with fair use.
2. Find a court case that dealt PRIMARILY with transformative use.
3. Find a court case that dealt PRIMARILY with the use of images.
4. Find a court case that dealt PRIMARILY with the use of music or sound recordings.
5. Find a court case that dealt PRIMARILY with [*insert copyright concept or topic here*].
6. Find a court case that had teachers as either the plaintiff or the defendant.
7. Find a court case that had students as either the plaintiff or the defendant.
8. Find a court case that had [*insert type of person here, e.g., corporate, musician*] as either the plaintiff or the defendant.
9. Find a video that explains [*insert copyright concept here*].
10. Repeat #9, replacing "video" with the media type of your choice.

Moderate

Moderate items ask students to locate multiple concept items, combining the concept with the type of information it contains or explains. The addition of a specific topic and source type adds a level of complexity to the clue items.

1. Find a primary source of information that explains [*insert copyright concept here*].
2. Find a secondary source of information explaining [*insert copyright concept here*].
3. Find a US Supreme Court case that PRIMARILY dealt with [*insert copyright concept here*].
4. Find an appellate court case that PRIMARILY dealt with [*insert copyright concept here*].
5. Find any court case that dealt with [*insert first copyright concept here*] and [*insert second copyright concept here*].

Complex

Complex items ask students to locate multiple concept items, combining more than two different concepts or have more than two types of constraints placed upon the clue.

1. Find a [*insert type of court case here*] that dealt with [*insert first copyright concept here*] and [*insert second copyright concept here*].
2. Find a [*insert type of court case here*] that had [*insert type of person, e.g., teacher, student, musician here*], and dealt PRIMARILY with [*insert copyright concept here*].
3. Repeat #2 and add additional copyright concepts as desired.
4. Find two [three, four, etc., as desired] court cases that contain similar findings regarding [*insert copyright concept here*].
5. Find two court cases at different levels (US Supreme Court and appellate, for example) that have similar findings but are not versions of themselves. That is, the higher-level case shouldn't be a further version of the same suit from a lower court.
6. Repeat #5, replacing "similar" with "different" or "conflicting."
7. Find two different secondary information sources that describe similar interpretations of any court case that dealt with [*insert copyright concept here*].
8. Repeat #7, replacing "similar" with "different" or "conflicting."

Appendix I
Sample Bingo Card and Concentration Game Concept Pairs

The pairs indicated here can be used either as called clues in the bingo game or as the cell contents on bingo cards created by the teacher. This list is created assuming that the question/answer format of bingo cards is the preferred format for the game. The concept pairs listed here are not exhaustive. Teachers should feel free to modify the pairs as needed to account for differences in reading levels, understanding levels, and the depth of instruction provided in the lessons.

Question (***Back of Bingobaker card***)	**Answer** (***Cell content on bingo card***)
Court Cases	
A & M Records, Inc. v. Napster	Downloading of music files is an infringement of copyright. Right of Distribution. Right of Reproduction. Fair Use; Napster (online file-sharing site) permitted the up- and downloading of digital music files.
Allman v. Capricorn Records	Violators can only be sued for breach of contract for using licensed materials; the record company accused of violating the scope of licenses in the reproduction and distribution of records.
Author's Guild v. Google, Inc.	Landmark Case; Transformative Use; scanning portions of work to include in search results is permitted under fair use; portions of copyrighted books were scanned so that users could discover them in online searches.
Author's Guild v. Hathi Trust	Scanning of print materials for visually impaired users and creating adaptations for accessibility is considered to be fair use. Adaptation for accessibility; public domain as well as copyright-protected works, can be scanned to be made available to users with print-disabilities.
Berlin v. E.C. Pubs. Inc.	Parody is considered to be fair use. Fair use; parody; satiric parodies of song lyrics published.
Blanch v. Koons	Other factors in addition to the four fair use factors can be considered in total fair use determination. The rights of author/creator must be balanced with the rights of user. Transformative use; fair use; portions of a photograph used as part of a separately contracted work.
Campbell v. Acuff Rose Music	Landmark case; Pretty Woman Case; parody can be considered fair use in spite of potential commercial nature. Fair use; parody; music group created a song as a parody of the "Oh, Pretty Woman" song by Roy Orbison.

Question (*Back of Bingobaker card*)	Answer (*Cell content on bingo card*)
Carter v. Helmsley-Spear, Inc.	Moral rights; murals have VARA protections; work made for hire; VARA; The permission to install murals on a building was retracted by the new management of said building, and when artists retained copyright of the murals.
Clean Flicks of Colo. V. Soderbergh	Redacting offensive content from films; redactions are not fair use; adaptation; fair use; transformative use; objectionable content (profanity, drugs, sexual references, etc.) removed from films, and then the films were sold.
Cohen v. G & M Realty L.P.	Graffiti is eligible for VARA protections in certain circumstances; the medium of "visual art" should be liberally interpreted; VARA; graffiti work on a public building was painted over in NY.
Disney Enter's Inc. v. Vid Angel	Redacting offensive content from films; streaming redacted movies is not fair use; adaptation; fair use; objectionable content (profanity, drugs, sexual references, etc.) removed from digital films, and then resulting products were streamed; copyright control measures were circumvented to remove the material.
DynaStudy Inc. v. Houston Independent School District	Administrators can be held responsible for the actions of teachers in their buildings; removal of copyright notification demonstrates willful infringement; reproduction; distribution; adaptation; willful infringement; vicarious infringement; a teacher scanned copyrighted test preparation materials and then posted the results on a public website. Administrators knew about it and did not take action to prevent it.
Eldred v. Ashcroft	Challenge to the CTEA; inspired the creation of Creative Commons; even though long, the finite term of copyright protection satisfies the "limited time" provision for protection. Creative Commons; CTEA.
Fairey v. Assoc. Press	Adaptation of format through the digital scanning process creates a derivative work and is protected by copyright.
Faulkner Press LLC v. Class Notes	Enrollment in class is an implied license to take notes; packaged class notes are derivative works; selling packaged class notes is murky (as of 2010).
Feist Publ'ns v. Rural Telephone Services Co.	Landmark case; minimum levels of creativity required to get copyright protection; "white pages" (simple alphabetical listing of names, addresses, etc.) does not meet creativity threshold.
Harper & Row, Pubs v. Nation Enterprises	Landmark case; unpublished status of work protects from fair use of that work; using too much of a work removes fair use eligibility.
Hearn v. Meyer	Slavish copying does not require sufficient creativity to grant fair use protections; Meyer copied, using exacting technique, illustrations owned by Hearn. "Slavish reproduction" is the generation of something using the exact same technique to the point where the reproduction appears essentially the same as the original. One example would be "tracing" an illustration and then transferring that tracing to a different publication.

Question (*Back of Bingobaker card*)	Answer (*Cell content on bingo card*)
Hines v. Overstock	Terms and conditions of websites are enforceable because the "agreement" to them is demonstrated through the use of the website. Hines objected to restocking fees for returned merchandise.
Kirtsaeng v. John Wiley & Sons	Landmark case; First Sale doctrine applies even if the sale is first completed outside of the United States. Kirtsaeng purchased books from international booksellers and then resold those same books inside the United States.
Molinell-Freytas v. Univ. of Puerto Rico	Work completed during non-working hours can still be considered a work made for hire. If work is substantially similar to work as a part of the employee's job, that work can be considered work made for hire.
Naruto v. Slater	Non-humans do not have standing to assert copyright ownership. Copyright law does not give animals the right to claim ownership. PETA sued Slater on behalf of a monkey (Naruto) for copyright infringement of photos that were taken when Naruto triggered a camera that had been left unattended in the wild.
Nat'l Assoc. of the Deaf v. Netflix	Website-only businesses are subject to ADA services. Netflix argued that they didn't need to provide captioning because they aren't in a physical location. Netflix was determined to be a "place of business."
Pearson v. Ishayev	Text-based links are not infringing on copyright. Ishayev sold copyrighted works and distributed them by using hyperlinks inside emails, as well as attached zip files in some cases; copyrightable materials.
Philpot v. WOS	When using licensed materials, users must adhere to the terms of the license, or the use cannot be considered fair use; Creative Commons licensing.
Recording Industry Ass'n of Am v. Diamond Multimedia	Space shifting (creating "mix tapes" or "playlists") is fair use only if the originals of the items are physically owned by the person making the new mix/playlist. Items cannot be recorded from a streaming service; Audio Home Recording Act; time shifting/space shifting.
San Francisco Arts v. Athletics v. U.S. Olympic Comm.	Translations; adaptation; derivative works.
Shaul v. Cherry Valley-Springfield	The copyright protection for works-made-for-hire is owned by the employer, not the employee; works made for hire.
Sony Corp of Am. v. Universal City	Betamax Case; recording publicly (off-air recording in this case) for time-shifting purposes is fair use.
Tresona Multimedia v. Burbank H.S.	Vocal director created a performance using various portions of protected works. This use was determined to be fair use, transformative use, and educational use.
Vernor v. Autodesk	Software "purchases" do not result in ownership, as software is licensed. Licenses can restrict otherwise fair use. First Sale not applicable to licensed materials; license; distribution; first sale.

Question (*Back of Bingobaker card*)	Answer (*Cell content on bingo card*)
Viacom v. YouTube	Landmark case; willful blindness needs to be proven in order for an ISP to be held liable for copyright infringement; burden of enforcing copyright rests with the copyright owner.
Woodson v. Atl City Bd of Educ.	Time limit exists for suing for copyright damages; work performed outside of work that is also substantially different from work duties is not work made for hire; copyright v. plagiarism.
Conceptual Pairs and Definitions	
Fair use	Nature of use; purpose and character of use; proportionality of amount being used; effect of use on market or value of the item; affirmative defense; using copyrighted works without gaining permission in certain circumstances.
Transformative use	Adding new purpose or meaning to an item; one consideration with regard to the purpose and character of the use in a fair use assessment.
Reproduction	An exclusive right of a copyright owner; making copies of an item, whether mechanically or through the functionality of some form of technology.
Distribution	An exclusive right of a copyright owner; causing an item or reproduction of an item to be "passed around" or "given out" to other people, either by hand or through the functionality of some form of technology.
Adaptation	An exclusive right of a copyright owner; changing the form or format of an item, such as from analog to digital; making a revision through the addition or deletion of content; creating a new item using an original as a portion of it.
Public performance	An exclusive right of a copyright owner: "playing" or "showing" an item such as a movie, song, or theater production (any item that requires the passage of time in order to perceive it) in a place open to the public, whether virtual or physical.
Public display	An exclusive right of a copyright owner; "hanging up," "showing," or allowing to be seen an item such as a sculpture, images, or webpages (any item that is static and can be perceived visually) in a place open to the public, whether virtual or physical.
Public performance of digital audio transmissions	An exclusive right of a copyright owner: "playing" or "streaming" digital audio content, especially via the internet or other digital means.
Public domain	An absence of copyright protection for an item; a type of Creative Commons license that content creators can attach to an item, permitting any use at all for that item by other people.
Creative Commons	A type of license that content creators can attach to an item that permits certain types of specific uses for those items by other people; a non-profit organization created in response to a failed Supreme Court case that challenged the constitutionality of the CTEA; created by Lawrence Lessig and Eric Eldred; founded in 2001.

Question (*Back of Bingobaker card*)	Answer (*Cell content on bingo card*)
License	A set of rules that govern the use of content; the set of rules that users agree to follow when registering for or signing up for certain websites, tools, or services; rules that take precedence over fair use when determining the permissibility of some uses of copyrighted material.
Infringement	Violation of one of the six exclusive rights of a copyright owner.
Innocent infringement	Infringement while believing to the best of one's knowledge that a particular use of copyrighted material is permitted; least severe type of copyright infringement.
Willful infringement	Infringement with certain knowledge that a particular use of copyrighted material is not permitted; using copyrighted material in contravention of conditions communicated after requesting permission; purposeful use of copyrighted material with the knowledge such that use is not permitted.
Vicarious infringement	An indirect form of infringement; being in a position to profit from and having the ability or power to stop a person's use of copyrighted material and failing to do so.
Contributory infringement	An indirect form of infringement; assisting a person with the infringement of copyrighted material.
Cease-and-desist letter	A legal letter telling someone to halt infringing activity is usually the first consequence levied against an infringer.
Copyright	One of the three types of intellectual property; intellectual property for creative content that requires authorship.
Derivative	A type of adaptation of a copyrighted work; a new work based on an older protected work; a different version of a copyright-protected work, such as movies of books, theatre productions of movies, translations, etc. Works that may have additional copyright protection for the new and added elements to an original copyrighted work.
Public	A type of place or space that is open to the public and where people may gather who are outside of a group of close friends or family; spaces such as restaurants, classrooms, stores, and the internet.

Appendix J
Multimedia Guidelines Cheat Sheet

Note: a downloadable version of this checklist is available at the text website.

Directions: Use this cheat sheet to help you decide whether your use of copyrighted material in your project is within the scope of the multi-media guidelines. List the amounts of each type of media that you intend to use in your project in the last column of the table to be sure that your use is permitted.

First, be sure to include a copyright notice on the first slide/page of your project.
These samples come from Simpson and Wolf (2021), p 163.

> NOTICE: The following presentation contains copyrighted materials used under the Multimedia Guidelines and Fair Use exemptions of U.S. Copyright Law. Further use is prohibited.
>
> NOTICE: I borrowed other people's stuff to create my project. I followed the rules. Please don't copy my project.

Media Type	Limits	My Use in My Project
Motion Media	10% or 3 minutes, whichever is less	
Text	10% or 1,000 words, whichever is less. Entirety of short poems (<250 words) 3 per poet 5 from an anthology Long poems (>250 words) 3 excerpts per poet 5 excerpts from an anthology	
Music, lyrics, and music video	10%, not more than 30 seconds from single work or combination of excerpts from that work Maintain basic characteristic of original if altered	
Illustrations, cartoons, and photographs	Whole images permitted, no more than 5 per artist/photographer. Whole images, no more than 10% or 15 from an anthology	
Numerical data sets	10 % or 2,500 fields/cells	

Appendix K
Guidelines and Laws Quick Reference

How To Use This Quick Reference Table

One of the more confusing aspects of the various guidelines that exist for the use of copyrighted works is that there sometimes is overlap between one set of guidelines and another. Additionally, there are some use cases that are controlled by explicit instruction provided in the copyright law itself. Is it any wonder that students especially, but truly, any lay person wishing to use copyrighted materials in a particular way, might be confused as to what is or is not permitted?

To give you a very high-level look at the source of this confusion, consider the following chart:

		Print	Image	Visual Art	Music	Audio-visual	Multi-Media
Guidelines	Print	●			●		●
	Music				●	●	●
	Audio-Visual	●	●		●	●	●
	Multi media	●	●	●	●	●	●
Laws	VARA		●	●		●	
	DMCA	●	●		●	●	●
	MTIA	●				●	●
	MMA				●		●
	CTEA	●	●	●	●	●	●
	TEACH	●	●		●	●	●

As you can see, depending on the type of copyrighted work that is intended to be used, there are several laws and guidelines that describe possible acceptable limits to its use.

In order to make the most appropriate decision regarding how one might be permitted to use a particular type of copyrighted work, I've collected and summarized the guidelines for the laws and guidelines above in the table below. Remember, limits described by **guidelines** do not have the force of law. Additionally, some stakeholder organizations consider the guidelines to be too restrictive. However, the guidelines as described are agreed-upon limits between rights holders and various industries. On the other hand, **laws** describe certain limits and timelines that affect the length of time copyrighted works are protected, the ways in which some copyrighted works can be used, and other permissions affecting the use of copyrighted works.

What does this mean for teachers and students, though? When it comes right down to it, most teachers and students simply want to be able to answer questions such as:

- How many pictures can I put into my project?
- How much music am I allowed to use for the show?
- Do I need to get permission to be able to use a "lot" of images?

This quick reference table is intended to assist users in determining whether their intended use of copyright-protected items can be considered fair use. Refer to the fair use lesson for a more detailed suggestion for teaching about the fair use concept and application.

The first column, with a shaded background, indicates the TYPE of copyrighted work that a user intends to include in a project. That column corresponds to the header row with icons in the table at the beginning of this appendix.

The second column names the set of guidelines or name of the law that describe the limits to using a particular type of copyrighted work.

The third column, the widest one on the right side of the table, lists the various limits to using that particular type of copyrighted work.

For instance, if a student wanted to use a passage of text from one of the Harry Potter books in a project analyzing the use of figurative language by literary characters, she sees that there are two sets of guidelines (print and multimedia) that describe limits to the use of text. She would notice that the print guidelines speak to teacher use of text, while the multimedia guidelines include student use, that is, they are not limited to teacher use. Finally, she would see that she could include up to 1,000 words, or 10 percent (whichever is less), from that Harry Potter book in her project and be confident that her use would be considered to be fair use. Of course, she would also need to provide appropriate citations according to her teacher's requirements so that she would also avoid possible plagiarism in her project.

There is no need for this student to memorize these limits. She can use the chart as a ready-reference item.

Print	Print Guidelines	Single copies by teachers: • One chapter • One article • One short story • One chart, graph, illustration, etc. May not change or alter. • May use for study or teaching • NO consumables • NO replacement of buying collections or anthologies Multiple copies by teachers: • Must include copyright notification from original • Poetry: 250 words on fewer than 2 pages • Short Prose: 2,500 words • Long Prose: 1,000 words or 10 percent, whichever is less • All Prose: up to 500 words • Picture Books: two pages as long as less than 10 percent of total All Copying by Teachers: • Must be spontaneous: initiated at direction of teacher; not directed by "higher up"; unable to get permission in time; use once, then must get permission • May not violate cumulative effect prohibition: may not create anthology; only use for one course or grade; only three items from single author, three items from single volume of journal/magazine; current events ok to use • May not charge students $ beyond actual cost for photocopying; may only copy nine total items per class per term.
	Multimedia Guidelines	Teachers may retain two copies, or one per creator. of final versions of multimedia projects. User limits: • Text (prose): 10 percent or 1,000 words, whichever is less • Poetry: up to 250 words, able to finish a line • Poetry: three per author or five per anthology • Longer Poetry: 3 excerpts (250 words) per author; 5 excerpts per anthology
Music	Print Guidelines	Printed music scores are also controlled by print guidelines.
	Music Guidelines	Teachers MAY: • Make emergency copies when replacements won't arrive on time for use in performances • Up to 10 percent of a work that is not a performable unit, and only for non-performance purposes • Once purchased, may simplify or edit, keeping the style the same • Once purchased may NOT alter lyrics (add, delete, or change) • Record performances of the choir/band for later analysis or instruction • Copy recordings for testing purposes
	Multimedia Guidelines	Teachers may retain two copies, or one per creator, of final versions of multimedia projects • 10 percent up to 30 seconds per work, even in combination • Fundamental melody and character must be maintained
	MMA	Extended copyright protection for certain sound recordings. Total Length of Protection for . . . • Pre 1923 pub = 12/31/2021 • 1923–1946 = 100 total years protection • 1947–1956 = 110 total years protection • 1957–2/15/1972 = protection ends 2/15/2067

Audiovisual	**Audiovisual Guidelines**	Must meet five requirements: • Be for non-profit or educational use • Shown in classroom or similar location (library, gym) • Shown only to enrolled students and teacher • Must be legal copy. Check those license agreements for streaming services! • Must be in face-to-face instruction. See section 110 for the definition of face-to-face instruction. May NOT: • Change format of original • Show for reward or entertainment
	Multimedia Guidelines	Teachers may retain two copies, or one per creator, of final versions of multimedia projects; 10 percent up to 3 minutes, whichever is less
Multimedia	**Multimedia Guidelines**	Teachers may retain two copies, or one per creator, of final versions of multimedia projects In/On Productions or Projects: • Must include copyright statement on the first screen/slide • Must cite/attribute all uses of copyrighted works
Visual Arts	**Multimedia Guidelines**	**Data sets:** 10 percent or 2,500 fields/cells, whichever is less
	VARA	• Permits artist to attach name if misappropriated • Permits artist to remove name if harmful to reputation • Permits artist to prevent modification or destruction of work if it's of recognized stature • Not transferrable to anyone else, unlike six exclusive rights
Print, Images, Music, Audiovisual, Multimedia, Visual Arts	**TEACH**	Use must be: • Directly connected to the lesson at hand • Only for enrolled students • Removed quickly • Institution must protect the copyright of owners • Available only for a discrete and confined period of time • Integrated into lecture-like whole • Mediated use; resembling regular class sessions May NOT: • scan or upload long or complete works • store works on open websites • permit access at will, no ending limit to access
	MTIA	• Applies to all types of works • Updated language to be more scalable in light of possible technology advancements (accessible format vs. specialized format) • Persons with wider range of accessibility needs benefit (blind, visual impairment, physical or motor limitations that prevent accessing work as a non-disabled person would)

Print, Images, Music, Audiovisual, Multimedia, Visual Arts	**CTEA**	• Applies to all types of works • Extended copyright protection to life of author +70 years • Works from 1928 entered the public domain on Jan 1, 2024; each year, another year's worth of works will enter • 1923 sound recordings entered public domain on Jan 1, 2024; each year, another year's worth of sound recordings will enter
	DMCA	• Many responsibilities for institutions and OSP • Applies to all types of works, but particularly those in digital or other technology facilitated format • May not break copyright protection if in place • Schools must have a copyright agent registered who will handle complaints and compliance • Must pay to webcast sound recordings • Must include copyright notice for any protected material used • MAY break copyright protection if needed to make items accessible to disabled people • MAY break copyright protection if no other available format is accessible, only for teaching, documentary, or parody remixes • MAY use clips of movies for digital and literacy education programs

Appendix L
Questions for Plicker Cards or Poll Everywhere Activities

Plicker cards and Poll Everywhere are two tools that teachers can use to increase student engagement during didactic instructional activities such as lectures. Each of these tools also can be used to stimulate small group discussion through the use of anonymous polling. The questions presented here are designed to function as formative assessment items that teachers can use to indicate the progress students make in their understanding of concepts being presented. As such, they are designed to be as unambiguous as possible. For items reflecting a more nuanced picture of student understanding, please consult the Test Bank (within this text or in the online resources) where a greater number and variety of questions are located. As you review these questions, you'll see that the correct answer is in bolded text. Some items do not have any correct answer indicated. Those represent items in which there is no one correct answer. Rather, all answers have elements of correctness or are intended to prompt students to justify their answers through discussion. The questions shown here have been embedded in the presentation that is intended to be used for Lesson #1. They are also able to be used in other presentations at the teacher's discretion. Unlike the objective test items, though, these questions are intended to elicit student responses during a lesson and act as formative assessment items rather than summative ones.

Which one of these is NOT one of the exclusive rights of copyright holders?

A. Right of reproduction

B. Right of public display

C. Right of monetary gain

D. Right of distribution

Which one of these groups contains ONLY exclusive rights of copyright holders?

A. Right of: distribution, display, derivation

B. Right of: adaptation, public display, distribution

C. Right of: public performance, public distribution, public display

D. Right of: attribution, commercial benefit, digital audio transmission

The Fair Use provision of the copyright law says that . . .

A. Teachers can use whatever resources they want for their teaching, since schools have so little money.

B. In certain circumstances, people can use copyrighted materials without asking permission from the copyright owner.

C. As long as the copyright material is used fairly across all groups of people, you don't have to get permission from the copyright owner to use it.

Which of the following are the four tests of fair use?

A. Nature of the user; Amount being used; Payment made to owner; What is being used

B. Reason for use; Where being used; Who is receiving content; How much paid for it

C. Purpose of Use; Nature of original item; Proportion being used; Effect of use on market for original item

D. Why being used; What is being used; How much is being used; How bad is the use

Note: Both C and D could be considered correct answers. If you would like a less ambiguous question, replace "D" with another distractor of your choice.

As part of the annual convocation, the ROTC unit recites the school creed as the opening activity/welcome for the students. Is this activity permissible under the copyright law?

A. Yes

B. No

As a part of your lesson on figurative language, the teacher would like students to analyze written passages during which they would identify examples of imagery, metaphor, simile, and anthropomorphism. Which of the following is the best example of fair use of written materials by this teacher?

A. Complete copies of Mary Shelley's book *Frankenstein*, one for each student

B. Copies of one-half of George R. R. Martin's book *Song of Ice and Fire*, one for each small group (three to five) of students

C. Copies of a set of three pages from J. K. Rowling's book *Harry Potter and the Sorcerer's Stone*, one set per student

D. Copies of a random selection of ten sentences taken from within J. R. R. Tolkien's book *The Hobbit*, one copy displayed for the entire class to see

You want to post an informative news article (related to your department's mission) on your department's webpage (so that current and future visitors to your page can read it right from your page without having to download anything), and have written to the publisher for permission to do so. It has been four weeks since you requested permission, and you have not heard anything. Do you post the article (which of the following choices is the best/safest option)?

A. Yes, without hesitation

B. No, no way!

C. No, but I post a synopsis and citation

D. Yes, but if I hear from the publisher that the answer is "no," I will take it down.

In your work with the student grievance committee, you hear that a college class about the "methods of teaching" requires students to create lessons and lesson ideas on a variety of topics. Students are mandated/required to submit those ideas for grading via a published and publicly accessible website owned/managed by the professor. Is the publication requirement of the assignment a copyright infringement?

A. Yes, absolutely. No other way to look at it.

B. No, it's perfectly fine.

C. No, but it might be problematic according to some other law.

D. Yes, but there might be a way students could protect their work.

As part of the transition to a new student information system, you ask a member of the faculty to design, develop, and implement the training for all personnel who will access the new system. You pay the faculty member for her work above and beyond her regular salary. When the initial training during transition is complete, your office asks her to turn over all training documents that she created so that they can be used by members of the HR training staff for the onboarding of future employees. She declines to share the documentation, asserting that she is the copyright owner and should be able to keep them. Is she correct?

A. Yes

B. No

C. Maybe. I need more information to decide (and, this is the information I need: _______)

Either display the video for the 4 chord song (https://youtu.be/oOlDewpCfZQ?si=PtRgamKh2S9X6tlW) or play the video so that students can only hear the song. Note: The song is six minutes long if played in its entirety. Playing only a portion of the video or song will be sufficient for the purposes of this question.

Based on what you saw/heard, the band Axis of Awesome should be concerned that they have violated the copyright of the writers and artists who wrote and performed the original songs used in the *4 chord song*.

A. True, they used so many other songs that they've violated the proportionality test of fair use (test #3).

B. False, they have created an original work using extremely small snippets of original songs.

C. True, they are publicly performing a large number of songs written by other people.

D. False, they put their video on YouTube, so it's not really being publicly performed.

References

Anderson, L. & Krathwohl, D. (2001). *A taxonomy for learning, teaching, and assessing: A revision of Bloom's taxonomy of educational objectives.* Addison Wesley Longman, Inc.

Bloom, B. S. (Ed.), Engelhart, M.D., Furst, E. J., Hill, W. H., & Krathwohl, D. R. (1956). *Taxonomy of educational objectives: Handbook I: Cognitive domain.* David McKay Company, Inc.

Butler, R. (2004). *Copyright for teachers and librarians.* Neal-Schuman Publishers.

Butler, R. (2014). *Copyright for academic librarians and professionals.* American Library Association.

Creative Commons. (2020). *Creative commons for educators and librarians.* ALA Editions. (Licensed CC BY 4.0).

Creative Commons. (2024). *A history of Creative Commons.* https://creativecommons.org/timeline/ (Licensed CC BY 4.0).

Crews, K. D. (2020). *Copyright law for librarians and educators: Creative strategies & practical solutions* (4th ed.). American Library Association.

Facing History & Ourselves. (June 17, 2017). *Gallery walk.* https://www.facinghistory.org/resource-library/gallery-walk-0

Heer, R. (2021). *A model of learning objectives–based on A taxonomy for learning, teaching, and assessing: A revision of Bloom's taxonomy of educational objectives.* https://www.celt.iastate.edu/wp-content/uploads/2015/09/RevisedBloomsHandout-1.pdf (Licensed CC BY SA 4.0).

Iowa State University Center for Excellence in Learning and Teaching. *Revised Bloom's taxonomy.* http://www.celt.iastate.edu/teaching-resources/effective-practice/revised-blooms-taxonomy/

Justia. (2024). *Our company.* https://company.justia.com/

Oyez. (2024). *About Oyez.* https://www.oyez.org/about

Russell, C. (2023). *Complete copyright for librarians and educators* (2nd ed.). American Library Association. (Licensed CC BY NC SA 3.0).

Simpson, C. & Wolf, S. E. (2021). *Copyright for schools: A practical guide* (6th ed.). ABC-CLIO.

Smith, K. & Macklin, L. (2014). *A framework for analyzing any U.S. copyright problem.* Creative Commons. https://kuscholarworks.ku.edu/bitstream/handle/1808/22723/Smith_Copyright_Analysis_Framework.pdf?sequence=1&isAllowed=y (Licensed CC BY SA 4.0).

Smith, P. & Ragan, T. (2005). *Instructional design* (3rd ed.). Wiley.

The Heritage Foundation. (2024). *The heritage guide to the constitution.* Retrieved May 3, 2024, from https://www.heritage.org/constitution

U. S. Copyright Office. (2023, November). *U.S. Copyright Office fair use index.* https://www.copyright.gov/fair-use/

Wolston, M. (2018). *A brief history of Creative Commons.* https://vimeo.com/251525073 (Licensed CC BY 4.0).

Zook, K. (2001). *Instructional design for classroom teaching and learning.* Houghton Mifflin.

Index

Note 1: Bolded page numbers indicate locations of lesson topics.

Note 2: Consult the concordance chapter for specific locations within the test bank, scenario bank, and court case appendix for individual topics and concepts.